OVER HERE

OVER HERE

Raymond Seitz

Weidenfeld & Nicolson
London

First published in Great Britain in 1998
by Weidenfeld & Nicolson

A catalogue reference for this book
is available from the British Library

ISBN 0 297 81598 9

Typeset by Selwood Systems,
Midsomer Norton
Printed in Great Britain by
Butler & Tanner Ltd, Frome
and London

Weidenfeld & Nicolson
The Orion Publishing Group Ltd
Orion House
5 Upper Saint Martin's Lane
London, WC2H 9EA

Caroline

CONTENTS

PREFACE

I don't think any two nations have had their relationship poked at and picked over more than the United States and the United Kingdom. Everyone seems to have something to say.

Book after book describes the historic connections between the two countries, starting from well before the American Revolution and continuing up to the present. There is at least a book a year on transatlantic politics. W. H. Allen probably wrote the definitive work, a labour of love which he published in 1950 in the afterglow of the Allied victory in the Second World War. His analysis of relations in the eighteenth and nineteenth century is particularly comprehensive. Once he arrives in the middle of this century, however, Allen welcomes America's rise to world power without noticing Britain's decline, so his look into the future is deceptively rosy.

Travellers have also been fond of writing down their impressions. Dickens, Wilde, Matthew Arnold and Frances Trollope all had a go at the Americans. The United States in the nineteenth century played a gangling straight man to their biting wit. From the other side, Thomas Jefferson recorded his horror at British tyranny, but Ralph Waldo Emerson and Mark Twain both waxed rhapsodic in their accounts of British life. In those days, the American literati for the most part didn't seem to mind standing at the end of the long British nose.

Just when you think the subject has been exhausted, new travellers arrive on the scene. Paul Theroux wrote a none too flattering book about the Kingdom in 1983, and Christopher Hitchens recently returned the favour with an account of his experiences in America. Bill Bryson has gently covered the highways and byways of both countries. Novelists can't resist either. Alison Lurie and Martin Amis come to mind as contemporary writers on each other's ground. Henry James stands alone as the ultimate transatlanticist of fiction.

Even former ambassadors succumb to the temptation to publish. James Bryce, who served as Her Majesty's representative in Washington early in this century, wrote two volumes about what makes Yankees tick. Robin Renwick, who departed Washington in 1995, has written an excellent survey of post-war relations. Two of my predecessors at the Court of St James's put pen to paper: Richard Rush and John Winant. The diaries of Abigail Adams, who was America's first official hostess in London, are renowned, and Henry Adams wrote *The Education of Henry Adams* based in part on his years at the embassy in the middle of the last century.

There seems to be something so intriguing about what transpires across the Atlantic – regardless of which side you happen to be on – that you simply have to put it down in black and white. The urge is even more irresistible because the Americans and British find each other just strange enough to be exotic and just familiar enough to be comprehensible. So we never hesitate to comment on each other.

With plenty of literary anthropology already on the shelves, I nonetheless decided to go ahead with my own rendition. There were several reasons. I have been in and out of Britain over the last quarter-century, and as an itinerant diplomat at the American embassy I enjoyed an unusual vantage point for looking at the Kingdom and marking the milestones of its progression. My stint as ambassador also happened to coincide with the last gasps of the Cold War. This change in international circumstances made Britain's choices about the future more difficult and stark, and it was hard for me to escape the feeling that Britain in the 1990s was loitering at a strategic crossroads.

Britain has also been going through a period of intense domestic change, and still is. 'Intense' may be the wrong word – Britain is rarely intense about anything – but the United Kingdom has changed a lot since I first lived here in the mid-1970s. Most of this is positive. The economy is different. So is the social structure. But the process of change has been awkward and uncomfortable.

The British have gained much but also lost some. The assault on Britain's handsome red telephone boxes, for instance, or the disappearance of the sturdy, hardback British passport may seem trivial, but they represent a plaining down of Britain. And things which the British always got right they now sometimes get wrong. When the Queen Mother's Gates were unveiled at Hyde Park Corner, they looked like an explosion had gone off in an aluminium factory.

There were bigger things too. The evidence of serious drought in this once reliably rainy country suggested that not even Mother Nature was in a good mood when thinking about Britain. The Channel Tunnel, which makes perfectly good economic sense, nonetheless reversed a natural act of geography which had long been a source of national comfort. In fact, connecting to Europe in any fashion doesn't come easy for this island race. The handover of Hong Kong to the Chinese signalled that the British imperial era was well and truly over. The British had never done anything so well as their Empire – not always and not everywhere, perhaps, but now this too was finished for all time. To an outsider, the tribulations of the Royal Family often seemed like burlesque. But the convulsive reaction to the death of Diana, Princess of Wales, churned so deep that this most sensible of nations sometimes seemed to take leave of its senses, and there were moments when the British did not appear to recognize each other.

Britain's past has taken a lot of blame for Britain's present. The country is said to be too preoccupied with tradition, too fuddy-duddy. This is ironic for Americans because tradition is what we admire most about the British, largely because we have so little of it ourselves. But the idea that the past is the cause of Britain's woes has seeped into the national consciousness with barely a respectable word of dissent, as if the place were in need of a wholesale deracination.

So when I was at the London embassy as ambassador, the Kingdom seemed a little disoriented. National institutions didn't fit quite so snugly as before. There weren't too many examples of the old phlegm and pluck. The country seemed to be suffering from a kind of institutional melancholy – the monarchy, the parliament, the church, the unions, the constitution – which made the British appear out of sorts with themselves. An opinion poll in 1993 reported that half the population, given the opportunity, would emigrate. I didn't believe this. But the British did.

Anyway, there is a lot to say about the British, as there always has been. But I should mention one other motivation behind these pages. After years of on-and-off living in Britain, I think I understand my own country better. The parallels and differences between the United Kingdom and the United States always make for stimulating parlour games, but comparing our respective national lives has given me a clearer vision of my home and why it is my home. In learning about Britain I have learned about America.

Everything about Britain is intertwined, and so are many things about the transatlantic relationship. Once you try to separate them into consumable morsels, you lose something of the flavour. Nonetheless, I divided this book into five loose parts, starting with my earliest encounters with things British and ending up with my conclusions about the fundamental nature of the Anglo-American relationship. Along the way I cover such treacherous territory as cricket, class and politics.

Finding the right proportion was hard, particularly because proportion itself is such a British characteristic. I didn't have the inclination to rehash old events and I didn't have the temerity to compose a memoir. I didn't want to be too ponderous and I didn't want to be too light. So often I fell back on Cole Porter's guidance. When he was asked which came first, the music or the words, he said, 'The dry martini.'

The book took longer than I expected, and at one point I thought it would qualify as a Millennium project. It also took longer than my publisher Ion Trewin thought necessary or my agent Jonathan Lloyd thought prudent or my editor Elsbeth Lindner thought possible. But they were remarkably patient. The exercise also required the forbearance of my new banking colleagues at Lehman Brothers, who benignly overlooked my late arrivals at work.

This book reflects many conversations with many friends over many years. I am thankful for all that, and especially for the chance to know about this fine land and the people who live in it.

London
September 1997

PART ONE

Slouching
Towards Albion

Kiss and Tell

My wife Caroline once said she would go with me anywhere on earth so long as there was a Bloomingdale's. She didn't mean this. Not exactly. She doesn't even like Bloomingdale's. And shopping is at the bottom of her list of interests. But Caroline was, as we say, 'kidding on the square'. As a woman devoted to family, friends, privacy and the grace notes of civilization, the footloose ways of a diplomatic life held few intrinsic attractions for her.

I once wrote a poem for Caroline:

> It's not so hard for a diplomat
> To lead the life of a philobat;
> But what is hard to reconcile
> Is falling in love with an ocnophile.

Caroline overlooked my poetry and tolerated my foreign service career. In fact, she has always put up with a lot, and, for all her exacting standards, she has been the best possible partner.

What is most lost in the following chapters is the role Caroline played at the London embassy. One reason I enjoyed the job of ambassador is that she and I were able to do so much of it together. I'm not sure she would make precisely the same statement. Acting as ambassadorial consort can often seem intrusive, repetitive, vapid or simply exhausting. Plotting out a schedule six months in advance did not sit well with Caroline's spontaneity, and there was many a diplomatic occasion when, given the choice, she would have preferred an appendectomy. But, whatever the vagaries, she was part of virtually everything.

Caroline had no more reason to turn up in London than I did. Perhaps less. She was born and raised in Union, South Carolina, a small, hardscrabble mill town in the upper part of the state. People there are open, devout, self-reliant and hard to move. They are politely proud they gave the British a good thrashing in the Revolutionary War, and they are equally proud the Yankees got the same treatment during the Civil War (which the genteel folk of the region call 'the late unpleasantness'). With its rural culture, extended clans, studied manners, social classes, sharp whiskey, boiled vegetables, horse races and literary elegance, the South has more in common with Britain than any other region in the United States. And, unlike most of America, the South also enjoys an acute sense of irony, which helps explain Caroline's view of the human condition.

As a girl she led a Norman Rockwell life, with white picket fences and peanut-butter sandwiches and a swimming hole down by the creek for hot summer days. She walked to school in the morning and sat on the verandah in the evening. Though she has not lived in South Carolina for a long time, her rooted background makes it a miracle she ever left the state at all.

When she was older, Caroline bridled under the strict social dictum of the magnolia South: 'Pretty if you can, but pleasant if it kills you.' As it turned out, she was both. While chatelaine of Winfield House, the grand Residence of the American ambassador, she constructed the menus and chose the flowers – white flowers, always white – and negotiated the social intricacies that are so much a part of London. But her pleasure came from the cavalcade of people she encountered. She delighted in knowing them, and her judgement of character was uncanny. She always welcomed guests (almost always), some of whom were old friends and some of whom came through the door uncertain what they would find. She gave people, whoever they might be, her undivided attention, and her warmth and humour usually melted the stiffest British reserve.

Caroline is indisputably a talker, a teller of stories. Her voice by now has lost much of the lilting Carolina accent, but none of the charm. Because conversation is so much a way of life among the British, London was an ideal home for her verbal vitality and wit. Her directness could sometimes startle a stranger, and often, as I would take my place at my end of the ambassadorial table, I would smile to myself at the thought of what was in store for the dinner partners on Caroline's right and left.

After the guests had gone home, and Winfield House had closed down for the night, we would lie in the bed of the cavernous master suite, usually with a dog or two between us, and mull over the day. And while I might relate that I had spent my time figuring out Labour's position on devolution or teasing out what Her Majesty's Government was likely to do next in Bosnia, she would tell me about this minister's peculiar childhood or that author's deepest jealousy. She had a way of getting to the heart of things.

For Caroline, the written word is as important as the spoken word. All her life, she has feasted on English literature. Stanzas of poetry seem to float on the surface of her mind like lilies on a pond. Her own letters deserve publication because they are so observant and funny. She is a grammarian who can be withering about a misplaced apostrophe, and she has never quite recovered from a misspelling she came across in the porter's lodge at Trinity Hall in Cambridge. Her stylistic puritanism, however, did not deter her from a daily review of the British tabloids to see what the various vicars and royals were getting up to. 'Listen to this!' she would exclaim. She loves the absurdities of life, with all its colour, and British farce made her laugh.

She could be acerbic, never so much as when commenting on the government I was meant to be representing. Her attitude to foreign policy is that countries should stay out of each other's business, and usually she is right. On the whole, she thinks politics is not a serious occupation for grown-ups. Once she threatened to leave me if she ever heard the word 'Maastricht' again.

Caroline didn't care much for the trappings of office nor the people who did. If she complained about anything, it was usually about excess, pomp or privilege, and as a general proposition she preferred the cinema at Whiteley's or a chat at the vet's to the social run of London. She was happiest when catching up with one of our three children – Barr, Hillary and Thomas – who looked on Winfield House as an oasis in their nomadic lives.

Occasionally she would reconsider her modest stance. One day a discerning London taxi driver, having inspected her outfit of blue jeans, anorak and sneakers, refused to deposit her at the front door of Winfield House. This gave her pause. Still, she was ever vigilant that the little pretences to which I was naturally given did not go unchecked. A conductor who once arrived late for dinner explained to me in a farrago of apologies that his Mozart rehearsal had run over. 'Ah, Mozart,' I said with a sophisticated tilt of my head. 'I think there are only two categories of composers: first, Mozart, and second, all the rest,' at which point I heard a voice behind me say, 'What about Marvin Gaye?'

I have listened to many a man in public life try to acknowledge the role of his wife. They rarely succeed and almost always sound perfunctory. But I could not imagine my job without such a sublime companion. Diplomacy, of course, was my chosen profession. I sought to do it, and in a manner of speaking I was paid to do it. This was not the case for Caroline. But she did it anyway. I can truthfully say of her that I do not know a more insightful person nor a sharper wit nor a warmer refuge nor a finer friend nor any American who has a deeper affection for Britain. The government of the United States never got a better deal.

Sticks and Stones

I never planned to get mixed up with the British. It just happened that way.

Life, I have discovered, is a pretty random experience, and mine has seemed as accidental as most. I never benefited from an overall plan or grand design or even a particular set of ambitions. More often than not, I followed the counsel of Yogi Bera, the great philosopher of American baseball, who once advised, 'When you come to a fork in the road, take it.'

But the forks always seemed to lead to London. Only towards the end of my diplomatic career, when I became American ambassador to the Court of St James's, could I glance over my shoulder and discern a pattern in what had gone before.

Almost all my working years as a diplomat were spent inside the roomy structure of the Anglo-American relationship. I entered the foreign service in 1966 anticipating a career that would take me to exotic corners of the earth where diplomats wore white linen suits in dusty souks and spies hung out in dim cafés. I expected to send off despatches about my midnight conversations with sultans, beys and pashas, and to explore the back roads of Sarawak and the back alleys of Katmandu. Instead, like Yankee Doodle, I mostly went to London. Three times, in fact: once as a first secretary in the 1970s, again as minister in the 1980s, and finally as ambassador.

In between these assignments to the embassy in Grosvenor Square, I worked in the State Department in Washington where the British popped up in the middle of most equations. Whatever the foreign policy issue, there was almost always a British angle. But even in Washington I had no particular ambition to plot the course of Anglo-American relations. Throughout my years in Foggy Bottom (as the State Department is affectionately if sardonically known), I clung to only one overriding objective: to make sure that whatever position I held brought with it a parking pass to the basement garage.

Most of my State Department work took place on the rarefied Seventh Floor in the private office of a succession of Secretaries of State. This meant I continued to see a lot of the British, who almost alone among the foreign representatives in Washington enjoyed easy access to the upper reaches of America's foreign policy establishment. The British looked at the making of American foreign policy the way a professional musician might look at the cacophonous tribulations of a high school orchestra. They often dropped by the rehearsals to offer a little advice here or a tip there, and also to get across their own point of view. They always tried to make themselves part of American decision-making, and in our wide-open system they often were. No one seemed to mind much because the British usually knew what they were talking about, and what we were talking about as well.

Still, from my various offices in Foggy Bottom I would occasionally gaze out the window, past the Lincoln Memorial, at the straight run of the Potomac River and daydream about how swiftly flowed the Orinoco and how broadly flowed the Nile. But when it came time to pack up and head overseas again I ended up back on the banks of the Thames. At the start of my diplomatic career, I was posted to Montreal, Nairobi and Bukavu (in eastern Congo), but from 1972 until I resigned from the foreign service in 1994 I served only in London or Washington, alternating back and forth between the two capitals, a transatlantic metronome. This was an unusual pattern for any diplomat. I never did own a white linen suit.

Having spent so much time in the United Kingdom, I am naturally identified by the British as an Anglophile. I suppose I am. But I never liked the term applied to me, and I used to cringe whenever I saw the word in a newspaper or heard it in an introduction.

I was always surprised the British used the label at all. Unlike Americans, the British have never expended much energy trying to convince you that their country and its inhabitants have particular appeal. You're supposed to know that already. Nor will they proffer too many apologies for their shortcomings, even if they willingly acknowledge them. Americans are far more eager than the British to know whether they are liked or not. We are more touchy if we are not appreciated and more tickled if we are. For us, complex foreign policy issues are often reduced to a question of which foreign leader is portrayed as pro-American and which as anti-American. And sometimes Americans accuse each other of being unAmerican. Until recently, anyway, the British never seemed too bothered what you thought of them one way or the other, and Britishness was a loose enough concept that it was difficult to be unBritish even if you wanted to be.

I used to think the British knew themselves very well. But today they seem to know mainly what they used to be. In the past British self-confidence meant that foreign opinion was just so much lint to be flicked off the English sleeve. Nowadays, however, the British are more restless about their own direction and more interested in what outsiders think. They feel less in control of events than they have in centuries, and for a nation accustomed to taking history by the scruff of the neck, this is a major adjustment.

The British now spend a lot of time trying to figure out whether what they used to be is what they still ought to be. The national press is full of national introspection. There are books galore on the subject. Conferences and seminars are organized to ponder the national identity. Sometimes it seems as if the whole country has stretched itself out on a psychiatrist's couch, recounting its earliest memories and describing its deepest anxieties. Comments from outsiders are a little more welcome than once was the case. If the opinion is critical, the British will usually nod in agreement. And if it is approving, the British will usually doubt you know what you're talking about. An outsider's approval or disapproval, however, is not the point. Instead it's whether you share a genuine concern for the nation's considerable travails and eventual wellbeing. I did, and I think this is why I was called an Anglophile.

To be an Anglophile, you need imagination, because imagination is a fundamental part of British life. The British like to pretend, which is one reason why they make such good writers, actors and spies. There always seems to be a little bit of make-believe about the place. For the British, the show does go on – the play is the thing – and they seem to prize few things so much as a good performance. Politics, cricket, history, conversation, monarchy, manners, religion and so forth are mainly performing arts.

To be British, you have to act the part. High Court judges and Eton schoolboys, when recently given the option, decided to keep their distinctive costumes. And nothing is more British than doing one's duty and not letting down the side. The courageous fireman, the devoted nurse, the eccentric don, the brave soldier, the bashful bowler, the chatty cabbie, the humble priest, the witty guest, the gracious prince, the noble lord, the loutish lad, the plucky schoolboy, the demure schoolgirl, the dotty aunt or the faithful dog are all discharging their prescribed roles.

The British have played these roles for generations, always with style and verve. And if a role is sometimes over-acted or histrionic or flubbed, the British will fall down laughing at themselves. Britain is only part serious theatre; the rest is music hall. This all takes a lot of imagination, and it's the best part of being an Anglophile.

Because I admire the British, it is difficult to explain my discomfort with the word Anglophile. I suppose I find it a little patronizing in both directions. I also find it inaccurate as a matter of lexicography, which is odd in a country dedicated to linguistic precision. Anglophilia means you like things English. Things Welsh, Scottish or Irish are left out, or tacked on at the bottom like the tail of a kite. To be more comprehensive, you would have to say 'Britophile'. But this lacks resonance.

In fact, all the basic terminology about the people who live on these islands is unsatisfactory. There is no single, functional word to describe a subject of the Kingdom (which, over the last two centuries, has been a Queendom as much as a Kingdom). 'Britisher' doesn't work and no one really tries to use it. 'Briton' seems a little forced and has never caught on except in the driest kind of writing. And 'Brit', though it is used, is too flip and too much like slang to be respectable.

There aren't even any good pejorative words which foreigners can hurl at inhabitants of the United Kingdom. As epithets go, 'limey' is pretty mild, and even this means only the English. In fact, the insult gap is one notable shortcoming in the glossary of Anglo-American relations. An American doesn't mind being called a 'Yank' – rather likes it in fact. So we each have to amplify our insults by calling in reinforcements – 'a bloody Yankee bastard', for example, or 'a limey son-of-a-bitch'. You would think after all these years we could have come up with something spicier.

The primary cause of the linguistic awkwardness in describing the people of the United Kingdom is England's disproportionate size compared to the other parts of the country. As it happens, this is also the cause of many of Britain's other problems today. England's bulk in relation to Scotland, Wales or Northern Ireland did not matter much when there was a huge empire to compensate. But the imperial cushion has largely disappeared, and England now overwhelms the rest of the country. It is as if the United States were suddenly reduced to a combination of Texas plus Rhode Island, Delaware and Idaho. England's disproportionate position within the Kingdom often makes the English seem neglectful of their British brethren. When Lord Nelson at Trafalgar uttered Britain's unofficial motto – 'England expects that every man will do his duty' – he forgot to mention what Wales or Scotland expected.

So when the English say 'the United Kingdom', they usually mean 'England and all the other bits'. I've asked many English friends whether the Northern Irish are British. The answer, after some hesitation, is normally yes, but the response is conveyed as a technicality. One friend helpfully explained: 'Half the Irish in Ulster are British because they think they're British. The other half aren't because they don't. But no one on the mainland really thinks any of them is British.'

Because Wales was long ago absorbed into the great English sponge, most English seem to think of the Welsh in cultural terms: rugby, coal, choirs and consonants. When you read about a new law or an education report or a statistical survey, it is often expressed as applying to 'England and Wales'. But this is not really intended to distinguish Wales so much as to differentiate Scotland.

When it comes to the question of what is British and what is

Scottish, the Scots are especially prickly and the English especially clumsy. For practical guidance, I was once told that, if a Scot loses an international competition, he is Scottish. If he wins, he is British. My private theory, however, is that the English are subconsciously frightened of the Scots and like to pretend they aren't there at all. This is sensible. As fighters and financiers the Scots have few equals, and therefore the best thing that has ever happened to the English is that there haven't been very many Scots. But pretending the Scots don't exist often leads the English to stumble over the delicacies of national usage and to confuse 'English', 'Scottish' and 'British'. Foreigners do this too, but for outsiders the Scots are forgiving. For the English they are not.

The term 'British' does offer a particular new advantage. No one ever refers to the descendants of non-white immigrants in the United Kingdom as English, Scottish, Welsh or Irish, even if they have lived in those regions for a couple of generations. In the United States two generations are enough to turn an immigrant into an American, though some like to hang on to a hyphen. But the quadripartite nature of the United Kingdom makes it difficult for non-white residents to establish a sense of nationality in the United Kingdom. The term 'British', however, is just malleable enough to be helpful. So the boxer Frank Bruno or the runner Linford Christie are British, and in that sense are more genuinely national champions than most other athletes in the United Kingdom.

The imprecision in this simple, national terminology is not very important. But it is peculiar that the United Kingdom doesn't quite have the vocabulary to describe its natives. Broadly, I suppose, the terms English, Scottish, Welsh and Irish are based on blood whereas the word 'British' is based on territory; but there are also enough exceptions to this observation to limit its value. As a rule of thumb I found it is best not to pay too much attention to defining what is British and what is not. The word 'Anglophile', I suppose, refers to something more than just English but not quite everything that is British. It's a little sloppy but will have to do. I ducked it when I could.

There is another reason why being called an 'Anglophile' always made me uncomfortable. I don't like Anglophiles. Or at least I don't like those Anglophiles who are almost slavish in their devotion to things English. I am an Anglophilophobe.

There is, alas, a breed of American for whom the allure of English manners, English vowels and English titles seems to cast a spell. They come to Britain often and too obviously envy the effortless elitism and easy erudition of the well-bred Englishman. They seem to hanker after class by association, as if to say that if the United States also had an aristocratic order they would naturally be members. The mere mention of the Duke of This or the Marquess of That turns their knees to jelly, and there's nothing more titillating for them than rubbing Savile Row shoulders in the Royal Enclosure at Ascot.

This kind of Anglo-delirium follows a long transatlantic tradition, but at bottom the phenomenon is not much more than vicarious snobbery, with a bit of Miniver-Cheevery thrown in. You can be snooty in Britain and get away with it. It's much harder to pull off in a republic. Excessive Anglophilia is harmless enough, I suppose, but I always found it embarrassing when I came across it and could not resist a twinge of contempt. Mercifully, the number of my countrymen who are terminally Anglophiliac is dwindling. Enough remain, however, that I never wanted to be confused with one.

A third reason I resisted the attribute of Anglophilia was professional. For a diplomat there is a fine line between educating your own government about another government's point of view and becoming an advocate for that same point of view. In the language of Foggy Bottom, this is called 'clientitis'.

British diplomats rarely succumb to this disease because they have practised the diplomatic craft for centuries and have built up an immunity. But even well-developed professionalism is no guarantee against infection. Arabists, for example, are notoriously susceptible. At the Foreign Office and the State Department, Arabists are called the Burnous Brigade or the Camel Corps. An Arabist may become so absorbed by the language, culture and mysteries of Araby that he ends up promoting Arab interests more than the interests of his own country. Every Secretary of State I have known, at one point or another, has erupted with anger at some ambassador in the field who has psychologically defected to the other side.

Clientitis is an understandable if unforgivable sin. After all, if you live in a foreign country, mingle with its people, read its newspapers, feel its pressures, appreciate is problems and talk to its politicians and officials, it is hard to resist adopting a sympathetic perspective. As they say in Washington, 'Where you sit is where you stand.' Moreover, a foreign government cannot be blamed for attempting to seduce the representatives of other countries in order to bring them around to its viewpoint. That is what the game is all about. Diplomats are by nature inclined to please, and in American diplomacy this is particularly true of political appointees who are likely to be solicitous of a government to which they are assigned and anxious for local popularity. But many career diplomats succumb as well, especially those who spend most of their years overseas without the sobering benefit of an occasional cold shower in their own home capital. The descent into clientitis can be so subtle that you scarcely recognize it's happening.

Despite my many years in Britain, I don't think I ever lost track of why I was here. Only once was I accused of going over to the other side, and this was in my last year as ambassador when my American colleague in Dublin put it about in Washington that I was in the pocket of the British. But that's a later story. My only point here is that for an American diplomat in London to be called an Anglophile is hardly a professional credential.

So adding together all these considerations, I never liked to be known as an Anglophile and the description never gave me much pleasure. I therefore found myself in the ludicrous position of disclaiming what was perfectly obvious to everyone else: that I am an Anglophile. I respect Britain and I like the British. This confession is a kind of self-outing. Anglophilia just crept up on me. I couldn't help it.

Fittings and Fixtures

The serendipitous route by which I arrived at this unexpected state of Anglophilia still puzzles me. I have no particular ancestral attachment to Britain, no genealogical line that I can trace back to a charming old parish in Somerset or East Anglia, and no distant cousins in Glasgow or Cardiff. Like many Americans my blood is a European soup of German, French, English, Dutch and Irish stirred together in haphazard proportions. The British usually mispronounce my surname or assume it is 'Sykes'. And I was raised a Catholic, which is not the best starting point for a sympathetic relationship with the British.

For some unaccountable reason I was brought up on the to-*mah*-to side of America's Linguistic Divide instead of the to-*may*-to side, but this was a family quirk rather than a deliberate preference and not as unusual as most British seem to think. As a child I received the prescribed dose of English nursery rhymes and Christopher Robin stories, but, like vaccinations, these were simply part of growing up in America. Nor was I one of those troops of American students who spent an undergraduate year at a British university or took a postgraduate degree at Oxford or Cambridge.

A twice-removed cousin of mine named Stuart Johnson served as the aide to the American ambassador in London in the latter part of the 1920s, but he died in an automobile accident outside Cairo well before I was born. My mother, when she was nineteen years old, visited him in London in the spring of 1927. She was presented at Court in the days when those things fluttered the heart of an American girl. I can only imagine the correspondence that whisked back and forth across the Atlantic in preparation for this event, but no account has survived except some yellowed newspaper clippings glued into the loose pages of a leather scrapbook.

My mother died when I was eleven, and I never asked her about her moment at the Palace. I have a photograph of her taken in a London studio the day before her presentation. She is standing in a white, three-quarter-length gown with a short train trailing behind her. A long loop of pearls hangs from her neck. A fold of fabric is wrapped around her forehead in the fetching fashion of the Twenties, and a little ostrich feather pops up from the back. She is erect and poised and elegant. When, in later years, one occasion or another would take me to Buckingham Palace, I would sometimes think that my mother had wandered along these same corridors decades before, and I regretted we never had a chance to talk about what it was like to be Yankees at Court.

Like countless other boys growing up in the English-speaking world, I was captivated by the handsome model soldiers manufactured by Britains Limited. I collected American models as well, but the central part of my military coalition was British. Fusiliers, grenadiers, hussars, lancers and lifeguards marched or charged their way through my youthful imagination for many years. This was an immense relief to all my relatives because there was never any question what gift I wanted for Christmas or for my birthday, and, sure enough, when these occasions rolled around, I would find gathered under the lighted tree in the living room or stacked before the cake on the dining-room table a sumptuous pile of long narrow boxes. Their shape would fill most boys with foreboding because they looked so much like necktie boxes. But for me they betokened new recruits for the Grand Army I was assembling upstairs. I can recall the excitement of lifting the lid to discover a squad of Black Watch or Coldstream Guards, each figure firmly strapped against the inside cardboard by little bands of elastic.

I spent hours and hours with these soldiers, distributing victory and defeat with an absolute authority I was never again to enjoy. I recreated many of Britain's most distinguished military disasters (I created a few disasters of my own as well, as when I once cut out the cups of my mother's brassières in order to supply parachutes to my detachment of American paratroopers). Most of my British soldiers were nineteenth-century figures. They fought at Waterloo, Sebastopol, Isandhlwana, Omdurman and Lucknow, almost always against American Indians. The Welsh were the bravest, the English the cleverest, the Scots the fiercest. Whether winning or losing, they were always glorious. If I had collected model ships instead of model soldiers, my youthful impression of Britain's military fortunes would have been more positive, but because I came from an army family I doubt my father would have permitted a naval vessel in the house.

At the end of these long battles that unfolded across the carpet of my bedroom, I promoted the figures who had demonstrated conspicuous leadership or courage in the face of the enemy or under the paws of our family dog. I painted tiny chevrons on the sleeves of their uniforms, and for those who had acquitted them-selves with particular gallantry I would daub little dots of coloured paint on the breasts of their tunics.

Some years later, I gave away these war-weary troops. This was a mistake. There must have been a couple of thousand. But I did hold back a few, and these I have kept with me through the years. In Grosvenor Square, I lined up the remnant of my military legions in a corner of a bookcase in my office where they mounted an ambassadorial guard for three years. All this explains why I never fail to feel a frisson of delight when the scarlet ranks of the Guards wheel into Horse Guards Parade at the Trooping the Colour, or whenever I come across the Horse Guards practising their paces in the early-morning light of Hyde Park. Of all British institutions, none has commanded my respect more than the professionalism and dash of the British army, even though it had suffered many reverses and innumerable casualties on my bedroom floor.

I remember my first glimpse of England. It was through a porthole on a clear morning in the summer of 1949. My father – at the time a colonel in the army – was assigned to return to Germany to command again the same regiment he had led on to the Normandy beaches five years earlier. The regiment, part of the First Division, was garrisoned in Bamberg, not far from Nuremberg.

By 1949 the Allied occupation of Germany had come to an official end, but the Cold War had set in hard in Central Europe, and American soldiers were headed back across the ocean to a continent that didn't seem to know how to stay out of trouble.

My father, mother, sister, brother and I sailed from one of the Manhattan quays on the Hudson River. Embarking on a transatlantic voyage was still a festive affair in those days, full of steamer trunks and romantic promise, even for an eight-year-old. I recall the bulky, two-stack liner, the *Sandy Patch*, drifting out to the middle of the river and slowly swinging its bow eastwards. We churned past the Statue of Liberty, cast off the tugboat lines, blasted our horn on any excuse and slipped in to the Verrazano Narrows just as the sun was setting and the galaxy of the New York skyline flickered into light. The ship headed into the open sea, leaving a flat avenue of white water behind, and that night, my first on the broad and blue Atlantic, I came down with measles.

I spent the crossing confined to sickbay. Only my parents and the medical staff were allowed into the ward. I passed the hours looking out the porthole, gazing at the grey swells and the white spray. Oceans, after a while, are boring, at least if you are young. My parents and the nurses tried to keep up my morale by telling me to stay on the lookout for the White Cliffs of Dover, because I could then tell we were almost at our destination. My parents sang the famous song and so did the doctors and nurses. Everyone seemed to know the words. Years later, when I met Vera Lynn and heard her sing about the white cliffs, I thought of my miserable shipboard confinement. And sure enough, one sunny day in June, as the *Sandy Patch* ploughed its way into the choppy English Channel, there they were, chalky white and gleaming along the distant edge of the water like a long smile. That was England, and through the porthole England was blue, green, white and round.

For most of my youth, Britain remained a place on the horizon. It rarely intruded into my world. Occasionally, the British would feature in overheard conversations between my father and his army friends, not always favourably. These old comrades reassured each other repeatedly that the war in Europe would have been over a lot sooner if Montgomery had just gotten off his ass. The British Tommy was superb, the veterans acknowledged with genuine admiration, but those hoity-toity generals of theirs couldn't put together a goddamn two-car funeral. And so forth. The British government, they also thought, was always borrowing money and never paying it back. The British, it seemed, were deadbeats. This opinion won general approval in my father's circle, and a small stereotype stuck in my mind. I thought of this years later when I read Tom Wolfe's *Bonfire of the Vanities*, in which an English journalist one evening offers to pick up the bill in a New York restaurant. Everyone else in the restaurant stands up and applauds.

My father was not a literary man, unless you count the mysteries of Erle Stanley Gardner. But, wherever we happened to be at the time, he kept on his bedside table a small leather-bound edition of Kipling's poem *If*. The precepts and platitudes of our household derived largely from an English poet, albeit a poet who had married an American and spent a lot of time in the United States. When Kipling urged Christendom to 'take up the white man's burden', he was trying to persuade Americans to accept colonial responsibility for the Philippines, and for a few brief colonial decades in the first half of this century the Philippines were for the American army what the Indian Raj had always been for the British army. In the Philippines, young officers chased rebels in the morning, played polo in the afternoon and dressed for dinner in the evening, and my father, shortly after leaving West Point, had been one of these. As much as any man of that era, he lived by Kipling's code. Years later I discovered that my father-in-law had also kept a copy of *If* at home. Both men were morally decisive and forthright to the core, and in this Victorian atmosphere of black-and-white certitude, both my wife and I were raised.

I recall vividly another moment from my childhood. One day I came across my mother in tears. She was seated on a chaise longue in the bedroom of our house in Fort Meade, Maryland, listening to the hulking short-wave radio that stood on a nearby table. The curtains were drawn and the room was darkened. A crackling voice in a solemn English accent was describing the funeral of George VI. I do not know whether my mother was moved by the sorrowful words she heard, by the memories of her youthful excursion to London, or by all the emotions of her wartime years. But she sobbed and she mourned.

There is one other relevant thing I recollect from boyhood. It is a joke my father was fond of telling. My father had a good sense of humour, most richly appreciated by himself. He was not given to blurting out jokes without a context, however, and I cannot imagine how he managed to manoeuvre so many conversations around to the point where he could deliver his little riddle. But I overheard the joke often enough. It went like this: what is the difference between a buffalo and a bison? Answer: a buffalo is an animal that roamed the western plains of the United States. A bison is something an Englishman washes his hands in. Uproarious laughter. A number of years went by before I finally understood the punch line. Perhaps that's why I remember it. In the meantime, however, it conjured up some pretty grisly images of the English and their sanitary habits.

The remainder of my adolescent impressions of Britain came from school and the movies. At fourteen, when my father went to the Middle East, I was sent off to boarding school in upstate New York. The headmaster was a tall, white-haired, angular man with piercing blue eyes and a ruddy beak of a nose. He was named Edward Pulling. He was English but had come to the United States after the First World War, and Millbrook School was his creation. The school had started in an old farm. There were several rambling, clapboard buildings and a big barn. Later, a few brick dormitories went up on either side of a grassy quadrangle with a white New England chapel at the top. In the autumn, when the leaves turned, the woods around the school blazed, and in the winter, the students laid down wooden boardwalks as pathways through the snow.

Pulling was a formidable figure, a man of granite rectitude. He detested the repressiveness of British boarding schools, which he thought suffocated the free spirit of youth. He was strict, but he encouraged an open system in which students would take responsibility for much of the day-to-day running of the school and for their own actions. Discipline, he believed, made sense only if its purpose was apparent. Above all, he thought education was a challenge to be enjoyed. On this last point I took an inordinately long time to come around to the same view, but in the end Pulling prevailed.

In those days – the late 1950s – the study of literature in America largely meant the study of English writers, or British writers. Other academic courses, such as mathematics and the sciences, had no particular nationality attached to them, and history was naturally taught from an American perspective. But, in the era before Dead White European Males were treated with suspicion in some American schools, the rich diet of literature we consumed at Millbrook was British – Chaucer at the start, Shakespeare every year and loads of Dickens, Brontë, Scott, Austen, Hardy and so forth. Occasionally, something by Melville or Hawthorne was thrown in, but the first taste of modern American writers, such as Hemingway and Faulkner, had to wait until the final year of secondary school. Poetry was overwhelmingly English.

At the time, this literary menu left me with three impressions. First, that English nineteenth-century novels were twice as long as they needed to be. Second, that reading stories about characters who lived in a faraway country of which I had no first-hand knowledge was a semi-colonial experience, and only later did I fully appreciate that I was studying heritage as much as literature. And, third, that in poetry and novels the British were exquisite writers. I suppose, if I had to choose one British influence in my early years, it would be the marvels of English literature which were revealed to me while sitting around the seminar table in Mr Pulling's office as he tutored a small number of easily distracted teenagers.

Many British I know received their earliest impressions of America through the movies. America, it seemed, was a larger-than-life place full of gangsters and gunslingers, tycoons and screwballs, hicks and hucksters. Wiseguys wisecracked. But a lot of Americans, at least adolescents my age, learned about Britain at the same time through the Saturday silver screen or movie repeats on late-night television, and the picture was just as distorted. It was immaterial whether the films were made in Hollywood or in one of the studios that flourished around London in the golden age of British cinema. In the early era of film, it was hard to tell the difference.

I had a particular advantage in appreciating this. My stepmother was an actress named Jessie Royce Landis. To marry an army general, as she did in 1956, was a leap of faith, in both directions, but she and my father made a glamorous couple and they somehow managed to cross the yawning divide between their respective professions. Perhaps this is because they always entered laughing. Royce was a born-in-a-trunk actress for whom life and the theatre were synonymous, and the little bit I know about movies and the stage I learned from her. From time to time she would park me on a high stool in the wings of a darkened theatre to watch her performance. For many years she played Broadway, off-Broadway, repertory and the splendid American invention of summer stock, and in the early 1950s she enjoyed a couple of successful seasons in London. Army life was a complication for an actress, and in her later career Royce switched to movies and television, which were more convenient if less satisfying. For her, the stages of New York and London remained the pinnacles of theatrical being. But she taught me a lot about the cinema as well.

Many of the movies I saw in my youth were about British characters, fictional or real, such as Robin Hood or Sir Walter Ralegh. Or they were based on British stories, such as *The Four Feathers* or *Wuthering Heights*. The world of the cinema mixed American and British cultures, and mangled them as well. Films about twentieth-century Britain invariably portrayed an island inhabited by a race of distressingly elegant people. The men wore black tie at the drop of a top hat and they carried slender silver cigarette cases. The women appeared in long satin gowns and feathery plumage. The English lived in grand houses and were almost always trailed by butlers. They were impossibly sophisticated, almost fey, like Noël Coward, or full of quick-witted pluck, like David Niven. And there were a lot of oleaginous smoothies such as George Sanders or handsome heart-stoppers such as Laurence Olivier.

In the early days, when American stars such as William Powell, Katharine Hepburn, John Barrymore or Barbara Stanwyck wanted to act worldly, they acted English, although they always had a little more snap. I never did figure out whether Douglas Fairbanks or Deborah Kerr or Ronald Colman were British or American, and I still scratch my head that two of the lead characters in *Gone with the Wind* were played by stars from across the sea. And Cary Grant, born in Britain and matured in the United States, was the perfect transatlantic blend of natural English charm and boyish American innocence. Long before the United States and the United Kingdom joined together in the serious business of geopolitical strategy, they had found a prosperous common ground in the cinema, and this remains the case. On the screen, we each perpetuated the other's stereotypes. But at least we saw something of one another, and I was usually in the front row.

It was not until the 1960s, during my university years at Yale and immediately afterwards, that Britain came to life for me. I had visited London once, and in a few summer days had traipsed through the customary tourist shrines. Until the 1960s, however, Britain for me was mainly archaeology: old museums, old actors, old books and old battles. But in that decade the country suddenly seemed to run amok through its own staid culture. I now understand better what happened then, but at the time, for an American, it seemed as if an earthquake had struck in a faraway place and a colossal tidal wave had swept across the ocean to burst upon the American shore, tossing up all manner of things from Carnaby Street and James Bond to mini-skirts and Mary Quant. Suddenly, inexplicably, Britain had zing.

Like millions of other post-Elvis Americans, I sat down in front of a television one evening in 1964 and gaped at the extraordinary figures from Liverpool who changed rock'n'roll overnight. Antic, cheeky and iconoclastic, the Beatles were much more than their music. They were definitely not Noël Coward. For the United States, the Beatles were the best British thing to happen to us since Cornwallis surrendered at Yorktown. Until 1964, an American never would have thought of calling Britain 'groovy'. But that's what it turned out to be, at least for a while. The Beatles and all the other vibrant pop phenomena of renaissance Britain in the mid-1960s shattered the image of a decrepit country full of musty castles and dusty bones.

And so, in 1965, after working for two years as a teacher in Texas, I went to Glasgow, bought a green Vespa motorscooter and strapped a guitar to the side. I spent a month searching for New Britannia. I worked my way across Scotland and then zigzagged south along the bed-and-breakfast trail. It rained almost every day. The cities and towns were unbearably dreary and shabby. Fried bread was the culinary highlight. Nothing seemed to have changed much from pre-Beatles times. Even in Swinging London, where I spent a fortnight on the prowl, no one ever swung anything new at me.

But I did learn a little more about the British along the way. I stayed a couple of nights at a farmhouse outside a village in Derbyshire whose name I have now forgotten. The owner was a widow, an expansive, red-cheeked, salt-of-the-earth woman of generous dimensions. Of my various encounters during the trip, she was the person I remembered most because she seemed so English. She was garrulous and cheery, and she saw it as her duty to set me straight on a few things. In my garret room at the top of the farmhouse there was a small, antique heater that required a two-shilling coin to operate the coils for a few minutes, during which time a thin vapour of warmth would exhale from the narrow red bars. When I asked the landlady for change to work the heater, she sighed disapprovingly. It was a dead give-away of my nationality. A person of mettle wouldn't need such coddling, and certainly not an Englishman.

In the couple of days that followed, she went on to scold me pleasantly about every topic that cropped up, particularly when the subject concerned the inadequacies of the United States and how Americans might improve themselves. Americans had no sense of ceremony, for example. Americans were too rich. American children were spoiled. Americans were too loud. Over many cups of milky tea, she laid out this catalogue of national failure. When I asked her if she had ever been to America, she shook her head. England was a country where things were done right, so there wasn't much point in going anywhere else. I suspect she thought the Beatles were American.

These snippets pretty much constituted the sum of my youthful brushes with the British. They do not suggest a creeping Anglophilia nor do they give any indication that, as an adult, I would live as many years in Britain as at home. But, when I was older and could review the little accidents of life, it seemed apparent that even before joining the foreign service I was already slouching towards Albion.

Twists and Turns

I arrived in Washington DC in the spring of 1966 and, along with a score of other shiny new foreign service officers, began a brief training course designed to teach the basic diplomatic skills, the most important of which was how to finagle your next assignment. With my new colleagues, I immediately started to lobby for my first posting. Whenever I encountered anybody important – anybody important was anybody over thirty – I insisted there was no place on earth too dangerous, too dirty, too distant or too diseased that I would not go.

In those days, it was the genteel custom in the foreign service to conclude the training programme by inviting a senior figure to come to the lecture hall in Roslyn, Virginia to impart a few words of inspiration and then read out the first assignments for the assembly of fledgling diplomats. The senior figure was usually someone smart enough never to have set foot in any of the places he was about to send us. The list was announced by name in alphabetical order, so I came towards the end. Romantic visions danced before me as I listened to the exotic roll call: Rabat, Bangui, Rangoon, Montevideo and so on. When my name was finally called out, there was a tense pause. 'Montreal.' In a split second my mind raced around the globe on a desperate hunt for this destination of intrigue, adventure and mystery until, stunned, I realized I was bound for a place located several miles north of Plattsburg, New York.

I liked Canada, though it is a confusing country. The British and French heritages are strong and usually defined in juxtaposition to each other. When set beside the United States, however, this uneasy coexistence of two communities forms an amalgam of Canadianness. A wag once said that, of all the nations of the world, Canada at the beginning faced the best possible choices about its national future. It could have enjoyed British politics, American economics and French culture. But instead it ended up with British economics, French politics and American culture. Americans do tend to be neglectful of Canada, which is understandable given the disparities between the two countries. When Al Capone was once asked about Canada, he said, 'Canada? What street's that on?' Canadians have to live with this.

For two centuries Canada acted as a barometer of Anglo-American affairs, though at the time I was only dimly aware of this historic role. In the middle of the eighteenth century, when the British defeated the French in Canada, they removed the primary danger to the security of the American colonies and therefore the primary reason for the colonies to stay within the protective embrace of the British Empire. If France had remained dominant in Canada, the Americans would have found rebellion against their British overlords a more perilous proposition. And after American independence many of the tensions between London and Washington centred around Canadian issues – fishing rights, frontier disputes and so forth – with Canada acting as a British threat or an American hostage, depending on your point of view.

My time in Montreal was brief, but I suppose I learned a few things about the British Commonwealth as well as some of the legacies of the British Empire in North America. There was a governor general in Ottawa who represented the Queen, which meant that Canada didn't dally before heading off to European wars. And some of the social issues which plague the American polity – gun control or national health policy, for example – seem to have found equitable solutions just across our northern border, in large measure due to the British ethos.

In Quebec I also learned a lot about people who did not want to be British or British-like, and my first dramatic moment in international politics occurred when I stood in a crowd in the Place Ville Marie in downtown Montreal and heard General de Gaulle rally French-Canadians with his call of 'Vive le Québec Libre!' as if Quebec were occupied territory. But most of my time in Canada was spent either learning to distinguish between honest and dishonest visa applicants or shuttling official visitors in and out of the American Pavilion at the World's Fair called Expo 67. After eighteen months, I was ordered to return to Washington to study Swahili at the Foreign Service Institute.

From 1968 to 1970, I worked at the American embassy in Nairobi. As a junior political officer, I drafted grave reports about whether Kenya would hold together after Jomo Kenyatta passed from the scene. The expatriate community in Nairobi was almost entirely British, either the old coffee-planting settlers who had made the necessary adjustments to continue the good life after Kenyan independence or the newer arrivals who were there to make some money in a salubrious climate. In any event, the British were dominant. In matters of government, the British role had shifted from colonial to pro-consular, a position of favour which the British intended to protect from American encroachment as best they could. After all, the United States had not been especially supportive of Britain's colonial authority in Africa, or anywhere else for that matter, and American motivations were regarded with suspicion.

My counterpart at the British high commission was named Richard Edis, who years later became Her Majesty's ambassador in Mozambique and then Tunisia. He was the first British diplomat I encountered in my career. In Nairobi we were both third secretaries, but while I felt myself to be green and callow, Richard gave the impression of having been in the diplomatic game since the Treaty of Westphalia. He was composed, precise and Cambridge-confident, and he had a focused view of British interests in East Africa. We were both very serious about our responsibilities and initially a little guarded with each other. He said 'Keenya' and I said 'Kenya'. But, as often happens at these diplomatic outposts, we gravitated to one another because what we were up to was basically the same, and we ended by comparing notes on this or that after exhausting games of squash. And, as also often happens, I saw Richard again at subsequent times and in subsequent places throughout my foreign service life.

While a second secretary in Nairobi, I was concurrently assigned as vice consul in the Seychelles Islands. This glorious archipelago is located plunk in the middle of the Indian Ocean – 'A Thousand Miles from Nowhere', as the welcoming sign in Victoria said – and at that time was still a British colony. I was given a handsome parchment exequatar signed by Elizabeth Regina which authorized the practice of my consular talents on British territory. The US Air Force ran a satellite-tracking station there, a white geodesic dome that looked like a big golf ball teed up at the top of a green mountain on the principal island of Mahe, and tending to the consular needs of the American staff was my ostensible duty.

The British had also grouped together a number of scattered outlying islands, largely uninhabited, which they called the British Indian Ocean Territory, and the Americans had plans to develop a naval staging post and airstrip on a spit of sand named Diego Garcia. Years later, after the Soviets invaded Afghanistan, these plans were rapidly put into play in order to gird the Western position in the Persian Gulf. At the time, however, the blueprints were not much more than military doodles. Still, BIOT was my first brush with broad strategic co-operation between the United Kingdom and the United States. The British had the real estate and the Americans had the things to park on it. This huge quadrant of the Indian Ocean was a classic power vacuum, and both the British and Americans tried to maintain a minimum presence with a minimum of fuss. In the 1991 Gulf War, Diego Garcia finally proved its worth.

The Seychelles then was virtually inaccessible. There was no airport. Tramp steamers plying to and from Bombay occasionally called at Victoria. Because of the tracking station, however, the Air Force kept a government contract with Pan American for weekly flights to Mahe on an old HU-16 seaplane based in Mombasa. It carried mail, electronic parts, technicians on rotation and, once a quarter, the American vice consul. After six droning hours, the plane splashed down in Victoria's small harbour, where it discharged its few supplies and passengers and then returned to Mombasa at dawn the next morning. If you missed the next morning's departure, you stayed in the Seychelles until the following week. I always managed to miss it.

My consular duties mostly consisted of issuing birth certificates to babies born of liaisons between the tracking station technicians and the nubile women of the islands. The Seychelles was a friendly place and there was a lot of consular business. The rest of the time I talked to the British colonial officers, the politicians of the two competing political parties, the Grand Blancs plantation owners, who made their money from copra, cinnamon and patchouli leaves, and the strange assortment of international vagabonds who had pitched up on the islands at one time or another and decided to stay there.

Whenever I went to the Seychelles, I felt I had been cast in a Peter Sellers movie. The Governor lived in a big house with tall shuttered windows and ceiling fans. In the morning he climbed into the back of his Rolls-Royce and was driven fifty yards or so down the driveway to the little sentry box at the entrance to see whether anyone had signed the visitors' book the previous day, and after inspecting the pages, which were usually blank, he drove back up the hill. The formality of Government House was as stifling as the heat: dinner at eight o'clock sharp, always black tie, plenty of barefoot servants in starched white livery, a heavy decanter of port passed clockwise around the table after the ladies had withdrawn, coffee afterwards with designated conversation partners on rattan chairs in the front sitting room, and out the door precisely at ten-thirty on penalty of fifty lashes. All the buttoned-up formality of the British colonial authorities in this sultry island setting seemed like an English lampoon, but the British, I concluded, have a way of making the preposterous seem perfectly normal.

The politics of the Seychelles were equally curious. Everywhere else in the world, populations had been agitating for independence from their colonial masters and sometimes starting wars to achieve it. But in the Seychelles the politics were upside down. The colonial masters wanted to impose independence on the islands and the local politicians were doing everything they could to resist it. The Seychelles was one of the leftovers in Britain's withdrawal from east of Suez, but London had a problem shooing the Seychellois puppy from the imperial lap. The British no longer wanted responsibility for the islands because they had to spend too much money there, which is exactly why the islanders wanted to remain colonials.

These politics did not make much difference to the United States so long as the tracking station on top of the mountain could continue to emit and receive signals from outer space. The political parties naturally thought they could drive a better bargain with the British if they excited the Americans by threatening to close the station. I was regularly reassured by the local leaders that they didn't really mean it, but I learned that even little countries often tried to play off the Americans against the British and vice versa. In the end, the locals relented and accepted the inevitable inconvenience of independence. As a consolation prize, they received an airport from Her Majesty.

After two years in Nairobi, with periodic diversions in the Seychelles, I was assigned to reopen the American consulate in Bukavu, an unhappy town at the southern edge of Lake Kivu in the extreme eastern part of what was then the Congo, next Zaïre and is now the Congo again. The town had been ruined by rebellion, civil war and mercenary invasion ever since Belgium had granted independence to the country almost a decade before. Over the next two years, I managed to have much of the adventure I had once imagined. But even here I learned a thing or two about the British.

The first was this: if there is only one European living in the smallest village in the deepest jungle in the furthest region of a faraway land, he or she is likely to be British. The long-time manager of an isolated cassiterite mine in the central part of Kivu Province was British. One of two White Fathers at the Baraka mission station on Lake Tanganyika was British and he carried an AK-47 wherever he went. A bush pilot who operated a spit-and-string aircraft out of Kindu was British. A Catholic Relief Services nurse, who was the only European woman within a week's march of Kasongo, was British. And, in a more elevated position, the provincial distributor of the magic drink Guinness, which was almost hard currency in Kivu, was also British. All of these people had stayed at their posts through the brutal travails of the Congo. They were tough-minded, a little idiosyncratic and very individualistic.

So I learned that the British always turn up in the damnedest places. They are congenital explorers. In later years I called this characteristic the Quantum Theory of English Empiricism, which postulates that nothing really exists unless an Englishman has seen it. The British explore things because the things are there to be explored. If someone has climbed to the craggy top of a high mountain or sailed solo across a treacherous sea or trekked the frozen wastes to one of the poles, it is almost surely a Brit.*

The second observation I formed about the British when I lived in the Congo was that they are very good at running things, at least other people's things if not necessarily their own. This had not occurred to me when I lived in Nairobi, but once I was in the Congo the contrast between the relative order and stability of post-colonial Kenya and the sad self-destruction and backwardness of post-colonial Congo was sharp.

Shortly after arriving in Bukavu, I went back to Nairobi to pick up a Land Rover which I needed for my new duties. I drove out of town on the smooth highway that runs across the Rift Valley, and somewhere near Eldoret I was waved down by a Kenyan policeman for a minor traffic violation. The policeman was dressed in a uniform so crisply pressed that it looked like cardboard. He stepped from his car, and as he approached my Land Rover he suddenly halted, stomped his polished boots against the macadam and stiffened ramrod straight into a quivering salute. He begged my pardon for detaining me, pointed out the error of my vehicular ways and wished me a pleasant journey.

Two days later I was slogging along a broken road from Goma to Bukavu on the western escarpment of Lake Kivu. The surface of the road had long since lost its asphalt except for a few jagged chunks, and it hadn't seen a grader in years. The Land Rover lurched and squirmed through mud holes four feet deep. As I slipped into a bend in the road, another mud-splattered Land Rover suddenly appeared coming in the opposite direction. It also slithered to a halt so that the two vehicles faced each other only a few feet apart. After a moment, the passenger door of the oncoming Land Rover was flung open. Three or four empty beer bottles fell into the muck. Clinging to the door for support, a provincial policeman

---

* The British compulsion to explore fascinated me during my Africa years, and I read a lot about the nineteenth-century adventurers who tried to map the Dark Continent. I sometimes pictured myself lying feverish under a canvas tent, the mosquito netting slightly parted, and muttering, 'You must go on without me,' which, regrettably, the British would do.

of the Congolese government heaved himself out. His tan uniform was wrinkled and stained, his belly hung over his belt, his black sunglasses were askew and he held a pistol in his right hand. He weaved towards me, stumbling a couple of times in the mud, and in a mix of French and Swahili berated me for driving on the wrong side of a one-track road, all the while waving the gun over his head. After a few more moments of invective, he spun around and fired a shot at the lake. I was pretty sure this man had not attended a British police academy.

In the summer of 1972, I returned to Washington where I joined the Secretariat Staff of the Department of State, eventually becoming its director. I carried Henry Kissinger's luggage on his Middle Eastern shuttles, and during the oil embargo and Kissinger's ill-fated 'Year of Europe' I was more and more pulled into the swirl of European affairs and Alliance politics. In this period, too, the American position in Vietnam collapsed and Richard Nixon resigned the presidency. Washington was a turbulent place, full of dramatic events and political agony.

One evening in the spring of 1975 I received a telephone call from a foreign service friend who had recently gone to the embassy in London. He said there was a position opening unexpectedly in the political section, and if I moved quickly it could all be stitched up in a matter of days. The only problem was that the slot called for an expert in African affairs.

We both agreed with the maxim that an expert is somebody a long way from home, but I wasn't certain I wanted to be considered an Africa expert even if I knew I wasn't one. The political counsellor at the embassy also telephoned, and he assured me my portfolio could be jiggered to include some other responsibilities, for example following the fortunes of the Conservative Party. My background in tribal politics, he said, would come in handy. I thought it over briefly. There were no other interesting assignments on the horizon, I said to myself, and London was supposed to be a civilized place. I decided to go and the paperwork started to flow.

A couple of months later I began my first assignment to the United Kingdom. By chance, my foreign and domestic duties neatly dovetailed because African issues, especially Rhodesia/Zimbabwe, embroiled both the Labour government and the Tory opposition, and caused a lot of friction between London and Washington as well. So as a junior diplomat I ended up hobnobbing with a lot of bigwigs in the different camps. But when I departed Britain shortly after the Conservative election victory in 1979, I did not expect to return.

Another jumble of coincidences, however, brought me back in 1984, this time as minister, which was the most senior position for a career diplomat at the embassy. The Reagan–Thatcher partnership reached its zenith during the five years that followed, and the first signs that the Cold War was unravelling also appeared. Just before leaving to return to Washington in the summer of 1989, Caroline asked me whether I thought we would ever come back. We were walking along a shady pathway near Sonning, and the delectable countryside billowed up around us. It was one of those warm, blue English days when an invisible hand seems to squeeze your heart. 'Oh, no,' I answered. 'That's impossible. There's only one job left at the embassy, and the ambassador is always a political appointment.' I shook my head. 'Impossible.'

Extraordinary and Plenipotentiary

In an old market square near the centre of Brussels there is a bar called the St Jean. It is a modest establishment with a few tables arranged around a plank floor and a long brass-topped counter running the width of the room. There is nothing exceptional about the St Jean, and I'm not sure I could find it again if I tried. But I had just completed two days of tedious discussions at NATO Headquarters on the subject of short-range nuclear missiles in post-Cold War Europe, and I happened to repair to this tranquil haven one drizzling Friday evening at the end of February 1991, feeling in need of a few short-range missiles myself.

At the time, I was the Assistant Secretary of State for European Affairs, a job I had held since returning to Washington at the beginning of President Bush's administration. The following two years had been a diplomatic roller-coaster. After decades of Cold War, Europe changed from a divided, impacted continent of permanent tension into a free-flowing geography in which all the old givens were tossed out the window. In Washington you could almost hear the pages of history turning.

During this remarkable European chronicle I was a regular journeyman to Brussels. Sometimes I went there to talk to the European Commission but more often my purpose was to consult with the permanent representatives of the NATO allies who regularly gathered around their circular conference table at the Alliance Headquarters in Evere on the outskirts of the city. It was in the guest house of the American ambassador to NATO that I watched the extraordinary television pictures of young Germans dancing on top of the Berlin Wall.

On this particular February evening, I was in the company of good friends. Will Taft, the former Deputy Secretary of Defense and then the American ambassador to NATO, and Julia Taft, a tireless expert in refugee affairs, had chosen the St Jean as a suitable place for a plate of moules and a bottle of wine. We looked forward to a Friday night of relaxed conversation before I returned to Washington the next morning.

As we arrived at the St Jean, I was handed a message at the door: 'Call the Secretary of State in Washington right away.' While the Tafts found a place for us to sit, I made my way to the telephone at the bar. I was pretty sure I knew what Jim Baker wanted. He would probably instruct me to extend my trip in Europe and go on to Lithuania, Latvia and Estonia. This little gesture would be taken as a sign of support for those tentative regimes still nervous in the Soviet shadow. We had discussed the possibility before I left on my NATO trip, but I thought the idea had gone cold.

I did not want to go to see the Balts. It would mean two or three more days on the winter road. But I nonetheless started formulating an itinerary in my head: fly to Frankfurt or maybe Helsinki, find something to Tallinn, then overland to Vilnius and Riga, or some such combination. I would have to plan carefully because I could never remember which city was the capital of which country. I also started to rehearse the words I would use to explain to Caroline that I would miss yet another weekend at home, and I worried about how I could get my laundry washed at short notice. Over the last two years, I had learned a lot about excuses and dirty shirts.

The White House is proud of its telephone system. The network is called White House Switch or White House Signal, and a White House telephone installed in your home in the Washington suburbs is among the most prestigious power badges in the city. To be interrupted at a Washington dinner party by a call from White

House Switch is a social coup. The system is manned by young army specialists who punctuate their sentences with the word 'sir'. They can find you anywhere, as they proved that night.

The bartender insisted on placing the call himself. There were a couple of false starts. White House Switch, confused by a French-speaking bartender at the other end of the line, twice called back to verify the number. Eventually, Secretary Baker came on the line. He was calling from a small outer room next to the Oval Office, but this was not unusual because Baker spent as much time at the White House as he did at the State Department. It was one reason why he was such an effective Secretary of State.

We exchanged some words about my NATO talks before Baker shifted the subject. 'I wanted to let you know that President Bush is going to call you,' he said. 'The President is going to ask you to be his ambassador to the Court of St James's.' There was a pause as Baker let me absorb this information. In a response falling well short of the moment, I said, 'You mean the one in London?' This clarification was not entirely misplaced. Misunderstandings are common in the diplomatic game. There is an apocryphal story in Foggy Bottom lore of President Reagan making an ambassadorial telephone call to a political appointee who later showed up in Washington with his skis thinking the President had appointed him to Switzerland instead of Swaziland. Stunned as I was, I wanted to be sure I got it right.

Baker said I should consider the matter carefully. I asked how long it would be before the President called. 'Five minutes,' he replied. I put down the phone. I asked the bartender if I could call my wife in Washington. Caroline, I thought, was not going to like this. She wouldn't oppose the idea of returning to London. She was as fond of the place as I was. But she would resist the ways of Washington that demanded an instantaneous decision about something so important and so personally disruptive. I, on the other hand, knew that the ways of Washington meant the President's decision could unravel as quickly as it had been taken. This was no time to dawdle. When Caroline answered the phone, I blurted out the conversation with Baker. There was silence at the other end of the line. 'When the President calls,' I shouted over the din of the bar room, 'I'm going to say yes.' More silence. My consultations complete, I hung up.

White House Switch rang the bar two more times to be sure of the number. The bartender was increasingly alarmed. Finally, I was speaking to the President. In his matter-of-fact way, he explained that Henry Catto, the current ambassador in London, was returning to Washington to take up the directorship of the United States Information Agency. With Europe changing so rapidly, he said, and with a new prime minister in Britain, it would be good to have someone in London who was familiar with the issues and the personalities. Would I go there as ambassador? Bush said only a handful of people were aware of his call to me. We should keep the proposal under wraps until things were ready for a proper announcement, but he hoped I would take the job. I said I did not need any time to make up my mind and would be pleased to go to London as his ambassador. I added several grovelling expressions of dedication and gratitude. The conversation was over. The only person in the bar more astonished than I was the bartender.

Since the beginning of relations between the United States and the United Kingdom, the position of American ambassador to the Court of St James's had never been awarded to a career diplomat. Even Paris and Rome at one time or another have fallen into the hands of a professional, but the London embassy remained unassailable for more than 200 years. So established was this exclusive political preserve that the prospect that I might one day present my diplomatic credentials to the Queen never crept into my most ambitious fantasies. I judged the likelihood of my becoming ambassador to the United Kingdom on a par with an invitation to conduct the San Francisco Symphony or to represent the United States in the pole vault.

The usual way of selecting American envoys to go overseas is a curious process, full of politics, chance and mishaps. Most foreign governments find it hard to comprehend how Washington can be so quixotic in choosing its representatives abroad. A career foreign service, trained and experienced, would seem the natural pool from which to draw the guardians of the nation's interests in foreign lands, but it has never worked that way. Each new administration starts off with earnest pronouncements of its intention to select only the best-qualified individuals for these diplomatic positions before succumbing to the pressures that are ingrained in our political history. Andrew Jackson was the first President to bring political zeal to ambassadorial appointments, and it has remained that way, more or less, ever since.

Patronage is as old as politics. If America had developed a system of honorific titles, the way the British have, things might have been different. Lord Smith of Milwaukee or Lord Jones of Wichita could have sufficed as rewards for political service. But, as it is, the title of ambassador is one of the few prestigious ranks which a president can confer, and for a country which is short on political glamour and which customarily regards foreign affairs as a nuisance, passing out these titles is simple enough to do.

When a new administration sweeps triumphantly into Washington, however, selecting ambassadors is only a minor part of a much broader process. A president inherits a colossal structure of federal government. The bureaucracy is a little like The Blob That Ate Chicago. It oozes out from the White House in every direction, down Pennsylvania Avenue and along Constitution Avenue, which are crammed with government offices overseeing a multitude of government programmes. The bureaucratic mass slides across the Potomac to the Virginia bank of the river, and it seeps northwards across the state line into Maryland. And beyond the capital, the federal reach spreads out across the vast nation from Florida to Alaska and Hawaii to Maine. For a country congenitally opposed to government, there's a lot of it. How, a president wonders, can he make this thing work?

One answer is that a new president appoints the people who run it – legions of them. The federal system, with its separation of powers, means that the President doesn't form his government from the elected members of the Congress. The legislature is elected to legislate, not govern. Instead, the President can call on anyone, anywhere – who may never have been elected to anything – to join his administration. In fact, in the whole executive branch, the President and the Vice President are the only elected officials.

The contrast with Britain is striking. When there's a change of party in Whitehall, only the top card in the deck is switched. A handful of elected MPs move into their Cabinet or ministerial positions with barely a ripple, and the line between political office and the civil service is clearly defined and rarely transgressed. Even the civil servants in private offices remain, like the furniture, largely undisturbed. Most of the MPs, after years in the House of Commons, already know the ropes and are usually familiar with their portfolios. A change of government in Whitehall is an intimate affair, and what you see is what you get. The limited number of round pegs and round holes can be a political challenge for a prime minister, but the bureaucratic effect is unruffled continuity. The British ship of state carries a lot of ballast.

Not so in America. An American president always sinks his roots much deeper into the bureaucratic soil, and a new administration comes together in a frenzy of office-seeking and office-conferring. Theoretically, the President can call on the best and brightest in the land. And sometimes he does. But, if the President has to choose between ability and loyalty, there's seldom a contest.

The jostling and jockeying for government jobs are intense. The self-promotion is often shameless. Washington abounds with rumours. There are long lists and short lists, supporters and detractors, trial balloons and whispered phone calls late at night. This is all known as Potomac Fever, and as a new administration comes together it reaches epidemic proportions. It is a fraught business, and normal government is disrupted for months.

Some 3,000 jobs are annotated in Washington's notorious Plum Book, a compilation of juicy positions ripe for picking. There are Cabinet secretaries, deputy secretaries, under secretaries, assistant secretaries, assistants to secretaries and secretaries to secretaries; and there are agency heads, bureau chiefs, administrators, chairmen, directors and counsellors, and members of commissions, councils, regulatory bodies and advisory boards. And ambassadors to faraway and strange lands. From this constellation of appointments a new president creates his firmament of power.

The critical decision-makers at the outset are the thick-and-thin coterie of confidants who have seen the new President through the long, gruelling process of winning office. They set the tone. And the tone is relentlessly political. Often from the President's home state – Georgia or California or Arkansas – they are his anchor in the Washington cross-currents. But it is almost impossible for these election-hardened advisers to shift gear once the campaigning has stopped and the governing begins. They are, after all, the ones who gathered around the new President in his initial obscurity, stimulated him in his early ambitions, advised him in his tactics, encouraged him in his successes, coached him after his mistakes, consoled him in his disappointments and stood with him in the cold of New Hampshire and the heat of Nebraska. They know his secrets. They are political to the bone. They keep the ledgers of owing and being owed, and they control the triumphant new administration's job centre.

I recall the transition from the Ford administration to the Carter administration. The Carter entourage believed that anyone in the State Department who had worked for Henry Kissinger must have the political sensitivity of a Visigoth. It took many months before the new relationships settled down. And then, four years later, the Reaganauts came to town. Anyone who had worked in the Carter administration was regarded as a gooey stick of butter that had been left out in the sun too long. In both transitions, the atmosphere was uneasy and the road bumpy. For a career diplomat, it all goes with the territory, and the further up the career service you rise, the more vulnerable you are to the political storms that blow through Washington after almost every election.

In the heady atmosphere of a new administration, when power and glory are divvied up, most ambassadorial positions seem pretty insignificant. They have little profile in the grander political designs of Washington. Many embassies, after all, lie in inhospitable territory. Career diplomats can count on having the inside track to such destinations as Ndjamena, Dacca and Ulan Bator. As a general rule, only the fruitier posts are up for grabs. A handful of embassies, especially in Western Europe, are assumed almost automatically to be the preserve of political appointees. Perhaps 30 per cent of all American embassies around the world will go to individuals who have had no prior diplomatic experience. But of the important posts, where American interests are substantial, as many as half will go to outsiders. The career service fills the rest.*

In the diplomatic sweepstakes, the influence of the new Secretary of State is tested within his Department partly by how well he

---

* I recall Sir Antony Acland, then the permanent under secretary at the Foreign Office and subsequently ambassador in Washington, telling me one day that all the top jobs in Britain's diplomatic posts were now filled by career diplomats. It was a discouraging bit of news – for me, not for him.

defends the interests of the career foreign service. Any new Secretary will have much bigger things on his mind, but he may be the only personal link between the State Department and the fresh political mass gathering on Pennsylvania Avenue. Even after an administration is well under way, the selection of ambassadors remains contentious. The next election is never far away. When George Shultz was Secretary of State, he was regularly exasperated and often angered by the constant skirmishing and bargaining with the White House Personnel Office. The bickering resembled children trading baseball cards in a playground: 'I'll give you Jordan and Venezuela if you give me Australia.'

I have never objected to the idea of political appointments to ambassadorial jobs. The good ones are very good. David Bruce is perhaps the pre-eminent example of a political appointee who served so well in so many posts, including London, that he became, in effect, a professional statesman. Many other non-career ambassadors have proven their worth in the field. Good political appointees bring insight about the rambling reaches of the American government and experience in dealing with it. They can work confidently with a difficult Congress and their access to the President is often unimpeded. Despite the stories of used-car salesmen and pizza magnates embarking on diplomatic missions, most political appointees try to do a competent job, even if they often appear adrift in unfamiliar seas. Bad political appointees spend most of their time inflating themselves on ambassadorial air or, worse, interpreting their diplomatic appointment as a licence to practise an independent foreign policy of their own concoction. But the genuine fools are rare. When they do come along, however, the American government seems to have a remarkably elastic capacity for embarrassment.*

The most unsavoury part of this peculiar American system is money. Getting elected president is an expensive business, and too often political appointments to ambassadorial positions are merely pay-offs for financial support in the campaign. After an election, political invoices are issued and paid. The White House Personnel Office often seems like a political version of Sotheby's with posts

* The Labour Party has talked about appointing 'businessmen' to diplomatic jobs abroad. They should know better.

auctioned to the highest bidder. The Congress passed a law in 1980 prohibiting any ambassadorial nomination as a reward for campaign contributions, but this has done little to disrupt the connection between money and embassies. Democrats as well as Republicans invest in the same market, and some contributors make sure they bet on both parties. Among President Clinton's first selections, five ambassadors to Western European posts had written campaign cheques which together totalled over a million dollars. Only when money is no longer an imperative in American presidential elections will the system be susceptible to change, and that is likely to be never.

President Bush's decision to send me to London would have been unlikely in the normal circumstances of political Washington. But Bush, midway through his term, was at the height of his popularity, just after the Gulf War, and he had little need to cultivate the margins of favour in the Republican establishment. In the winter of 1991, his re-election was a foregone conclusion. Henry Catto's departure from London was unanticipated, so the customary political pressures for partisan indulgence did not have a chance to envelop the Oval Office, and in any event Bush was serious about foreign policy and had himself twice served as ambassador.

When it comes to secrets about people, Washington leaks like a colander. Word of the appointment was in the *Washington Post* the morning after the Brussels phone call. In the diplomatic world, it is good manners as well as good sense to check with the host government that an ambassador will be happily received at his prospective post before the news is public. This *agrément*, as it is called, is seldom refused, though governments have been known to wince at some of our selections. Bush telephoned John Major about my nomination, and informal approval from Buckingham Palace came back in a few days.

With that step in place, I began the tortuous process of completing the forms which are meant to determine one's suitability to assume the position of American ambassador. This exercise is now so involved and intrusive that it seems like bureaucratic proctoscopy. The FBI investigates your background, tracking down old school-mates and neighbours from the past to unearth any concealed episodes of alcoholism, drug addiction, promiscuity, immorality, criminality or conspiring with darkly suspicious characters. In another set of forms on financial disclosure, every personal asset and debt must be reported. Lawyers from the State Department, the Office of Government Ethics and the Legal Counsel's office in the White House pore over the records in order to identify, as required by law, not only any genuine conflict of interest but the *appearance* of a conflict of interest. In my case, there wasn't much to pore over.

Other questionnaires ask whether you have ever belonged to a club which discriminates in its membership or whether you have ever been annoyed by someone criticizing your drinking. The final confessional form is called 'The Supplement to Standard Form 86', and it asks plaintively, 'Is there anything in your life that could cause embarrassment to you or to the President if publicly known?' And then it says, 'Provide details.' Are you kidding?

The purpose of this microscopic scrutiny is not to assure that a President's choices are strait-laced and virtuous, but to narrow the target area for the Senate and the press once a nomination is public. Senior presidential appointments require confirmation by the full Senate after a review and recommendation by one of its committees. This can prove a treacherous road, particularly when the Senate is in the hands of one party and the White House in the hands of the other. There is always the danger that a presidential nominee, for whatever reason, might be stuck on a senatorial spit for roasting. Bush's nomination of Clarence Thomas to the Supreme Court became a lurid spectacle when considered by the Senate Judiciary Committee, and Clinton's intended nominations of Zoe Baird and Kimba Wood for attorney general turned into the sanctimonious farce of 'nannygate', even though the President's fellow Democrats were in control of the Senate.

Ambassadorial nominations are not often troublesome, but some have foundered in the process. The Senate hearing to confirm my nomination took place in April 1991 in the great, echoing chamber of the Senate Foreign Relations Committee, Senator Joseph Biden, Democrat of Delaware, presiding. Because my father was from Delaware and because I had attended eighth grade in Wilmington, Biden regarded me as a native son of the Blue Rooster State and I did nothing to disabuse him. The Senator was also chairman of the European sub-committee, and, while we seldom agreed, he and I had enjoyed many informal discussions in his office over the previous two years. Biden was ready to be helpful in briskly moving along my nomination so that I could be confirmed before the Queen's State Visit to the United States scheduled for May.

Having spent the previous two years in charge of European policy at the State Department, I expected some questions from the assembled Senators about the liberation of Eastern Europe or the collapse of the Soviet Union or the unification of Germany. But none of this came up. Nor was there much probing of the Anglo-American relationship. Senator Sarbanes, the Democrat from Maryland, asked several teasing questions about why a Republican president, of all people, would choose a career diplomat for a plum post. What unspeakable thing had I done to deserve this? Was I related to Bush? Was there a Yale connection? Had I written any big cheques lately?

Almost all the other senatorial questions dwelt on Northern Ireland. As the interrogation passed around the raised horseshoe dais, each Senator rang the Irish bell. This was all *pro forma* and for the record, the Senators asking the expected Irish questions and getting the expected Irish replies. But it was also a signal that, in the varied breadth of Anglo-American relations, the politics lay in things Irish.

The full Senate voted through my nomination a few days later with no dissenters. One step remained. On 1 May, in the grandiose rooms on the eighth floor of the State Department, Jim Baker conducted my swearing-in ceremony. Caroline held the bible and the chief of protocol administered the oath of office. Customarily, I would not have endorsed such an elaborate ceremony, but this after all was a major event in the history of the career foreign service. London had fallen.

The oath of office is the same formula of words which an American president swears when he is inaugurated or an American soldier when he is enlisted – 'to protect and defend the Constitution of the United States against all enemies, foreign and domestic'. It is a pretty big commitment. At that moment, I became an ambassador extraordinary and plenipotentiary, the former because I was the personal representative of the President and the latter because I possessed full powers to negotiate on behalf of my government. In theory. The reality is far more complicated.

I collected my letters of credence, my presidential commission and an envelope containing formal instructions from the Secretary of State. With my family, I paid a farewell call on President Bush in the Oval Office, and that evening I drank a toast to the bartender at the St Jean.

Time and Again

When I returned to Britain in 1991, it was the third time I had made the transatlantic transfer, and, naturally, the more often I have moved here the easier it is to do. Most Americans make the transition to British ways without too much bother. I suppose the reverse is true as well, though the British usually seem a little more apprehensive before moving to the United States and a little more shell-shocked once they have arrived.

The problem for an American coming to Britain is that most things seem familiar. But this familiarity is deceptive. Deep down, the dimensions which measure the American side of the ocean are different from those which shape the British side, and on the scores of occasions when my aircraft has circled over Heathrow before descending, I have felt inside me an automatic recalibration of my interior dials. I know I am crossing from one psychological zone into another.

Nowadays I barely notice this altered state when it happens. But arriving in Britain is a little like glancing into a curvy mirror at a carnival. The familiar dimensions are subtly distorted. This is especially true of the concept of time, which is elongated, and the concept of space, which is contracted. An outsider takes a while to appreciate this.

The American pop singer Bette Midler once said, 'When it's 3.00 p.m. in New York, it's 1938 in London.' She has a point. Time does seem to slow down when you come to Britain, even though the British control international time from just down the Thames at Greenwich.

Put another way, time is savoured here, like a rich chocolate dissolving on the roof of your mouth. But it's not just the tempo that changes. The British are more conscious of the flow of time – its depth and motion and endlessness – and they enjoy the fullness of time more than most Americans are likely to do. After all, Britain has been around for quite a while, and there is nothing very new under the sun. For the British, real value seems to come with the simple accumulation of time. Old is good. It is tried and proven. It is lasting, and, set against the measure of time, lasting is by itself an achievement worthy of respect.

Time in Britain is prestigious. Even things that are new are supposed to look old. The Houses of Parliament, which aren't much older than the Capitol in Washington, were built to look used and Gothic and ancient. An Italian ambassador once snootily commented to me that the British were in fact pretty recent arrivals in the antiquity game, so I suppose everything is relative. Maybe if you live by the Mediterranean, Britain looks modern. But the chronology is less important than the way a nation regards its past, and the British take their past personally.

The British are attached to each other by their history. They are a people descended. They have no starting date and there has been no real interruption in their history that has snipped the string of national time. Disraeli said that the British, unlike the Americans, could never start over. In Britain the generations are like the seasons: they come and they go in their own natural, fluid rhythm. The English lord in his English manor planted his avenue of English trees knowing their maturity would please later generations and not his own. Things in Britain are held in common, not so much with contemporaries as with those who went before and those who will come afterwards. There is a compact of preservation among British generations which treats time as a vertical phenomenon.

This continuity is the source of a lot of criticism about present-day Britain, not least from the British themselves. Britain is too slow to change, it is said, too mired in its past and too mesmerized by it. The nation can't take a step forward without looking over its shoulder. Stuck in its ways and arthritic in its habits, the Kingdom is overloaded with oldness. With so much past the British don't like to take chances with the future.

I suppose these criticisms are valid, though Britain's enchantment with its own past is what beguiles so many Americans. Henry James noted that the sheer oldness of Britain was liable to give Americans an 'aesthetic headache'. Caroline and I frequently suffered this syndrome.*

If time in Britain is vertical, time in America is horizontal. It spreads out sideways, and what came before and what will come afterwards are somebody else's business. In America each generation believes in its own uniqueness. The past is detachable. In fact, for most Americans, all history is ancient history, and the best thing about the past is that it's over. In America, there seems to be a nervy confidence that time is divided into chunks, and each piece is separate and different and belongs to you. Time isn't a compact the way it is in Britain; it's a temporal contract that can be renegotiated. Tomorrow's another day.

And just as the British adore what is old, Americans delight in what is new. New suggests change, and we like change not because it is necessarily better but just because it is new. America is, after all, the New World, a planet away from the past. We called places New York and New England, New Orleans and New Mexico, and our politicians have always promised a fresh beginning – a New Freedom, a New Deal, a New Frontier, a New World Order. In America, a new idea can always get an even break, and as Disraeli observed, you can always start over.

Because Americans fancy what is new, we also come in for a lot of criticism. We are often neglectful of the past, it is said, and can therefore seem untutored or naive. We sometimes seem a little reckless. And it is true that we are preoccupied by speed and self-improvement and instant reward. We often disparage what is old, especially the growing of it. Still, these characteristics which treat

* On the other hand, John Ruskin refused to go to the United States, he said, precisely for aesthetic reasons.

time as a vexation also make Americans original and willing to try new things, and I think this sense of edgy liberation is what excites the British about America.

So, if all the world's a stage, America is a one-act play, and the idea is that you perform the role you write yourself. Britain, on the other hand, is a saga, and you play the scene as it was written long ago.

The other dimension that distinguishes one country from the other is space. This is obvious to say. But it is different to feel. America rolls out in front of you. Britain closes in around you.

The vastness of America is hard for a British visitor to comprehend. The horizons seem infinitely expandable. When I fly over the country, especially the West, I look down in fascination at the stunning magnitude of the place. And when I think of pioneers in wagon trains toiling across the dry, rough prairies, I wonder how they did it and where they thought they were headed. America is big. Britain could comfortably fit inside a dozen different states with plenty of elbow room. Oregon alone is a little larger than all of Britain, and more than thirty-eight United Kingdoms could fit inside our national borders. America is a voluptuous country of volume.

A British friend once asked for my help in plotting his first trip to the United States. He had a whole week to spend there, he said, and he planned to rent a car in Boston, spend a day each in New York and Philadelphia, stop by Washington and then head south for a couple of days in Disney World and the beaches of Florida. His question was whether I thought he had enough time to visit the Grand Old Opry in Nashville, Tennessee. Even with a map in his hands, he could not comprehend the immensity of the country and the distance between points.

Gertrude Stein said: 'In the United States, there is more space where nobody is than where anybody is.' We are a loose society and a sprawling one. We can fill up the room around us with little regard for wasted space because there is always more of it. And so we are not rooted down nor are we particularly attached to place. Americans are always movin' on, metaphorically as well as physically. Our houses are free-standing, our population is free-floating and our attitude is free-wheeling.

Scale is important to Americans – the bigger the better. In the land of the Big Apple, the Big Mac, the big shot, the big sky and big bucks, we like talking big, thinking big and making it big. America is a big deal, a country of exaggeration, hyperbole and superlatives: the tallest, the longest, the deepest, the fastest. One of our mythical heroes is Paul Bunyon, the giant logger who stood higher than the forests of the Midwest. And Mount Rushmore in South Dakota, with its gigantic sculptures of four past presidents carved colossally into its stony face, would be hard to imagine in the Lake District. In America, the sky's the limit.

On the other hand, you can't swing a cat in Britain without knocking something over. An American in this country is always struck by how small and jammed up it is. Nothing is ever far away. Practically the first sign you see when you drive into a British town is the direction to the nearest crematorium. There's hardly enough room for the living.

Britain is more densely populated per square mile than China and about the same as India, and this human concentration increases sharply as you approach London and the south-east. The Empire must have been a kind of *Lebensraum* for the British, and I have sometimes wondered what the United Kingdom would have been like if all those colonial settlers who sailed the seas had instead stayed home and multiplied.

Arranging large numbers of people in a small amount of space requires delicate balances and well-defined conventions of behaviour. The famous British reserve, the closely guarded privacy, the complex of unspoken rules, the orderliness of everyday life are the natural features of a crowded society thrown upon itself. There is a good reason for lace curtains in British windows.

The British also seem bewitched by things in miniature. Antique stalls up and down the country are a clutter of Victorian miniatures – little things that fit into each other, and little silver boxes and little golden lockets, and piles of tiny bibelots, whatnots, doodads and thingamajigs. Queen Mary's doll's house in Windsor is a famous example of reduced ratios. Craftsmen used to make little cabinets and print little bibles, and artists painted miniature portraits. And British fantasy is inhabited by elves, fairies and pixies.

Because there isn't much space to spread out, things in Britain seem to cluster together. Britain is a nestling nation, a molecular place. Society operates in small, compartmentalized units, each fixing its spatial relationship with the other. I was once told that if I really wanted to understand Britain, I should study the façade of one of its great cathedrals, such as Wells or Lincoln, where everything is arranged in intricate patterns and ascending registers, each harmonizing with the other. And it is so.

When you look around in Britain, you find rank on rank of terraced houses fitted together in orderly uniformity. London is made up of narrow buildings arranged around little garden squares. The countryside is dotted with little villages, often only a mile or so apart, with little churches and little pubs and little houses with little doors behind little walls. The British army is subdivided into small, compact regiments that operate like building blocks, and ancient British universities are decentralized confederations of small, autonomous colleges. Barristers in England divide neatly into four Inns of Court, and politicians in the House of Commons represent 659 little constituencies. A profusion of small, professional football clubs move up and down the league tables, and there used to be almost a hundred separate trade unions in Britain. There are still about a hundred livery companies in the City of London and close to a hundred cosy clubs in the West End. All of this could be etched on the west face of Westminster Abbey.

So, whenever I leave the United States and arrive in the United Kingdom, I try to remember this: in Britain, there is a lot of time crammed into a little space.

Rank and File

Grosvenor Square has been the heart of the American community in London for many years. The Square was first laid out in 1725 when the metropolis was slowly expanding westwards. The gardens then were oval-shaped. A statue of the new Hanoverian king, George I, mounted on a great horse and swathed in Roman robes, was erected in the middle of the parterres by Sir Thomas Grosvenor, scion of the great landowning family whose descendants became the Dukes of Westminster. The statue was so damaged during the Jacobite disturbances twenty years later that it was removed. Even then, the English gave the Germans a hard time.

When John Adams arrived in London as the first American envoy to the Court of St James's, he took a house at the corner of Duke Street, where Grosvenor Square gives into Brook Street. It cost him £160 a year to rent. The house is still there, and it's the only original building left standing in the Square.

For the next century or so, American embassies and American ambassadors led itinerant lives, shifting from one location to another around central London. It was not until Walter Hines Page arrived, just before the First World War, and found the embassy headquarters in Victoria Street in deplorable condition, that America's diplomatic establishment returned to Grosvenor Square, this time to a hand-some Georgian-style building on the east side which now houses the Canadian High Commission.

In the decades afterwards, Grosvenor Square gradually developed the character of Little America. The American Club, the American Society, the American Chamber of Commerce were all located near by. The Society of American Women, founded by Jenny Jerome (Winston Churchill's mother) and Nancy Astor (the first woman Member of Parliament), worked out of a room next to the embassy. Maude Burke, the American who became Lady Cunard and one of London's most shimmering and fearsome hostesses in the inter-war years, asked that her ashes be spread in Grosvenor Square, which is one reason the grass is so green.

The serious Americanization of the Square occurred after the United States entered the Second World War. General Eisenhower made his headquarters on the north side of the Square, where the US Navy building is today. During the war, there were so many American servicemen in the vicinity that Londoners called the Square 'Eisenhowerplatz'. The American Church was located in North Audley Street and the Grosvenor Chapel, in South Audley Street, became the church of the American armed forces. A lot of Yanks married a lot of Brits in both places.

The American flavour of Grosvenor Square remains. On one side there is a statue of Franklin Delano Roosevelt standing erect with his famous cloak hanging in folds from his shoulders. A little plaza is laid out in front. Across the way is a memorial to the American Eagle squadrons who fought in the Battle of Britain, and beyond this, where the park exits to Grosvenor Street, is a bronze disc set in the pavement to commemorate the bicentennial of the Treaty of Paris which brought peace if not harmony to the Anglo-American relationship. On the west shoulder of the Square stands a statue of Eisenhower, donated by the people of his home state, Kansas, who were cajoled into making the gift by Charlie Price when he was ambassador.*

---

* Between the United States and the United Kingdom, there is a serious statue gap. In London alone there are statues to Washington, Lincoln, Roosevelt, Eisenhower and Kennedy. Winston Churchill looks across Massachusetts Avenue, in front of the British embassy in Washington, but I've never seen a statue of any other prime minister, and certainly not of a British king.

In 1960, the American embassy moved across the Square and into a new building which most Londoners still think resembles a multistorey carpark. On the top of the embassy, overlooking the treeline of the Square, is a gigantic gilded eagle measuring thirty-five feet from wing-tip to wing-tip. One MP, with the usual British penchant for understatement, called the bird a 'blatant monstrosity'. The building was designed by Eero Saarinen, and though the fretwork of anodized aluminium on the façade was meant to harmonize with the rest of the Square, it doesn't quite make the grade. Still, with the passage of time, I think the character of the building holds up much better than the eyesores which British architects regularly inflicted on the city in the same period. The United States doesn't own the land on which the embassy sits. The Duke of Westminster does, and the American Government pays His Grace one peppercorn per year. It seems likely Americans will remain around Grosvenor Square for a long time – the lease runs until Christmas Day, 2953.

On the ground floor of the embassy is an airy white atrium. There is also a low fountain into which visitors from time to time accidentally step. Carved on to the face of one wall is a gold-leaf list of the envoys who have represented the United States since the beginning of the official relationship. Over the years, the embassy has also assembled a collection of portraits of all ambassadors departed, and it has become traditional that an ambassador leaves behind a painting as a gift to the embassy. These too hang in the atrium. One evening, a few days after my arrival in London, I wandered through the atrium to read the roll of names and examine the gallery of portraits. I counted that I was the fifty-fifth ambassador,* and I concluded I had slipped in the back door of a pretty distinguished club.

The picture gallery makes up a stern crowd. Only Ann Armstrong's portrait lightens the masculine load. In recent years a few ambassadors have come from the hinterland of the United States, but the overwhelming majority represents America's East Coast

---

* American envoys to Britain were called 'minister' until 1893, and 'ambassador' thereafter. It was one of the little signals that relations were improving. For the purposes of this book, however, I have used the title 'ambassador' for all of them.

establishment. Fourteen predecessors came from Massachusetts alone (most people would not regard Massachusetts as a mirror of America; Jim Baker, of Texas, before he became secretary of state, was once asked if he had ever visited a communist country. 'No,' he replied, 'but I've been to Massachusetts'). Twenty-four ambassadors attended Harvard, Yale or Princeton, so almost half absorbed their higher learning at the Big Three Ivy League schools. More than half were trained as lawyers.

Five of the early envoys went on to become president of the United States. But London has not served as a catapult to the presidency since before the Civil War. John Davis, who held the post just after the First World War, ran as the Democratic nominee against Herbert Hoover in 1928. He was trounced. Joseph Kennedy barely disguised his aspirations for the White House, but his indiscretions while ambassador in London on the eve of the Second World War stewed his chances. He fell back to pursuing his ambitions vicariously through his sons. Either on the way to London or on the way back, four envoys served as vice president and ten as secretary of state.

Through the nineteenth century, many ambassadors saw their appointments as interludes in their political careers, most of them having held elective office of one kind or another. By the turn of the century, however, presidents began to draw from a wider if not deeper pool of individuals who had succeeded in other walks of life such as business or banking. Whitelaw Reid, Alanson Houghton, Andrew Mellon, Winthrop Aldrich, John Hay Whitney and Walter Annenberg read like a tycoons' Hall of Fame. If money talks, it can be very persuasive in Washington and downright eloquent in London, as in most places. Ambassador Annenberg donated the indoor swimming pool at the Prime Minister's official country home at Chequers (before departing my job, I reminded John Major of this and offered him a set of darts. He declined).

No American ambassador has ever been expelled from Great Britain. This would be an unremarkable record except that the reverse is not true. In this particular diplomatic game, usually played in tit-for-tat fashion, the Americans are currently winning by two goals. One British envoy was expelled from Washington for recruiting American citizens to fight in the British army during the Crimean War. The other was publicly trapped into endorsing Grover

Cleveland and the Democratic Party in the election of 1888.

Most American ambassadors would have found it hard to get expelled in nineteenth-century Britain because Her Majesty's Government usually treated them with indifference. In Washington, on the other hand, few opportunities were passed up to twist the tail of the British lion. The British were suspected of lurking behind every political rock, and they usually were. Nonetheless, there is an unbreachable rule of diplomacy that one country does not interfere in the internal affairs of another; and the corollary is that, if you do, you better not get caught.

Two American ambassadors served twice in London, a fact which makes optimists out of almost all of their departing successors. And in a rare American salute to hereditary competence, John Adams, John Quincy Adams and Charles Francis Adams – father, son and grandson – all came to London as ambassadors. In this century the post received its greatest infusion of dignity from Averell Harriman, who served in London for a shorter time than any of his predecessors, and David Bruce, who stayed longer than anyone else.

There have been a couple of notable strays in the ambassadorial fold, both of whom came to London when Ulysses S. Grant was president. One was a handsome Bostonian named John Motley, who never quite understood that he was expected to illuminate the opinions of the Grant administration instead of his own. Eventually ordered to return to Washington, Motley refused to step down and continued to press his own erratic views in the dwindling number of London salons where he was welcome. He left the embassy only on the day of his successor's arrival, and he never did go back to the United States. Instead he roamed around England for another six years until his death. He is buried in Kensal Green. Motley stands out among American ambassadors to the Court of St James's for having been considered *persona non grata* by both governments.

The other maverick was Robert Schenck, who may have made the most enduring contribution to the Anglo-American relationship. He despatched no reports or cables to Washington nor could he have been less interested in the great events of the day. Instead he was an acknowledged authority on the subject of draw poker and an accomplished practitioner of the game. The whist tables of London were cleared as the British, always a gambling race, learned a new way to lose their money. Schenck's tenure came to an abrupt end in a welter of financial scandals so characteristic of the Grant administration and he returned to the United States to find a good lawyer.

My predecessors had a few things in common to pass on – the dangers of chronic Anglophilia, for example, or Ireland, which has been a thorn in the side of the relationship almost from the beginning. Another recurring theme was the matter of money, either the lack of it or the abundance of it. The US Congress has always been stingy in appropriating funds for our embassies. It's not a popular way to spend the taxpayers' dollars, so ambassadors are often left to their own devices.

John Adams was discouraged that he didn't have the resources to cut a diplomatic swath in Court society. He found his relative penury humiliating. The expectations, he said, were simply too great to fulfil in a country where ceremony and substance were two sides of the same coin. Thomas Pinckney of South Carolina also complained about the meagre funds. 'I have in fact', he wrote home, 'been a constant and progressive loser, and at length am incapable of supplying the deficiencies of the public allowance.' James Buchanan found his expenses so great that he kept his bills as 'curiosities', and Edward Pierrepont packed up and went home.

The cure for this generic problem has been to circumvent the parsimonious Congress and instead appoint big men with deep pockets. There was none grander than Whitelaw Reid. Long covetous of the post, Reid was the embodiment of Teddy Roosevelt's bullishness as well as the new wealth and vigour of the United States. He had accumulated a fortune as the proprietor of the *New York Herald* and was perhaps the foremost of the great newspaper magnates such as Hearst, Pulitzer and Bennett who founded communications empires at the close of the nineteenth century. Reid arrived in London in the spring of 1905, shortly after Roosevelt's inauguration. He took over the great marble halls and panelled rooms of Dorchester House in Park Lane, where the Dorchester Hotel now stands, and in these sumptuous surroundings he entertained London society for seven lavish years. So great was his prestige that when he died in London – the only American envoy to expire with his ambassadorial boots on – His Majesty's Government assigned HMS *Natal* the stately mission of carrying the remains back to the United States.

Over the following years, there have been a few ambassadors without private means. Elliott Richardson, on arriving in London in 1975, informed London society that, when the money ran out, so would the drinks. When my appointment was announced, the British press fell on the question of how a career public servant could possibly manage the financial demands, a thought which had also crossed my mind. After all, Charlie Price, my gregarious predecessor but one, had already confessed publicly that his five years as ambassador had cost him at least $300,000 in unreimbursed official expenses. My own diplomatic indigence did turn out to be a struggle, but I was consoled by recalling the British saying in the Second World War that the Americans were 'over-paid, over-sexed and over here', and I said to myself that, in my case, two out of three wasn't bad.

Another thread in the ambassadorial fabric concerns dress. In 1855 Secretary of State Marcy sent a message to all America's envoys overseas directing them to appear at Court 'in the simple dress of an American citizen'. Marcy was trying to control a controversial issue that harassed American ambassadors in London well into this century. The United States was a stripped-down revolutionary republic and Americans should not appear to be something which they were not. For American politicians, it was almost subversive to have a representative in London publicly aping the sartorial conceits of an effete aristocracy.

James Monroe, already a reluctant envoy to London, quickly soured on the British after a run of snubs about his apparel. He spent as much time out of London as he could, taking a house in Cheltenham in order to avoid the ceremonies of Court. When he did attend the occasional levee, he did so conspicuously in the garb of democratic virtue. Most of Monroe's successors, however, were less ardent about their republican wardrobes.

George Bancroft, the historian and literary Anglophobe, was sent to London by President Polk because he was supposed to be 'flattery-proof', as Polk put it, but no sooner had Bancroft stepped off the boat than he stepped into silk stockings. James Buchanan had to negotiate his Court dress with the Master of Ceremonies at the Palace. So sensitive did the apparel issue become in American politics that the Congress got into the act and passed a resolution in 1867 requiring that America's representatives abroad should be characterized by plain dress as well as plain talk. A generation later, the elegant Ambassador Choate called this preoccupation with sartorial simplicity 'the most impertinent piece of swagger in the world'. Whitelaw Reid would have none of it either, and he paid as meticulous attention to wearing the right clothes on the right occasion as did the famously fastidious King Edward VII, with whom he was friends. Even Joe Kennedy fastened silver buckles to his shoes.

Edward Everett, the scholarly editor of the *North American Review*, came to London as ambassador in 1841, and he defended the extravagance of his outfits on the ground that others at the Court wore 'much fancier' dress, a view with which I came to sympathize. Standing at a diplomatic reception in Buckingham Palace, done up in my best finery, was a deflating experience. Surrounded by my fellow ambassadors in gold-braided diplomatic uniforms, all festooned with brilliant sashes across their fronts and glittery decorations the size of hub caps (the smaller the country, the bigger the medals), I felt pretty plain. I always attended these functions with a quiet apprehension that someone would mistake me for a footman and ask me to fetch him a drink.*

Another link which bound together these eminent emissaries was the British frustration with the independence of the American legislature. In Britain, the House of Commons does pretty much what the government tells it to do. But in America Congress has its own head. The nineteenth century is littered with treaties negotiated by an ambassador in London and subsequently rejected by the Senate in Washington.

In 1794 Thomas Pinckney and John Jay reached an agreement with the British government intended to smooth over some of the issues still unsettled after the American War of Independence. In those days both parties to an agreement always signed two originals, each to be sent home in a separate ship. Somehow, both copies of the Jay Treaty ended up on the same boat,

---

* James Buchanan had the same worry. He wore a sword to Court events in order to appear a little more up-market than the Palace staff.

which then sank in the crossing. So the agreement seemed doomed from the start. When a duplicate finally reached the United States, it was immediately denounced as a sell-out to the British and it died in the Senate. Major treaties with the British were similarly rejected in 1811, 1824, 1857 and 1910, usually on the principle that, if an American official could reach agreement with the British, there must be something wrong with the bargain. John Jay lamented, 'Such were the prejudices of the American people that no man could form a treaty with Great Britain, however advantageous it might be to the country.'

While not a bilateral treaty, the Versailles accords ending the First World War were also voted down by the Senate, which wanted nothing more to do with Europe in general and Britain in particular. When I was at the embassy in the 1980s, the Senate only narrowly approved an amendment to the Anglo-American extradition treaty, and in the 1990s the Congress passed resolutions and laws about Bosnia and Cuba which were contrary to the President's policy and frustrating for the British. The independent role of the US Congress means that an ambassador can represent his president but not necessarily his government.

Most of these former ambassadors would barely recognize the operation of today's embassy in Grosvenor Square. Until the Second World War, the embassy here was largely a man-and-a-dog establishment (some of the dogs were distinguished in their own right: Washington Irving was a secretary in the 1840s, Henry Adams assisted his father in the 1860s, and John Kennedy briefly worked for his father in 1939). The London embassy now is less like a traditional diplomatic post and more like a branch office of the federal government. Almost thirty departments or agencies shelter under the embassy umbrella, and one of the ambassador's jobs is to keep them from bumping into each other. It's hard to track what they're all up to.

In any given year, the cables going back and forth between London and Washington stack up to about one million pages. In the old days, a visa application was a major event requiring considerable deliberation, but now the embassy stamps out more than a 150,000 a year, and the visa queue still stretches around the block.* If nothing else, these figures demonstrate the modern density of Anglo-American relations.

If I were asked to officiate at an awards ceremony for all my predecessors, I would hand out the following prizes.

For Best Ambassador: Charles Francis Adams. During the American Civil War Adams had to contend with a British government that came close to giving hypocrisy a bad name. Largely through his own wits, Adams stopped the British from recognizing the Southern Confederacy. Had London done so, transatlantic history would have been profoundly and permanently transformed.

For Worst Ambassador, the prize must go to Joseph P. Kennedy. Most inept ambassadors do little real damage. But at the beginning of the Second World War Kennedy was reporting home that Britain was a worn-out, defeatist country and bound to lose to the Nazis. He also seemed eager for that result and did little to disguise his German sympathies. Roosevelt eased Kennedy out of London once the 1940 presidential election was safely behind him.

For Most Sensitive Ambassador, the winner is Walter Hines Page. Commenting on British cuisine, he said, 'They have only three vegetables and two of them are cabbages.'

For Most Observant representative, I would have to pick Nathaniel Hawthorne. Technically, Hawthorne should be disqualified from the competition because he served only as American consul in Liverpool in 1855. But the famous novelist had a good eye. He wrote this: 'They [the English] imagine us, in our collective capacity, a kind of wild beast, whose normal condition is savage fury, and are always looking for the moment when we shall break through the barriers of international law and comity, and compel the reasonable part of the world, with themselves at the head, to combine for the purpose of putting us in a stronger cage.' I think Hawthorne's statement would ring a bell with all American ambassadors who have been to the Court of St James's.

---

* The British don't need a visa to visit the United States, so most of this volume represents only the non-British who apply to the embassy.

Nickel and Dime

At Winfield House in Regent's Park, where American ambassadors have lived since 1955, the tall French doors in the state dining room lead into a rose garden, and there, set on a simple stone plinth, is a bronze statue of Barbara Hutton. Her legs are drawn up beneath her and she is wearing the filmy gown of a ballerina. Her chin is raised and she has the faraway, winsome look of an abandoned waif.

When Barbara Hutton turned twenty-one, she came into a fortune which in today's money would be worth about $800 million. Her grandfather had come up with the idea of a shop where any item could be purchased for five or ten cents, and by the time of his death there were more than 2,000 Woolworth stores strung out across the United States. Barbara's youth and wealth inspired Noël Coward's 'Poor Little Rich Girl' and Bing Crosby's 'Million Dollar Baby', and she was the centre of public attention all her unhappy, nomadic life. Thrice divorced by the time she was thirty-three, she went on to four more disastrous marriages. She died in a room at the Beverly Wilshire Hotel in Los Angeles in 1979, surrounded by booze, pills and cigarettes. She was physically emaciated and financially broke.

Hutton came to London in 1935 after her marriage to a manipulative Danish aristocrat named Count Haugwitz-Reventlow. Her only child was born the following year. At the time, the United States was in a panic about the kidnapping and murder of the baby of renowned aviator Charles Lindbergh, and Barbara feared she might be the target of a copycat crime. She was also looking for a house in London that would give architectural body to her social ambitions.

When a Crown property in Regent's Park came on the market, she bought it for $4.5 million. With the help of a New York architect, she designed a new house that could also double as a fortress. The high fence, the guard pavilions, the interior shutters made of steel and the metal grilles concealed in the cavities of the walls turned the house into a twentieth-century keep. Within a year, she moved in with her son, her Count, her two Rolls-Royces and her thirty-one retainers.

The derelict structure Hutton tore down to make way for her new creation was called St Dunstan's. At the height of the Regency, the farmland that would become Regent's Park was opened up for fashionable development, and the third Marquess of Hertford built the park's largest free-standing villa, after an exuberant, colonnaded design by Decimus Burton. The Marquess was a colourful figure about town and a former envoy to the Russian Court. He inspired a couple of characters in Disraeli's novels. In keeping with the high-born British tradition of plundering the continent, the Marquess amassed an enormous treasury of art, much of which can be seen today in the rooms of the Wallace Collection.

From the church of St Dunstan's in Fleet Street, Hertford bought the clock and bonging statues of Gog and Magog, which he installed in the gardens of his house. The villa was the scene of many extravagant entertainments. The Marquess, a man of exotic and lavish tastes, hosted so many parties that he was known as the 'Caliph of Regent's Park'. So the place has always enjoyed a certain reputation. There must be something in the water.*

---

* Otto Kahn, the American banker and philanthropist, bought the house at the turn of the century, but later donated it to a society for the blind. When the St Dunstan's Society moved to less expensive quarters in the mid-1930s, the newspaper magnate Lord Rothermere moved in. But by now the house was decrepit, and after a fire Rothermere moved out. I once asked the present Lord Rothermere if by chance he recollected St Dunstan's House. He looked at me blankly. 'Oh,' he said, 'you must mean my grandfather. No, I don't remember it. He had many houses. Gave them away to his girlfriends.'

Hutton didn't last long in Regent's Park. In 1938 she divorced her Danish husband after a sensational trial in a London courtroom, which also put paid to her hopes of acceptance in polite society. The following year brought the European war. This was not what she had in mind for the safety of her son, and, packing up her considerable belongings, Hutton returned to the United States. She married the actor Cary Grant – a union dubbed 'Cash and Cary' – but the marriage was over before the war was.

By the time peace had returned, Hutton had no interest in resuming her residency in England, and in a paroxysm of patriotism she offered the house to the US government for the sum of one dollar. The federal bureaucracy at first hesitated (Washington has never been very good at budgets), but just as Hutton was about to withdraw the offer she received a cable from President Truman gratefully accepting. The embassy negotiated a ninety-nine-year lease with the Crown, Congress voted the necessary funds for repairs, the interior and exterior were put back in shape and Ambassador Winthrop Aldrich gave a ball for the Queen on the night he took up residence in February 1955.

Barbara Hutton had named her new residence Winfield House after her childhood home, Winfield Hall, a sixty-room, marble-clad estate in Glen Cove on the north shore of Long Island. Her grandfather's middle name was Winfield, the 'W' in 'F. W. Wool-worth'. This was a disappointing discovery for me. I had hoped the place was named after the Duke of Winfield or the Earl of Winfield, and I was let down to learn that Caroline and I would live in a house named after a five-and-ten-cent store.

Winfield House is a handsome, red-brick Georgian mansion. It's hard to believe the place was built as a private home. The rooms on the ground floor are airy and voluminous. Surely one of the most stunning interiors in London is the Green Room, whose creation is almost entirely due to the generosity of the Annenbergs. Running sixty feet from the polished oak doors of the hall to the French windows overlooking a side garden, the room is covered in the soft green patterns of hand-painted Chinese paper which had been found in an old Irish castle, laboriously peeled away and brought to London. With two shimmering chandeliers suspended from the ceiling and two huge Chippendale mirrors flanking the fireplace, the effect is elegant and dramatic.

The house stands in twelve acres of lawn and dells. The only private garden in London which is larger is at Buckingham Palace. A curving tree-line defines the boundary of Regent's Park, and except for the knobby finger of the Telecom Tower the eastern horizon is uninterrupted. At the far end of the lawn, just beyond the fence, there is a small aviary set beside the serpentine arm of a pond. Ducks and swans drift beneath a curtain of willow trees. Roosters crow in the morning and peacocks screech at twilight. On some evenings, cranes swoop down on the grass, and in the dim light look like ghostly apparitions.

At night the house is so quiet you can hear the strokes of Big Ben. There used to be scores of rabbits in the dells, and one morning I spooked a fox in the garden. In the spring a tributary of yellow daffodils winds along the southern margin of the lawn all the way to the pond, and in the summer white roses bloom off the terrace and behind the blinds of neatly clipped hedges. Winfield House is a country manor set right in the middle of the city.

Winfield House is also a little like New York: a nice place to visit but I wouldn't want to live there. It's not a pleasure dome, and Caroline and I always felt edgy when guests seemed to salivate over the cushy comforts of such a grand environment, a condition more apparent than real. In truth, there are a number of drawbacks, the first of which is having Uncle Sam as your landlord. The residence is a champagne house run on a beer budget. It costs a good bit more than a million dollars a year to maintain, but even this is not enough to keep up the basic fabric. Our stay there was a chronicle of roof leaks, faulty wiring, broken pipes, failed heating, torn upholstery and disintegrating curtains, and there was never enough money to fix them properly. It was hard to move around without stepping over a repairman or two, and their ministrations were inevitable gerry-rigged and stop-gap. Winfield House struggled along, wheezing and coughing, and in constant need of attention.

Living there we also felt cut off from London. Set in the park, the house has no neighbourhood, and we missed the newsagent around the corner and the clink of milk bottles at the front door we had known from earlier days in the city. The isolation is reinforced by the security arrangements. We lived in a plastic bubble, and there was little room for spontaneity. Security is a regrettable necessity these days, and getting to know our Special Branch escorts was one of the delights of our tenure, but psychologically we felt cauterized from everyday life. On a couple of occasions, when the alarms went off at night, we would go downstairs to find two or three Uzi-toting policemen in bullet-proof vests. This was a long way from a contented suburban life. And one day, early on, Caroline came across the emergency 'trauma kit', which left little to the imagination, though given the social pace at Winfield House a trauma kit didn't seem such a bad idea.

It was almost impossible to draw a line between our official lives and our private lives. With butlers, footmen, maids, cooks, g. ·ners and guards – all of whom were hard working and professiona - as well as innumerable visitors and house guests, it was hard to find a refuge. A clock-winder showed up once a week and had a flair for coming into a room at just the wrong moment. Our only significant contribution to the design of Winfield House was the installation of a miniature kitchen on the first floor in a room previously reserved for pressing. Here we would make morning coffee or feed the dogs or cook a hamburger on a Saturday night. After all the vast formality of the house, this small kitchen was like a cosy hut in the forest where we could keep in touch with our private reality.

As a base for official operations, however, Winfield House is incomparable, and we used it for that purpose until the foundations creaked. Overnight guests were easily accommodated, though when the President or Vice President stayed with us there were so many brawny Secret Service agents in tow that the house looked like a Marine barracks. And I also remember an overweight Senator who insisted on performing his semi-naked callisthenics in the first-floor corridor, which didn't sit well with Caroline's morning coffee, and the wife of a congressman who was discovered stuffing our towels into her suitcase. But usually overnight guests came and went without a ripple.

An American ambassador in London inherits a complicated framework of social expectations, and the challenge of the job is to discharge these obligations and still leave room to do the sorts of things you want to do. This is particularly difficult during the Season, a British phenomenon which has always been the subject of intense anthropological study.

Every summer, Londoners try to cram a year's worth of events into three months. Though the British are not a notably athletic race, many of these occasions involve large numbers of cool and elegant people watching small numbers of hot and sweaty people compete at tennis, rowing, horse racing or cricket. There are also gentler touches such as the opera at Glyndebourne, the flowers at Chelsea and the paintings at the Summer Exhibition. With the Queen's Birthday, Trooping the Colour and several mass-production garden parties at Buckingham Palace, the royal family is especially active during the Season. On the diplomatic circuit, an uncommon number of National Days fall in May, June and July (for these, my usual manoeuvre was to walk in the front door of an embassy, touch the opposite wall and then leave). And for light relief Parliament always careens to a close at this time, usually in a raggedy finale of treachery and mishaps. The whirlwind of the Season always produced a considerable backdraft at Winfield House.

But the Season is only a quarter of the year. Throughout the calendar, Caroline and I hosted innumerable receptions where Winfield House felt the feet of thousands of guests, many of whom neither the house nor we would never see again.

Receptions are hard. It was sometimes difficult for Caroline and me to screw up the discipline to stand again in a receiving line – smile set, hand outstretched, knees locked – and we occasionally recalled Groucho Marx's comment: 'I've had a wonderful evening, but this wasn't it.' Guests always seemed so pleased to be at Winfield House, however, that we would make it through the event on a second rush of adrenalin. We often had the help of a toastmaster, one of those red-coated border collies who know how to herd a gathering from one room to another and keep a function running smoothly. His name was Maurice Jack, a handsome man with a square jaw and the no-nonsense voice of a drill sergeant. He would station himself at the entryway between the hall and the stairwell, and after a quick exchange with an entering guest, turn to us and call out the name. Usually he got it right, but sometimes not, in which case he would offer a random selection of syllables.*

---

* Receiving lines require considerable concentration. On one occasion, the former secretary of state Alexander Haig – never a master of social detail – was standing with us, and when Maurice called out, 'Count Otto von Bismarck,' Haig said to the guest, 'Oh, and where are you from?'

The problem with a receiving line is keeping it going lest the queue start to build into an impatient backlog. If this happened, Maurice would step forward and whisper in my ear, 'Backed up to the door, sir,' as if he were describing an intestinal condition, and we would try to move things along. I always admired the ability of brisker hosts who knew how to take the hand of the guest and snap it along like a wrist shot. Douglas Hurd was so good at this that you felt you had been catapulted off the end of an aircraft carrier.

A diplomat is a person sent abroad to eat for his country, and at Winfield House there was a lot of eating. For dinner parties, the setting was both splendid and intimate, and in the evening the house glowed. Sometimes these shindigs were large affairs – forty or fifty people – but just as often the party was small, not more than a dozen. I probably spent as much time constructing guest lists as I did on any other single activity.

The object of the dinner party is to bring together interesting people, of whom London seems to have a limitless supply, and, over time, to appreciate the mood of the country, its preoccupations, worries and foibles. There is a kind of alchemy about a dinner party, and if the recipe is approximately right, with politicians and novelists, officials and journalists, bankers and actors, Winfield House can fairly sparkle. There are also countless pitfalls: visitors to be squeezed in at the last moment and guests who fall out the day before; the prickly business of etiquette and precedence; and making sure that ex-lovers are not seated together and deal-makers are.

This is not always successful. We once received a thank-you note from a journalist who said how much he had enjoyed the evening, even though one of his dinner partners was suing him for libel. On another occasion we innocently managed to place the adulterous co-respondent in a transatlantic divorce case at the same table as the wronged wife. But the degree to which the choreography of these affairs was flawless is largely a tribute to Victoria Legge-Bourke, who ran the embassy's Protocol Office. She was a magician of social intricacy, a one-person rescue squad, a superb friend, and she seemed to have the skinny on almost everyone in town.

But the meals didn't stop there. At some periods during the year, I would rotate myself through breakfast, lunch and dinner at

Winfield House, day after day. There were always individuals you wanted to see privately, and a meal at the residence was as good an opportunity for quiet conversation as any. And there were always visitors from Washington whom you wanted to put together with their British counterparts. It was at these little events that ideas, insights, excuses and a good bit of tittletattle were served up. The chefs in the kitchen sometimes felt they had become short-order cooks; and, with guests coming in one door and going out another, the butler, Graham Hartley, sometimes felt he was starring in a Monty Python sketch. But it worked. On the other hand, by the time I came to my final meal at the end of my tenure, I considered donating my body to the Museum of Natural History.

To assist us in our social duties, Caroline and I had three dogs. Two of them – Topsy and Scarlett – had spent the required six months in British quarantine. Committing them to this canine stalag was probably the hardest decision we had to make about returning to Britain, and I recall the feeling of gloom and guilt in Washington, knowing we were about to send our pets up the river. Topsy had been with us when I was minister, so she would be a two-time loser. Like all Labradors, Scarlett ran to fat – a condition she encouraged at every opportunity – and she needed regular exercise, which kennel pens cannot provide.

So Topsy and Scarlett went into the slammer. To bridge our bereavement, a golden retriever named Chloe joined us shortly after we moved into Winfield House. By Thanksgiving of our first year, the two imported dogs were released from their penal probation. We reserved a long weekend for the reunion, and all the household turned out for the great homecoming. Chloe, who had enjoyed the exclusive run of Winfield House and its broad gardens for an idyllic half-year, needed repeated reassurance that Topsy and Scarlett were indeed part of the family and not just another couple of official guests passing through. The prodigal two, on the other hand, needed comforting that we had not committed emotional adultery in bringing a third dog into the fold.

These three dogs – or the Girls, as they were known collectively – humanized the cool grandeur of Winfield House. They possessed remarkable charm and occasional grace. Not everyone who came to the residence found their presence endearing, but, for better or worse, they were an integral part of the operation and enjoyed the run of the place.

Chloe was a retriever in every sinew. At dinners she would gently remove the napkins from the laps of guests and disappear. She considered herself the sports director of the house, and on the marble top of a console table by the terrace doors we kept a ratty box of ground-down tennis balls which clashed aesthetically with the nineteenth-century bronze statuary. Most visitors were sooner or later accosted by her. John Major, as an avid cricketer, bowled balls down the gentle slope of the garden for Chloe, and George Bush, a baseball pitcher at Yale, limbered his arm in the same way. Chloe could cram three tennis balls into her mouth at once, and she would trot around the drawing room looking as if she were suffering from a bad case of mumps. And sooner or later, on one lap or another, these soggy things would be deposited.

Scarlett was both the sweetest and most mischievous of the three. She climbed into George Shultz's bath when George Shultz was in it. One female dinner guest, who had never been to Winfield House before and seemed a little anxious about the affair, made the mistake of removing her shoes beneath the veil of the table cloth in the grand dining room. When it came time to leave the table, her feet groped for her shoes. We found them a half-hour later in the rose garden. Scarlett's appetite was insatiable. She ate my wristwatch. She swallowed a guest's hearing aid. She ate the feathers off a viscountess's coat and the rim off a publisher's hat. She checked all the meal preparations in the kitchen and she patrolled the tables at dinner parties like a conscientious *maître d'hôtel*. When I once ushered some luncheon guests into our small dining room, we found Scarlett wagging her way along the top of the table as she finished off the last of a dozen breadrolls. And at receptions she managed to perfect the technique of a quick, leaping pirouette that would remove a canapé from between a guest's fingers, leaving only a damp mist of her thievery. Scarlett was trouble, but it would be hard to find a nicer dog anywhere.

But it was Topsy whom people most remembered. She was the doyenne of the household without a trace of embarrassment about her rude background. A mongrel from the back alleys of Brooklyn, she had been rescued by Caroline from the sure doom of a New York pound. Her narrow escape, however, had no effect on her confidence or social aplomb. Scraggly-haired with button eyes and revolving ears, Topsy's intelligence was well above that of her pure-bred siblings. At the innumerable receptions we hosted, the order of the receiving line would be: me, Caroline and Topsy. She would sniff the cuff or hem of each passing visitor and give a judgmental glance. When the Queen and Prince Philip came for dinner one evening, Topsy oversaw the greeting, and after dinner, when the Queen retired briefly upstairs, Topsy followed her to be sure everything was in proper order. As the Queen was about to close the door of a guest room, she turned and saw Topsy sitting attentively in the corridor. With a quick beckoning of her finger, the Queen invited Topsy to join her, and so she did. This gesture made a monarchist out of me. Topsy already was one.

Winfield House was the proverbial gilded cage, to be sure, but a wondrous place too. Doing the job would have been difficult without the assistance of this remarkable building. From my at-home office on the first floor, I would sometimes look down at the statue of the poor little rich girl who had created her modern castle in Regent's Park a half-century ago, and I would give a nod of thanks for the house that Hutton built.

Pomp and Circumstance

L ooking down from my office window on an overcast morning
in June 1991 I saw three landau carriages roll into Grosvenor
Square. In the first carriage sat the Marshal of the Diplomatic
Corps, Sir John Richards, and he was coming to fetch me. The
horses clip-clopped their way once around the square and drew up
in front of the wide steps descending from the main entrance of
the embassy.

With Caroline and eight senior members of the embassy staff, I
went down to the lobby to greet the Marshal. The men were
dressed in white tie, tailcoats and top hats, an unusual get-up
for mid-morning. But Sir John had earlier explained to me that
this was contemporary 'Court dress', and in monarchal Britain
you wore evening dress in the morning and morning dress in the
afternoon.

In my hand I clutched an envelope containing my diplomatic
credentials, in which the President asks the Queen to receive me
as his representative and to treat with me in the name of the United
States. These documents I was to present to Her Majesty at a
ceremony in Buckingham Palace at eleven o'clock that morning.
Once the Queen had accepted my letters of credence, I would
become a fully fledged, Government-approved, 100-watt ambassa-

dor to the Court of St James's.* For me, however, the object of the exercise was that I not make a fool of myself. After all, I was going to meet a sovereign monarch who could trace her bloodline back over sixty-two reigns to Egbert of Wessex. Egbert became the first King of the English in 829 when my ancestors were tanning bear hides in dank Alsatian caves.

The Marshal was a retired Royal Marine general, and when he stepped down from his gilded carriage I already knew I was in trouble. Tall, elegant, moustachioed, sashed and uniformed, with military ribbons and medals cascading down to his knees, Sir John climbed the stairs with his white-gloved hand resting nonchalantly on the hilt of his sword. He looked exactly as Hollywood would have ordained. I, on the other hand, had no medals, no sword, no moustache. When it comes to glamour and glitter, there's no beating the British.

The embassy's detachment of Marine guards formed a corridor from the door to the pavement where the carriages awaited. Most of the embassy staff had crowded on to the porch to watch the spectacle. After a few moments of hand-waving and hat-tipping, I settled myself into the first carriage, opposite Sir John. The other members of the party filled up the two remaining landaus. To the snorts of horses, the clatter of wheels and the cheers from the front steps of the embassy, the procession pulled away into London's confused traffic. Caroline wasn't part of the official event. She followed in an automobile, a kind of ceremonial codicil at the tail end of the entourage. This wouldn't be regarded as a high point in the history of the feminist movement, but in Britain there is no appeal in matters of protocol.

Along Park Lane, around Hyde Park Corner, down Constitution Hill the little cavalcade progressed. Pedestrians and tourists along the way waved and craned their necks to see who was inside. Maybe the Queen Mum. As we turned into the forecourt of the Palace, the band which accompanies the Changing of the Guard struck up 'Yankee Doodle Dandy'. Waiting at the entrance in the inner court

---

* Even the best educated British neglect to use the proper possessive form of St James's. Rarely are the natives so grammatically louche. What St James's possesses, however, is unclear. It's probably a reference to St James's Hospital (appropriately enough, a hospital for lepers), which used to stand where the Palace now is. In any case, credentials are nowadays presented in Buckingham Palace.

were David Airlie, the Lord Chamberlain, and the Queen's private secretary, Sir Robert Fellowes. Roger Hervey, the head of the Protocol Department at the Foreign Office, was also there, as was the Queen's young equerry. Footmen in livery padded in the background.

I was taken up the grand staircase and through a series of enfiladed rooms, one leading into the next like a chambered nautilus. My corner-eye caught the daytime gleam of gilt and crystal and bevelled mirrors. All the rooms seemed red and plush. Paintings and portraits the size of billboards hung on the flocked walls. Like following a labyrinth in ancient Thebes, our little party made its way, room by room, towards a central Presence.

Somewhere in the mysterious heart of all this architecture and grandeur stood the figure of British sovereignty. The intricate choreography, the interior space, the decorated escorts, the hovering attendants, even the silence were designed to amplify the sense of majesty and anticipation, of approaching the unapproachable. Kings and popes and tribal chiefs have managed to awe their subjects and guests in the same way since the beginning of time. The more barriers there are to surmount, the more stairs there are to climb, the more distance there is to traverse, the more doors there are to open, the more protocol there is to remember, the more special and apart is the object of all this elaboration.

The credentials patrol entered another in the series of great rooms, and here we were brought to a halt. The senior embassy staff, who would be presented after me, were corralled at the far end of the room, and Caroline, who had been taken up by a lady-in-waiting, was in another corner. With the Marshal of the Diplomatic Corps at my shoulder, I was positioned in front of a stratospheric double door. Looking as relaxed as possible, I went over in my mind the little minuet I would have to dance – was it two steps forward and one bow or two bows and one step? Do not offer your hand unless she offers hers first. Do not ask any personal questions such as 'How are the kids?'

At a signal, the doors swung open. In the middle of a cavernous, golden reception room, at a distance roughly the same as Chicago to Minneapolis, stood the Queen. She wore a simple day dress – no sceptre, no crown, no diamonds and not a throne or a jester in sight – and a little handbag dangled from her wrist. Posted at her side was the permanent under secretary at the Foreign Office, Sir Patrick Wright, immaculate in his dark-blue diplomatic uniform and cradling a great plumed hat across his front like a pet ostrich.

Bow. Two steps. Stop. Bow again. Stride across the infinite field of carpet. Stop. Bow. 'I have the honour, Your Majesty, to present the letter of recall of my predecessor and my letter of credential.' I knew my lips were moving but I wasn't certain any words were coming out. The Queen took the envelope and passed it to Sir Patrick. We then began a brief conversation, a little stilted perhaps, but a few casual words nonetheless. Sir Patrick was there to fill any indelicate gaps. But, for all the formality, protocol and ritual that separated the Queen from everyone else in the world, the substance of our exchange was as simple as a chance encounter on a street corner.

The Queen asked after President Bush, who would shortly be in London for the Economic Summit, and we talked a while about Mikhail Gorbachev, who would also be coming to the Summit for the first time. She asked for my opinion about the Soviet Union and I said I thought it was falling apart. Her questions were direct, but her voice seemed oddly tentative, and, while she listened to the replies, she did so with an eye that drifted to the middle distance. After all, in the course of forty years, the Queen had received and said farewell to some 2,000 ambassadors and high commissioners, and another 2,000 or so doubtless lay in her future.

I had been told that our conversation would last only a few minutes, and then the Queen, without a word, would somehow indicate she was ready to move on to the next stage of the ceremony. I was to watch for a telltale gesture, as if looking at a pheasant about to take flight. And so it happened. The Queen, with a shift of her weight and a slight exhalation, said, 'Well ...' You could hear the three dots, at which point I asked whether I could present the members of the embassy staff who had accompanied me.

At the regal nod, the doors swung open again, and there, queued in the corridor like a row of penguins, stood my eight embassy colleagues. One by one, step by step, bow by bow, each came forward and retreated, while I stood to the Queen's side making the introductions and briefly explaining the responsibilities of each officer. This proved awkward only when the CIA station chief came into the room. The Queen was rightly curious about the ambiguous title 'Political Liaison'. I mumbled something nonsensical about politically liaisoning and liaisoning politically, and so I managed to start off my official relationship with the constitutional monarch by a little act of deceit.

The formal credentials ceremony now completed, the doors closed again. I asked the Queen whether I might present my wife. With another nod from the Sovereign, the magic doors swung open for a third time. Curtseying where I had bowed, Caroline then came forward.

The curtsey is a tricky business. A far more arduous and potentially catastrophic exercise than a bow, the curtsey is also laden with heavy political overtones for an American. Some years earlier, when the Queen paid a visit to America, she was greeted at Andrews Air Force Base by Lee Annenberg, the wife of the former ambassador. Mrs Annenberg was then the chief of protocol in the Ford administration. The morning after the Queen's arrival, the *Washington Post* ran a front-page photograph of Mrs Annenberg prostrate on the runway in an effusive curtsey. For the American public, the curtsey came too close to a grovel, and Mrs Annenberg's tribute suggested not only servility but treason. If one is inclined to a royal curtsey on American soil, it would be far better to do so in front of the Kabaka of Uganda than the British Sovereign. There is, of course, a common-sense, when-in-Rome solution to the curtsey dilemma, and this is the rule Caroline followed.

But the political complications of the curtsey pale beside the physical challenge of trying not to tip over. In the event, Caroline executed the steps with the natural grace of a democratic swan. Another little conversation with the Queen ensued followed by another three dots. We said goodbye, turned in a final bow-and-curtsey combination at the doorway, and it was over.

On the return trip to the embassy, the carriages retraced the route beside Green Park and Hyde Park. Jostling along in my upholstered compartment, I had two thoughts. I recalled the report of John Adams, after he had presented his credentials to George III. Adams had immediately sent off a despatch to Washington describing his encounter with the English King, whose greatest sadness had been the loss of the American colonies. The King had confessed this to Adams, and the two had assured each other of their best efforts, despite the recent bitterness, to make the new relationship a success. Adams sent his detailed account to Washington for all the senior officials to read because the British monarch was the centre of power in the great British Empire. Each word would have been perused for significance and nuance. In contrast, I would send no message about my audience with the Queen. An administrative notice would record that my credentials had been delivered, but otherwise there would be no interest in my exchange with Her Majesty, so far had power slipped from the royal hands.

My second thought was of the credentials ceremonies I had occasionally attended at the White House when I was Assistant Secretary of State. The White House is usually a pretty informal place. President Nixon once tried to impose an imperial flourish by introducing a cohort of White House guards dressed in braided tunics and toy soldier hats, but they looked too much like extras from the *Nutcracker Suite* and were quickly laughed off stage.

In Washington the welcoming of new ambassadors is a mini-social event. President Bush would periodically clear a couple of hours from his schedule to receive the newcomers. A bevy of ambassadors, with their spouses and children, would gather in the West Room where drinks or tea were served and a string ensemble played light music. At a sign from a presidential aide, I would gather up an ambassadorial family and escort them to the next room where we found President and Mrs Bush seated on a sofa. The President would leap up and I would make the introductions, and then we would all sit down for a little chit-chat while sipping whatever was in our hands. Another aide would eventually interrupt the conversation, and one of my colleagues would prepare to bring in the next family. The event was always informal and relaxed, as if the new ambassador had simply found himself in the neighbourhood that afternoon and decided to drop by to say hello. An ambassador from an important country – China, Britain, Israel and so forth – was received separately, but the emphasis was always on the informality of the occasion. There is a lot of distance between the White House and Buckingham Palace.

My credentials procession of gilded carriages made one more clattering loop around Grosvenor Square and pulled up in front of the embassy, where we had begun. A tray of silver cups emerged from the crowd and I handed shots of brandy to the drivers and footmen who had skilfully negotiated the London streets, and I then took a flower basket full of carrots and fed the horses. Like the Queen, the horses had the distracted look of one ceremony and one ambassador too many.

PART TWO

Britain Is a Duck

Grace and Favour

The monarchy and the royal family played a small role in my day-to-day life in London. Throughout the calendar, there was a scattering of events or ceremonies where Caroline and I would encounter a Windsor; but, with a couple of special exceptions, our official and social lives only occasionally intersected with royalty. This was a disappointment for many of our friends at home who expected we would dine with the Queen every Friday night.

Still, there is never any doubt that Britain is a kingdom. The monarchy today is like an intricate tapestry that hangs in the background of everyday events. The British government takes action 'On Her Majesty's Service'. Currency and coins bear the Queen's portrait, and the Queen's picture is stamped in the corner of letters sent through the post. The Queen is toasted on any pretext, and God is regularly enjoined to save her. Parliament sits at the Queen's pleasure, considers the legislative programme laid out in the Queen's Speech, and passes bills for the Queen's assent. The entryways of fashionable shops in London are adorned with the seal of the Queen's patronage, and most organizations in town seem to be the Royal This or the Royal That. Queen's Counsel prosecute criminals in the courts of law. Army officers receive the Queen's commission and bishops hold the Queen's warrant. The Queen's official calendar is reported daily in the Court circular of the broadsheet press. So the monarchy, in the person of the Queen, provides the framework of legitimacy for British life, and in that respect the monarchal omnipresence is so pervasive that it is difficult to imagine untangling the structure if suddenly there were no monarchy at all.

When I arrived in London in 1991, I didn't expect the Crown would become a matter of controversy and speculation. If I had thought about it at all, I would have said the monarchy, like the Mississippi, would just keep rolling along. I would still say that, but with less confidence. Too many faults in the structure have been discovered in the last few years. The Queen, at the end of 1992, spoke of her 'annus horribilis', meaning especially the separation of the Prince and Princess of Wales and the spectacular fire at Windsor Castle. But she also meant the general disrepute that had begun to undermine the monarchy and the questions about its relevance in contemporary British life. When Diana, Princess of Wales, died in 1997, an uncomfortable void opened up between the royal family and the grieving British public. Like the Albert Memorial monument, which is part reliquary and part meringue, the monarchy had been slowly rusting on the inside. And once the Crown is broken, it is hard to repair.

For an American, a monarchy, even a constitutional one, cannot be easily reconciled with a modern democracy. Some Americans nonetheless retain an umbilical sentimentality towards the House of Windsor. My mother was that way, and so too were many of her generation. But they are fewer and fewer with each passing year. When I accompanied the Queen on her state visit to the United States in 1991, I watched the faces of the crowds that gathered round in the cities where our itinerary took us. Americans, I thought, were interested, perhaps intrigued, certainly curious and almost always respectful. But they were disconnected from what they saw. The Queen, as a present manifestation of our own national origins, has become a pretty remote notion, especially the further west you go.

Nonetheless the fairyland of carriages and coronets excites the American imagination. The glitter of a royal wedding or the glamour of an unhappy princess are the stuff of gossip and Harlequin romances, and they have a diverting appeal for bare-bone republicans. American tourists flock to the Changing of the Guard at Buckingham Palace and stand three deep to watch the Trooping the Colour on a June morning. We are impressed by the antiquity of the throne, its sheer durability. But in the end, for Americans, the British monarchy is a long-running curiosity. Like *The Mousetrap*, everyone should see it once. A young American friend of mine, when asked to translate the royal motto 'Dieu et Mon Droit', absently replied, 'God is my finger,' which proves that Americans have a long way to go when it comes to British royalty (and the French language).

The serious role of the monarchy in Britain is, I think, overlooked by most Americans. Perhaps, nowadays, the British overlook it too. It's all so vague. Americans would be impatient with a system that operates largely on precedent and habit. A fog of convention surrounds the monarchy, with so much unwritten and often unspoken. This creates an obscurity at the centre of the British constitution which would be intolerable in America, where we insist on spelling out all the rules in black and white.

British constitutional scholars have attempted to give some shape to the formless role of the monarchy. But Burke, Bagehot, Dicey, Jennings all write as if they were describing the aurora borealis. Walter Bagehot is the most often quoted. He summons up the 'magic' of the Crown and wisely urges that not too much light intrude upon it. He lays out the powers of the monarch as 'to warn, to encourage, to be consulted', whatever that means. But this vagueness also accounts for the resilience and adaptability of the British monarchy. No one knows precisely what the role of the Crown is, and a strict definition is left for the time when a strict definition might be needed. If a definition is not needed now, there is no reason to give one.

Trying to sort through the candy floss, I ended up accepting that there were several attributes of the Crown which I would never wholly comprehend. Virtually all of these royal roles are hard to translate into an American context. The nature of dynasties, and especially the hereditary principle, is simply alien to the American soul, and the search for American equivalents inevitably ends in frustration. The Crown, for all its institutional splendour, is too supple a commodity, and it's never very clear to an outsider where the individual who wears the crown leaves off and the institution which preserves the crown begins. And that is how it is meant to be.

The first attribute of the monarchy seems to be spiritual. This is puzzling for an American, especially when looking at an institution whose trappings are so lavishly temporal and at a society which is so determinedly secular. But the British have always seemed to me a spiritual race, both in the uplifting as well as the messianic sense of the word. They are not particularly virtuous, but they are moralistic. And in contemporary Britain, where religious spirituality is not a conspicuous trait, the Crown embodies this important ingredient of Britishness.

It's been a long time since the last Coronation. In this solemn rite of investiture, however, the new monarch sits in Westminster Abbey, on the throne of Edward the Confessor and surrounded by the tombs of kings and queens departed. The monarch is crowned by the hand of man in the name of God and daubed with holy oil. Like the administration of a sacrament, the Coronation suggests that the monarchy is still divine in origin. Part of the Coronation is also primal because the ancient, tribal dynasty links the people to their ancestral past. This numinous incarnation of mystical design is a little embarrassing today. And vulnerable. But I think it lies at the centre of the British monarchy. And this Queen takes it very seriously.

Early one winter evening, when the rector of St Margaret's Church, the worldly Canon Donald Gray, was showing me around the shadowy recesses of Westminster Abbey, I asked whether he thought the Queen might one day abdicate in favour of her long-attendant son. 'Oh no,' he responded without a trace of hesitation. 'You see, she's been anointed.' We Americans have nothing like this – a few marble monuments to fallen heroes, perhaps, but that's all.

The spirituality of the monarchy is distinct from its ecclesiastical role. Until I lived in Britain, I suppose I thought the Church of England had broken away from Rome lock, stock and barrel. But, it seems, Henry VIII's rebellion was more like a palace coup. He simply wrested the supervisory apparatus from the Pope. So the Church of England was disestablished and then immediately re-established under new management. Instead of a foreign pope calling the shots, there was an English king, and the administration of the Church of England wasn't any more self-governing than it had been before. Genuine breaking away was left to the Methodists and Presbyterians and other non-conformists. And so the British monarch is also the Supreme Governor of the Church of England and 'Defender of the Faith'. (This 'F.D.' is engraved on all British coinage, though the initials do not appear on paper currency, suggesting that religious considerations are a little less important when serious money is involved.)

An American finds it peculiar that the Queen, who reigns over all her subjects, is head of a national church to which a sizeable minority of her subjects does not belong. In fact, the practical delicacy these days is that the Church of England is not a majority religion anywhere in the United Kingdom except England itself. And important urban concentrations in England are not even Christian. Parliament approves ecclesiastical legislation sent to it by the General Synod, so theoretically all the country has a democratic say. But that is governance, not religion. In any case, an American scratches his pate on discovering that the Queen is head of a distinct national church which isn't national.

Americans are grounded in the belief that Church and State must be kept strictly separate (keeping religion and politics apart is a different matter). So it is surprising to see, for example, the temporal body of the House of Commons deliberating on the question of whether women can be ordained in the Anglican Church. This hardly seems an appropriate matter for government, as perfunctory as Parliament's role may be. Nor does it seem quite right that the Prime Minister should be in the business of selecting bishops for approval by the Queen. But that's the way it is. In America, Caesar and God are not supposed to be seen in the same room together, let alone chatting with each other. But, for the British Crown, the church and the state are two faces of the same coin.

On two counts, at least – the spiritual and the ecclesiastical – Americans can therefore make little psychological connection with the Crown and can draw no institutional parallels. But, even in looking at the monarchy's constitutional role, Americans remain puzzled. The monarch is head of state. In giving assent to the laws of government, the monarch is the source of government legitimacy in the realm. And the convergence of the spiritual, ecclesiastical and constitutional authorities in the person of the Queen makes Britain start to look suspiciously like a theocracy.

The constitutional responsibility of the monarch is, by now, a pretty nebulous business. Because the constitution is unwritten, the temporal authority of the Queen is a complex of conventions, precedents, anomalies and accidents. She is a kind of constitutional palimpsest. She is, in theory, apolitical, or at least impartial. In fact, one of the persuasive arguments in favour of a hereditary head of state, as opposed to an elected one, is that birth is an apolitical act (except, possibly, in Northern Ireland). This permits the monarch to remain insulated from the grit and grime of politics and class, a kind of Grand Protector or Chief Umpire, the guarantor of the people's rights and the guardian against the abuse of government. And the monarch arrives at this position by the favour of genealogy and not the whim of political mood.

The reality is that the monarch's authority today is largely fictitious. This Queen performs innumerable little symbolic acts of sovereignty, day in and day out, year after year, but the Crown seems to be mainly a constitutional convenience. The real decision-making authority of the monarchy has withered to an ambiguous set of reserve powers called the Royal Prerogative.

An outsider eventually learns that the principal Royal Prerogative is the raised eyebrow. On the odd occasion when the Queen betrays the slightest displeasure about a government decision, the government is likely to think again. In Britain today there is still no political advantage anywhere in incurring the Queen's disfavour. So when that little arch or reservation rises on the royal brow, a silent shudder runs through Whitehall.

Among her more formal prerogatives, the Queen may dissolve Parliament. And she may send for a political leader to form a government. But these decisions are normally perfunctory and predetermined, a constitutional pantomime. In extraordinary circumstances, however, the judgment of the Queen would come into play. In the 1992 election, I recall many pundits expected a hung Parliament. Some even hoped for an inconclusive outcome just to see what would happen. In the event of no obvious majority, the Queen, guided by few rules and fewer precedents, would have relied on the counsel of the great and the good, and simply felt her way forward.

And 'feeling your way forward' is today as good a constitutional definition of the British monarchy as one is likely to find.

For an American, this all seems hopelessly murky. While Church and State may be separate in the United States, the roles of head of state and head of government are combined. Some presidents are better at the former role, such as Ronald Reagan, and some are better at the latter, such as Lyndon Johnson. Some are not very good at either, such as Jimmy Carter. But the authorities of the President are spelled out in a written constitution, and if there are voids or contradictions the Supreme Court is there to resolve them. If a president dies in office, for example, everyone knows exactly what would happen in the succession. If a prime minister dies in office, no one knows exactly what would happen, except the Queen would do something because the Queen would be expected to do something.

To me, one of the attractive features of the British monarchy, floating like a fuzzy cloud in the constitutional sky, is that it tends to put government in its place, a little further down in the order of things. For all the simplicity of its trappings, the American presidency is prone to fits of arrogance. But in Britain the government itself is not supreme. It is always an unpretentious cut below the Royal Household. When I went to John Smith's funeral in Edinburgh in the spring of 1994, I was struck that the Prime Minister, John Major, as the head of government, was placed in a pew several rows back from the Queen's representative, and so far back that he was in the pew just in front of me. As silly as precedence and protocol can sometimes seem, I rather like a system that ranks politicians somewhere below the pinnacle of state, and this the British royal system does.

The fourth attribute of the Crown is the Queen's role as head of the Commonwealth. This too has no American equivalent. Ever since the Monroe Doctrine, the United States has claimed a certain status as leader and protector in our own hemisphere. It is a patronizing if realistic assertion that is resented by most of the countries to which it is meant to apply. American hemispheric leadership is largely geopolitical in nature, however, and there is no solid foundation of common heritage, language or constitutional history to bind the Latin neighbours together with the Colossus of the North.

The Commonwealth, on the other hand, is a relatively new organization built on the much older structural pilings of British imperialism. It is an imprint of Empire, a little like a film negative where the outlines appear only when held up to the light. All the states except Britain have one thing in common: they were all British colonies. I assume the United States could qualify for membership, though I never raised the subject. Because the Commonwealth is loose in concept and unambitious in practice, it manages to survive in a world where other institutions seem so frequently to stumble over their purposes. The Queen is the head, but this is not an inherited role. It is by invitation. The Queen, however, is also head of state in sixteen of the member countries, so the British monarch would seem to have the inside track for the job.

The Queen takes her position as head of the Commonwealth very seriously. The royal family annually logs many miles in visits to member countries, where they are photographed eating peculiar things and watching dusty dances. The Queen sees the Secretary General regularly, and high commissioners from Commonwealth countries are accorded special places at royal events. On controversial issues, the Commonwealth tries hard not to divide along racial lines, which the Queen knows would be disastrous for its longevity. The royal eyebrow almost touched the royal coronet when Mrs Thatcher was hell-bent on recognizing the Rhodesian internal settlement and relaxing sanctions against South Africa.

Given the Queen's interest it does seem curious that the Royal Household, where the monarch is free to make appointments as she wishes, is so thoroughly white and British in its composition. But perhaps this is an instinct not to make the Commonwealth or the Queen's role more than it is. In any event the Commonwealth accords the Queen an exceptional international status which no other country can emulate.

I don't suppose continuity should necessarily be considered a virtue. But for the British it is. And continuity is the fifth attribute of the monarchy and perhaps the most British. The continuity which the Queen personifies is much more than just hanging on. The British monarchy is the chalice of state, and the royal vessel is meant to contain the undisturbed essence of Britishness, a kind of concentrate of nationhood, passed from royal hand to royal hand over generations. If it is dropped, or even fumbled, the point is lost. Presidents on the other hand come and go, and politics easily dilutes the symbolism of the office. The presidency is a pretty simple device when set beside the effulgence of a monarchy.

For the Crown today, it is the continuity which counts especially. Like an old clock, the beat matters. The other roles – spiritual, ecclesiastical, constitutional and international – would lose much of their reason and lustre without it. Continuity therefore becomes a purpose in itself, the single remaining source of renewable magic.

All this makes the monarchy sound an awesome invention, especially if it's mainly held together by illusion. And so the illusion is reinforced by distance. American presidents are meant to be accessible, but British monarchs are meant to be inaccessible, or at least separated by an encrusted façade. Paradoxically the pomp of royal office has expanded as the power of royal office has contracted. It seems that the less authority there is the more ritual there must be, and only the British have the self-assurance to pull it off.

Caroline and I had to learn many little contrivances of royal deference and Court courtesy. When you are invited to a royal event, for example, it is 'in the presence of' the Queen, suggesting a kind of majestic apparition for which you must arrive at least fifteen minutes early. A blank page in a guest book is reserved for the solitary signature of a royal. You are not introduced to the Queen but 'presented'. The conversational address for the Queen is always 'Ma'am' (sounding very close to 'Mom'), and even the definite article in the phrase 'the Queen' is supposed to be spelled with a capital T. This protocol makes for a stiff confection. And there are many other conventions of apartness. No civil or criminal suit may be brought against the monarch, and in that sense she is above the law. The Queen is not even required to have a driver's licence when she goes out for a spin. A Queen is different because she is supposed to be.

After a while, I came to understand that many of these rigorous conventions are meant to protect both the monarch and the national illusion. As much as possible the public life of the monarch is separated from the private one, so everyone can pretend. But it was here, at this critical frontier between public and private, that the British monarchy suddenly found itself in trouble.

During my time as ambassador the controversy surrounding the royal family turned so tawdry that the value of the monarchy itself came into question. Longtime misgivings about other aspects of the system seeped to the surface, and even the most ardent supporters of the royal line had to concede there was more to it than just a few articles in the tabloid press. After the Windsor fire the Heritage Secretary, Peter Brooke, blithely announced in Parliament that the taxpayer would foot the bill. But the taxpayer said no and the government immediately retreated. Instead, the question became whether the Queen herself should any longer enjoy an exemption from income taxes, and the Royal Household hastily cobbled together an understanding with the Treasury that required the Queen to pay her fair share.

These were insignificant issues, important only as symptoms. I detected no animus directed towards the Queen herself. In fact, everyone believes the United Kingdom could do no better than to have Elizabeth II on the throne, and the longer she reigns, the longer some of the fundamental issues about the monarchy can be postponed. Even the most rabid republican agrees that the Queen is dignified and dutiful beyond an Englishman's wildest dreams. She has gracefully presided over the nation's painful transition from imperial glory. She has spent almost all her isolated life saying the right thing in the right place at the right time, and never putting a royal foot wrong. She has faithfully, doggedly kept up her side of the bargain. Indeed, it is the prospect of the après-moi succession that has acted as a catalyst for public disenchantment.

When Walter Bagehot wrote that daylight should not be allowed to intrude upon the magic, he didn't anticipate flash bulbs and arc lights. Mouths agape Caroline and I happened to have watched the royal edition of the television game show *It's a Knockout* in the summer of 1987. The spectacle of the younger royals scampering about performing slapstick stunts in front of the cameras was lasting. It was a little as if Chelsea Clinton had agreed to take top billing on a mud-wrestling show. The intention, I suppose, was to prove to the nation that the young royals, far from being remote or stuffy, were fun-loving, with-it and up to date. But the effect was simply silly and trivial. The programme made it clear, even to an outsider, that the young royals were burdened by very little judgment about the consequences of their own actions, and this indeed proved to be the pattern. You could almost hear Bagehot spinning.

By the time we returned to London in 1991, the old conventions between the monarchy and the media had broken down into a kind of royal peepshow. The notorious 'Squidgy' and 'Camillagate' tapes were stunning exposures of arrested social development. Peekaboo photographs of the Princess of Wales in her gymnasium titillated the public, and pictures of the 'financial adviser' to the Duchess of York ministering to the royal toes added some smut to the proceedings – amateur by American standards, perhaps, but nonetheless impressive in royal annals. With the separation of the Duke and Duchess of York, all the royal marriages of the younger generation had come apart, hardly what one has in mind when contemplating continuity.

Whenever I was travelling in the United States, delivering myself of profound ambassadorial pronouncements on the state of transatlantic relations, the first question from the audience was usually, 'Do you think Chuck and Di will get back together?' The grand pageant of the monarchy had degenerated into daytime soap opera, live and in colour. You couldn't pass a news shop in the United States, let alone the United Kingdom, without seeing at least two or three mellow portraits of Princess Diana staring from the magazine stands or book racks. Rather than recoiling from the media muck, the royals seemed to wade deeper into it. Andrew Morton's book *Diana: Her True Story* appeared in 1992 and described the Princess as a bulimic, suicidal innocent abandoned by her husband and a martyr in the monarchal cause. The Prince of Wales riposted in a 1994 documentary which depicted him as bullied in childhood, pressed into a loveless marriage, adulterous by default and deeply misunderstood. Diana retaliated a few months later with a plaintive BBC television interview in which, doe-eyed and vulnerable, she confessed her own extra-marital affair and, I thought, managed to humiliate everyone in the sordid story, including herself. By the mid-1990s 'Honi soit qui mal y pense' had acquired a new spin.

For an American it seemed as if the public relations of the younger generation of royals had been handed over to Oprah Winfrey. Let-it-all-hang-out is an American form of therapy, and public confession is a familiar characteristic of the American media, and to a lesser extent of American politics. But you don't expect to find it in a thousand-year-old monarchy. It seemed so common and counter-British.

As I went about my London business I saw that the more traditional part of the Establishment was increasingly alarmed by the chain of royal exposés and fiascos. The Queen finally commanded a royal divorce between the Prince and Princess of Wales, just the way she might direct the shooting of a horse with a broken leg. The government found it harder to explain the legal considerations of succession and the church found it harder to explain the religious implications. Social London seemed to divide into two camps, each pitching its tent and raising its colours whenever the conversation turned to the future of the monarchy. There was the party of the Prince and the party of the Princess, one demanding loyalty and the other sympathy, one describing the Princess as cunning, manipulative and publicity-hungry and the other calling the Prince naive, whimsical and self-pitying. Had all this occurred a couple of centuries earlier, Londoners would have tucked daggers in their belts and scurried along darkened corridors.

Diana's senseless death in the eerie yellow glow of a Paris underpass ended all this intramural backbiting. A combustible mix of shock, guilt, anger and sympathy produced extraordinary scenes of bereavement throughout Britain, an outpouring of inchoate emotion that was genuine and moving. And strange. Transmogrified by her death, the celebrity-princess became an overnight icon, a tabernacle of national catharsis. Whether Diana's record merited this adulation or whether her glamour had conjured up a national gossamer were unsettling questions. But the royal family, in the testudinal remove of Balmoral, seemed initially to misread the swollen mood of the people, and the task of mending the connection between the monarchy and its subjects will take a long time.

Intrigue and gossip have always been part of the royal scenery. But as a diplomat in London I also heard many more serious complaints about the monarchy. The travesties of the younger generation of royals simply gave the criticisms more credibility.

The problem with the monarchy, I often heard, is that Great Britain cannot be shaken out of its twentieth-century insensibility unless the institution is at least reformed and possibly eliminated. This is not merely an attempt to resolve the constitutional paradox of a blue-blooded monarchy in a full-blooded democracy. It is more specifically British. In all its elaboration the Crown is accused of perpetuating a British self-image that is no longer relevant, and the nation cannot come to terms with itself, either economically or socially, unless the weight of the Crown is relieved. The anachronism of monarchy, it is said, preserves a Britannia in aspic.

The monarchy does not even do its job very well, the critics maintain. The United Kingdom is less united now than it has been in 200 years. The average Scot has little time for the royals from the far south and the Welsh have shown as much interest in the Crown as the Prince of Wales has shown in Wales. There is a generational divide as well, with the older part of British society fondly collecting jubilee chinaware, but the younger generation largely indifferent. Moreover, the very concept of a royal sovereignty is incompatible with the requirements of European unity and the Crown is therefore said to be an obstacle to Britain's manifest future.

On top of this, the critique continues, the monarchy is the capstone of the British class system. It is the shimmering apex of a hierarchical pyramid that sanctions social division and encourages social deference. Rooted in the Crown and spreading outwards like a tangle of fruity vinery is a fawning system of nobles and knights, lords and ladies, ranks and orders, wigs and ermine, bows and curtseys which still permeates British habits and British values. So the monarchy stifles the kind of egalitarianism on which a modern state should be based.

Finally, and most scathingly, the monarchy is said to be inappropriate. The scale of the institution is an expensive pretension to grandeur that can no longer be justified by Britain's contemporary circumstances. As a Texan would say, the monarchy today is 'all hat and no cattle'. There is about the monarchy a kind of institutional obesity that does not fit well in leaner times. The sumptuous palaces, the rituals and totems of ceremony, the royals major and the royals minor, the backward-walking viziers and all the paraphernalia, filigree and flummery of royalty are too calorific a concoction for the modern taste and unsuitable for Britain's more modest place in the world.

These are harsh articles of indictment perhaps one day to be nailed to the door of Buckingham Palace.

I often sensed this estrangement between the monarchy and the nation, an uneasiness which had brought forward many questions about the Crown that would normally lie dormant and undisturbed. The royal shenanigans put the monarchy on the defensive, a posture exacerbated by Diana's death. If the Crown these days must be justified on analytical or logical grounds, it is not a persuasive case to make. Opinion polls regularly report that as many as one-third of the British public believe the monarchy should be abolished once Elizabeth II has set aside her sceptre. Dedicated republicans and ardent left-wingers no longer seem quite the isolated, ranting minority that has been their usual lot. One woman, a monarchist to the bone and a longtime courtier, remarked to me one evening with a heavy sigh, 'Well, maybe the time has come.'

Much of the criticism of the royal family has been about style, either the hi-jinks and low-jinks of the royal youth or the indulgence and expense of the royal progress. Without much authority, the Crown depends on respect, and this is precisely the intangible treasure which the boisterous young royals squandered. The American presidency is always capable of regeneration, no matter how disappointing or undignified the incumbent, but, once the respect for the royal family is wasted, it is difficult to retrieve. And if the Crown becomes risible, it has lost everything.

To me the monarchy does seem too isolated from good judgment and good advice and too ornate in many of its manifestations. And it would be far better if the Crown were seen to initiate its own adaptations rather than having them pressed upon the institution by Parliament or an overwhelming expression of public opinion. As an organic institution, the monarchy should not change so rapidly that it appears merely fashionable nor so slowly that it seems reactionary. But I think it does need to trim its stately sails and bring a little discipline to the crew.

As a foreigner who can only dimly understand the British monarchy, my own conclusion about the Crown is another paradox: the Crown is not a necessary part of day-to-day life in Britain but it is an essential part. I doubt whether any substitute could provide for the same quality of legitimacy or sovereignty which the monarchy embodies. Nor do I think the British have the will or the appetite for an epic constitutional overhaul. For better or worse, for richer or poorer, in good times and bad, the United Kingdom is wedded to the Crown, and until the country is energetically ready for a constitutional upheaval, it will remain so. The succession will go forward, as the constitution provides, because that is how the monarchy is supposed to work. Continuity, after all, is the point, and for the British to propose otherwise is to misunderstand their own constitution. And I suspect King Charles III will make a pretty good king anyway.

More fundamental than constitutional and housekeeping debates, however, the Crown seems to me deeply embedded in the identity of the English people, if not all the British people. The monarchy reinforces the sense of English uniqueness, and British uniqueness too, especially now that other western monarchies have disappeared or been reduced to constitutional toys. My sense is that removing the British Crown would be akin to psychological amputation. Perhaps the British would find this liberating, or, as others would argue, it would force the British to confront their own realities instead of wallowing in the embellishments of the past. But I doubt it. The monarchy is too much wrapped up in the British character: the worship of time, the respect for continuity, the sense of duty, the love of theatre, the romance of tradition and the spirit of pragmatism. The monarchy represents what the British are.

Airs and Graces

Class lies at the core of virtually every analysis of Britain today, and most of my discussions about the state of the country usually ended up at this sociological destination, however circuitous the conversational route. The subject seems inexhaustible. Like Original Sin, class is the universal explanation for the nation's ills.

For an outsider, the insignia of class are not so easy to identify these days. In the streets of London it's rare to spot a bowler hat or a cloth cap. If you're from the upper stratum of British society, you might deny that class exists at all. An English friend of mine once said, 'There really isn't any such thing as class any more. For example, you don't say "servants" nowadays. You say "staff".' I suppose that's progress of a sort. On the other hand, if you're from a less fortunate echelon of British society, the conspiracy of class lurks behind everything from a change of government to a change of weather.

The rules of British class are opaque, and a foreigner is never certain when they come into play. Americans tend to simplify class in Britain as a contrast between the sophisticated aristocracy and the toiling masses, a kind of upstairs–downstairs drama on a grand national scale. Much of what Americans still glimpse or read about class in Britain – whether the frolicking toffs or the mean-street toughs – reinforces this passing impression of separate classes with little in between. But British class these days is a more elusive concept, even for the British, and, like a greased watermelon, just when you've grabbed hold of the thing, it squirts away.

America has a class structure too, just as every other society has. We have WASPs listed in the Social Register or the Blue Book, and the British always remind you of this. But class in America doesn't hang over the country like a dark, brooding cloud. Nor has it shaped our cross-class politics. The real divisions of social attitude in America run along racial lines, and, as unhappy as this may be, it's not the same thing.

Moreover, the word 'class' suggests something different in America. It implies material status attained by an individual rather than social status conferred by society as a whole. An American family dynasty is a rare phenomenon, and in any case is unlikely to run more than three generations before petering out. The gilded plutocracy of the Vanderbilts, Morgans and Carnegies had evaporated by the middle of this century, and the period when top-drawer society aped the manners of the British has long since disappeared. American class today is kaleidoscopic. People come and go, rise and fall, and, in contrast to Britain, little is predetermined. In the society at large an American is more admired for achievements in his own lifetime than for any legacy of birth. The distance travelled is the critical calculation, not the position at the starting gate.

One day on a visit to the Knole estate I heard a story from the sixth baron, Lord Sackville, which illuminates the difference between class in Britain and class in the United States. Some years ago, Sackville recounted, he flew to Houston, Texas for a meeting where he was to represent a British corporation on whose board he served as a letterhead lord. He was met at the airport by a caricature Texan – big, open and hearty – who was president of a successful Houston oil company. The Texan had invited Sackville to stay the weekend at his ranch, and sitting together in the front of a white Cadillac that seemed the size of a small Boeing, they drove into the endless, piney reaches of east Texas.

In Texas fashion the driveway to the ranch was a journey in itself, but halfway along Sackville's new friend slammed on the brakes and announced, 'I want to show you something.' The car pulled off the main road and followed a dirt track for a couple of miles before again coming to a halt. There, in a nearby clump of trees, stood a dilapidated wooden shack, weathered by the years and long ago abandoned. The Texan leaned over the steering wheel and gazed for a moment at the shanty. 'That', he finally said with a sweep of his arm, 'is where I was born.'

The crooked shanty and the humble origins it represented were a source of immense pride for the Texan, a kind of personal trophy which demonstrated the magnitude of his rags-to-riches achievement. For an Englishman in similar circumstances, the shack would have been an embarrassment, an unwelcome reminder of rude social roots which success could not disguise too rapidly. It would have been ploughed under and the earth salted.

There is no scientific explanation for the British class system. Or perhaps there is. I have heard the observation that the class system has run so deep in British society for so long that generations of preferential nutrition have resulted in an upper class which is taller than the lower class. This is hard to believe, especially considering the quality of food dished up in private schools and private clubs. On the other hand, I have also run across a lot of tall Englishmen in important places.

Asa Briggs, the eminent scholar of Britain's social past, speculates that the division of class goes all the way back to the conquering Normans and the subjugated Saxons. For a thousand years there has been one class which has done the telling and one class which has done the doing. Another measure says that class is simply the economic difference between those who employ and those who are employed. But no sooner is this proposition put forward today than it breaks down. In contemporary Britain, even the classiest have to make a living.

Nancy Mitford was less analytical on the subject and more intuitive. In the hey-day of the class system, she divided people between 'U' and 'Non-U'. You were or you weren't, and it pretty much came down to how you managed your way through an artichoke. Other theories suggest the class system is an external phenomenon – you are what you are invited to.

This is all very complicated. To deal with class, I found I had to fall back on deductive reasoning, which says that if it looks like a duck, walks like a duck and quacks like a duck, then it must be a duck. Class in Britain is a duck.

One evening at dinner I sat next to a duchess. She was the matriarch of a great family home in the shires north of London. She asked me if I would like to visit one weekend. 'Yes,' I replied. 'Then you must come this autumn,' she said. 'With pleasure,' I agreed. There was a pause and a little frown as she mulled over the prospect of a Yankee on a ducal demesne. Then she said, 'You do shoot, don't you?' 'No,' I answered. There was another pause. 'Then you must come in the summer,' she said. For the British aristocracy, there is a time to live and a time to die, and a proper time to do most things.

Today's older generation of aristocrats is the last one that remembers Britain in the days of imperial grandeur and worldly sway. It is surely the last one that can collectively recall a privileged past of footmen in the front hall and nannies in the nursery. There are a few great nobles for whom nothing much has changed at all. With the Duke of Abercorn in his Irish eyrie or the Duke of Argyll in his Scottish lair, one can still imagine an older Britain when the titled class controlled every important aspect of the country. But this is a mirage. Lineage alone does not guarantee much of substance now, and the age when aristocratic status automatically conferred unquestioned influence is over. Few noble hands have a grip on the levers of political and economic power any more.

These days the British aristocracy is influential not for doing but for being. It derives its legitimacy from the Crown, though its prestige is its own. The royal family, after all, descends from Germans who were imported into Britain as a matter of constitutional convenience a scant three centuries ago. The real heart of the British nobility reaches back much further to ancient halls and feudal fires. The aristocracy is admired for its antiquity but also because it has survived the twentieth century more or less intact. Every so often I read in the newspapers of another great estate dissolved in financial crisis or another noble line trickling away into oblivion. Holding on isn't easy. But at least the form of the aristocracy has remained in place if not its substance, and that seems to be enough.

It is hard for me to explain why the aristocracy has never really been challenged. I've never thought of the British as docile. In fact, the British in my experience can be very feisty. But the titled nobles ruled the country without serious challenge or disruption through most of the Kingdom's history. It is commonplace for social critics to point out that Britain never suffered the same sort of foreign invasion or domestic upheaval which afflicted virtually every country on the European continent. Things might have changed if it had. Still, I doubt whether Britain today would be much different if Napoleon had marched on York or if the guillotine had flashed at Tyburn.

Perhaps it is true that the Empire acted as a safety valve, allowing the steam of internal discontent to escape to faraway lands. But more often in British history the aristocracy reacted to pressure from below with a nimbleness that eluded the more elaborate nobilities across the Channel. The British aristocracy has always been flexible and open to newcomers who have proved themselves, which usually meant making a lot of money. In Britain adjustments or reforms seemed to come just in the nick of time, and the noble class survived.

Perhaps another reason is that by the eighteenth century, when Britain was still a collection of regions rather than a single nation, the aristocracy was as close to a social definition of 'Britain' as one was likely to find. It had developed a code of behaviour and a manner of speech that were detached from regional identity and were distinctly its own. Aristocrats intermarried and interbred, and those sons who did not succeed to the estates ran the other institutions of the country – the government, the Empire, the church and the military. Class, wealth, power and nationality were all coincident. America never had anything like it, except possibly the Mafia.

So the aristocracy became an adaptable, tightly knit hierarchy that held together the constituent parts of the Kingdom. Different regions of England retained their native characteristics, and Scotland, Ireland and Wales still possessed the features of separate states. But the aristocracy, like tree branches that intertwine overhead, formed a single, solid canopy covering the whole. The aristocracy was British before anyone else was. And with common ways and common interests, the nobility naturally developed an awesome confidence in its God-given destiny.

The decline of the aristocracy in this century has been distinctly British because it has been distinctly gradual, even if a little bumpy. Much of Britain's recent history has been the story of the slow restructuring of national power and the hollowing out of the old governing class. Without the tumultuous events of a great domestic drama, the privilege and authority of the aristocracy were under almost constant assault for a hundred years, either by the mandate of new legislation or by the steady deterioration of the old economy.

The series of Reform Acts in the nineteenth century, like the waves of a democratic tide, eroded the political dominance of the old order. The Parliament Act of 1911 undermined the institutional grasp of entrenched aristocratic interests in the House of Lords. Land values also plummeted. And, on a horrific scale, the carnage of the First World War decimated the youthful heirs to the nobility and drained away its blood in foreign mire. If death did not touch all the titled families, taxes did. The landed nobles became a class of patrons without much patronage. From 1880 to 1920 so many calamities struck the established aristocracy that it must have seemed like a plague of locusts had been let loose on the estates. In the brief span of two generations or so, Europe's most durable, confident, dominant and natural possessors of power saw it all run suddenly and irreversibly through their aristocratic fingers.

America had little to do with this social metamorphosis. It was mainly just another country with bad manners. A remarkable number of British grandees attempted to retrieve their financial fortunes by importing American heiresses to subsidize the unproductive assets of their class, and a lot of wealthy Americans believed that old titles could dignify new money. In the span of a generation or so there were some 300 of these transatlantic marital mergers. Depleted of cash and talent, two dukes of Marlborough married American heiresses to staunch the financial haemorrhage of their gargantuan estate at Blenheim. The eighth Duke married an American and acquired central heating in the deal. On securing his ample marriage contract with Consuelo Vanderbilt, the ninth Duke wired home the romantic news that the lake beside the great house could now be dredged. There were a few beneficial by-products of these brokered unions, such as Winston Churchill, but for the most part the trade in blue blood and greenbacks was not a very respectable chapter in Anglo-American relations.

More broadly, America was seen by the ruling class of Britain as a centre of crude subversion, happily distant but still a hotbed of distasteful ideas and social experiments which vaguely menaced the old order of Europe. Turn-of-the-century America in all its burgeoning, cocky adolescence represented the values and characteristics which the nobility of Britain found unbearable. America was chaotically democratic and contemptuous of tradition. There, money was king and the measure of all things. America was proof of the turmoil and mediocrity that inevitably follow a deliberate break with the past. American wheat undermined the agricultural base of the aristocracy and American women undermined its genealogical grandeur. America was new and therefore vulgar; it was populist and therefore unruly; it was violent and therefore uncivil. Even as the century matured, America arrived unspeakably late at European wars, and it was no surprise that Mrs Wallis Simpson from Baltimore precipitated the ruin of a monarch. If America was a premonition of the future, the ruling class of Britain despaired. Some of these attitudes are still around.

During my years in London, my encounters with the old landed nobility were rare. In the day-to-day life of the nation, the aristocracy seems to be a subdued presence, never very prominent but always there. Occasionally, however, I could imagine the way it once was, and through one friend I sometimes glimpsed down a tunnel of time another era that Britain used to know but America never did.

Over four centuries the Cecil family has woven itself in and out of Britain's public life. The master of the family is the Marquess of Salisbury, and the marquesses of Salisbury have always sat at the high table of British authority. Robert Cecil is today's heir to the title. When he took a seat in the House of Commons as an MP, Robert was the seventh successive Cecil to do so. Perhaps he never would have entered politics in the first place were it not for the weighty traditions of his family, though he has all the ability and affability that would make politics a natural calling.

Robert abandoned his parliamentary seat in 1987, but through some genealogical jujitsu which hardly anyone understood, he moved to the Lords, even though his father was still breathing, and there he soon became the Prime Minister's Leader of the upper house. When Robert eventually becomes marquess, he will preside over the Elizabethan magnificence of Hatfield House in Hertfordshire, whence he will supervise the family estates so that he in turn can pass them on to his son. That's the way it works.

For the moment, however, Robert is Lord Cranborne, and he lives at Cranborne Chase in Dorset. This medieval brick manor is as comfortable and scruffy as an old shoe. At Cranborne Chase the past seems only yesterday. From a central baronial hall with a fireplace as big as a garage, the house shambles outwards into various chambers and towers reached by narrow passageways and turreted stairwells. When Caroline and I stayed there one night, another guest was so cold in the draughty old place that she borrowed one of our dogs to put in her bed.

The manor house stands in tufted fields which were once a royal hunting ground, or chase, and Robert Cranborne tells stories of catching poachers late at night when the moon picks up the limestone light of the surrounding hills. Scattered about the estate are little stone cottages rented to farmers who tip their hats when Lord Cranborne passes by and come to consult him about issues affecting the wellbeing of the community. On frosty winter weekends the local hunt assembles at the gates of the house and the forecourt fills up with snorting horses and yapping dogs. On other weekends Cranborne conducts a wellington-boot salon for his many political friends. And on Sunday mornings he takes his place in the family pew at the church across the low, stone wall where he leads the singing of the hymns. If you squint your eyes in Cranborne Chase, you are in another century.

Cranborne is among the few exceptions of younger nobles secure in their aristocratic status and, in return, conscious of their public obligations. In Britain this is an old contract between noble and nation. In the best part of patrician aristocracy, there was an ethos of service in which privilege was exchanged for duty. Most Conservative prime ministers in this century, for example, have had an aristocratic connection of one kind or another.

Of the various hereditary peers whom I have known in the House of Lords, Peter Carrington is the paradigm of this old trade-off between the fortune of birth and the responsibility of state. As soldier, diplomat and server of causes, the formidable Lord Carrington has always mixed the wry detachment of his aristocratic perspective with a selfless dedication to his country. Any nation would be lucky to have one of him. But he is the rearguard of a rare breed. In contemporary Britain there is no longer much room for such bargains, and the younger Robert Cecils of Britain's modern political world can be counted on the fingers of your hand.

For an American, the British nobility is like a complicated grammar with a bewildering array of declensions, none of which reveals very much about the labyrinthine nature of the aristocratic system.*

First and even second impressions are invariably wrong. There seems to be an exception to every rule. It's hard to remember that a baronetcy is hereditary but not noble. And when aristocratic son succeeds aristocratic father, one title is shed and another one assumed. If you don't know how to pronounce 'Cholmondeley' (Chumley) or 'Buccleuch' (B'cloo), you have failed a preliminary aptitude test.† The Duke of Devonshire told me once that the silliest question he is asked is why he doesn't live in Devon, and I nodded sympathetically without any idea of the answer.

Without consulting a manual, or just 'knowing', I could not tell the difference between an hereditary peer and a life peer. They don't seem to walk differently. Or perhaps they do. Nor could I ever remember whether an earl outranks a viscount or the other way around. Not even those in the know can sort out the tangles of who is related to whom. If you assume that everybody in the aristocracy is a cousin of everybody else, it is a wise precaution. But someone is always shuffling the deck.

These accumulated quirks are like the knots of a gnarled oak. Answers mostly come from instinct. The idiosyncrasies of the aristocratic class are meant to be absorbed through a process of social osmosis. And the simple intuition about these things is one of the imperceptible dividing lines between those who belong to the British nobility and all the rest. The truth is that most members of the British aristocracy are themselves confused about these intricacies, and in most instances seem not to care too much. But

* *Burke's Peerage* and *Debrett's* are more like publications of the Audubon Society.

† The pronunciation of names led to my worst *faux pas* among the English. I once commented to the dean of British novelists, Anthony Powell (pronounced 'Pole'), that he might be more widely read in America if he pronounced his name properly. This was a feeble joke, but Powell was so put out he recorded the incident in his diaries.

it is one thing for an aristocrat to stumble over a social nicety and quite another for an outsider to do so, especially an American. I never addressed an envelope with confidence.

There are few generalities which sensibly apply to the hereditary aristocracy. It is too disparate now, too much like a collection of souvenirs tucked away in the national attic. Some nobles have become economic prisoners in their costly country estates. A few have managed their property ingeniously and shrewdly controlled their more liquid assets. Some have hired tax lawyers as their new estate managers. Others have sold off bits and pieces of the family treasure. But the last several decades have been a trauma.

Despite the changes, however, many institutions in Britain still retain an aristocratic flavour. The nobility has hardly gone to ground. The Manorial Society, the Court of Claims and the Court of Lord Lyon still settle quaint questions of succession with a gravity far exceeding the substance, and the College of Arms conducts its serious business as if nothing much has happened. The Crown is still the 'magic circle', and each county has its lord lieutenant ceremoniously representing the royal interest. Commissions, trusts and corporate boards still appoint dignified personages of ancient title. Fox hunting and shooting parties continue to take place on brambly weekends, and if there is a great titled house in the vicinity, its occupants still enjoy the respect and sometimes deference of the village community.

Most noticeably, the House of Lords, in its olympian setting, vaguely oversees the general welfare of the nation. Her Majesty's Government is still arranged in such a fashion that each ministry must have a peer in residence who is answerable in the House of Lords. But, for the hereditary peers, this seems to be mainly a contrivance. Only a handful of born aristocrats play an active role in the upper chamber, let alone in the government. Attrition is naturally working away at the hereditary principle, and the dwindling noble ranks are rarely replenished. The Labour government elected in May 1997 says it will eliminate all hereditary peers from the Lords – one more blow to be absorbed. In the meantime, the House of Lords, in all its Gothic grandeur, stands by the Thames, a remembrance of things past.

Britain's social commentators are like zoologists peering through the bars and taking notes on the behaviour of this unique species that has somehow made its way through a social ice age. There is still plenty to gawp at. If any of his direct descendants had been in charge, the first Duke of Marlborough would surely have lost each of his glorious battles. None of Britain's first families seems to have so consistently and convincingly established the case against the hereditary principle. The Marquess of Blandford, the current heir to the dukedom, comes across as a helpless dissolute who regularly appears in the tabloid press after one drug bust or another. The present Marquess of Bath is a more colourful character, but the wiring of his chromosomes also seems to have gone awry. An erratic, ageing hippy with a leering smile and multiple wifelets, he lives at Longleat, an elegant stone house commanding a sweeping view of the Somerset countryside and now surrounded by a safari park, a cowboy fort and a small garden inhabited by roller-skating parrots. And the twelfth Duke of Manchester ended up in a Florida jail. But none of this should be exaggerated. In the British aristocracy the gene pool always had a shallow end.

The melancholy saga of aristocratic decline has taken place in a very British way. Things have changed a lot without seeming to change much. For all its loss of power and position, the British aristocracy maintains the paraphernalia and mores of a distinct class. It goes through the motions. It keeps up appearances. But, if retreat is the most difficult manoeuvre in war, the British aristocracy has managed brilliantly to disengage itself from the stressful front of British social change, and in so doing to maintain its orderly formations and much of its equipment. Each successive shock to the political system has been accepted gracefully or grudgingly, and, no matter how reduced their fortunes, British nobles have become masters of interior tactics.

As the role of the nobility has receded, its place in the social order seems to have become safer. The titles and privileges and exceptions of the aristocracy could be abolished with a snap of the fingers. And it could be done without necessarily abolishing the monarchy. But there is no public cry for this. There are no learned journals, no noisy demonstrations, no radical manifestos that promote this solution. No serious political party has advocated getting rid of the titled class and none is likely to do so. In fact, the aristocracy is probably more secure now than at any time in the last three generations. Most of British life is a matter of proportion and balance, and, so long as the aristocracy does not exceed its place, things will be okay. It is a very British solution to a very British problem.

Today there seem to be two principal legacies from Britain's grand aristocratic past. First, it is customary to say that the British aristocracy, so set in its ways and so sure of its eminence, drowned the entrepreneurial spirit of the nation in a lily-padded pond of languor and complacency. A noble nonchalance prevented Britain from adapting to new circumstances when a quicker pace was necessary, and control of the land created a social immobilism.

It is equally true, however, that the decline of the aristocratic class and the decline of Britain as a whole occurred simultaneously, and it is not always clear which one was pushing the other down the slide. So long accustomed to the aristocracy for its political leadership, social order and international confidence, Britain seems now a little confused about where to find the same self-assurance. The fading of aristocratic influence has liberated the country beyond dispute, but the country has also lost something in the process. Britain today seems to look backwards from time to time to see what it was.

And second, so long as there is an hereditary aristocracy in Britain, there will be a class mentality. To claim otherwise is silly. A small number of people, listed in the books of social usage and ranked by precedence in the rolls of protocol, have by the simple randomness of birth been accorded a special place of superior status in a nation which cares very much about status. Willy-nilly one tranche of people is separated from the rest.

This may seem a curious anachronism now because the political power of the aristocracy has dissipated over the years and its wealth declined. But its simple status has remained like a post-imperial exhaust. This is gently reinforced in a multitude of trivial deferential gestures. There is a special language of address. A noble may not vote on election day. Where one stands and where one sits is keyed to whether a noble is in the same room. And in countless ways the aristocracy is a superstructure around the British monarchy, supporting the form and the substance of the Crown. So the aristocracy establishes a social order of class distinctions which cascades from the top of society to the bottom.

There is a lot about the aristocracy which I admire. I like the light touch, the poise, the aplomb, the unruffled confidence. I like the patrician attitude of public responsibility and duty, the comedy and sometimes even the arrogance. I think the British rather like their nobility too. And want to keep it. Despite all the gnashing criticism and rending introspection about the nation's place in the modern world, the British seem to find something comforting and reassuring in the steady, rhythmic, aristocratic flow. After all, the British aristocracy is a class act.

Prim and Proper

Once upon a time the upper class of Britain was also the ruling class, a definable caste made up of well-born individuals who could spot each other at twenty paces. This coincidence of authority and position made the identification of power in British society pretty easy. It was the apex of the 'class system'. By the end of my London years, however, I concluded that things were not so simple any more. In fact, I found the term 'class system' misleading. There may still be a lot of class in Britain today, I thought, but there wasn't much of a system.

The real ruling class – the Decision-Making Zone of British life – is now an amorphous mass of different elements, a kind of social plasma that is probably more fluid today than at any time since the early nineteenth century. Little now is fixed in the hierarchy of power, so the real 'system', such as it is, defies social definition and is full of contradictions. The Decision-Making Zone is rigid and flexible, steady and erratic, conformist and eccentric. It is British.

The old upper class hasn't been displaced. It has simply moved over to make room for a more recent arrival on the social scene: a middle-class urban gentry, well educated and professional, influential in forming national opinion and thoroughly comfortable with the exercise of economic and political power. An American might call this breed 'upwardly mobile', but, whatever the description, the shouldering forward of the new elite is what is sociologically different in Britain today, and the power-sharing at the top of British society is now a kind of Grand Compromise between the Old Establishment and the New Establishment, as only the British could engineer.

Picking out differences between these two intersecting orbits is difficult. They are not interchangeable but they overlap so widely that making distinctions, except on the fringes, is a hopeless exercise. Notting Hill isn't confused with Kensington, and the Groucho Club isn't exactly Boodle's, but this apparent duopoly means that the old-boy network is entangled with the new-boy network, and together they make things work.

To some degree each group imitates the other, so an outsider who relies on an old map quickly loses his direction. Moreover, the Decision-Making Zone as a whole is open to newcomers because it recognizes merit when it sees it, and has thus become the natural and expected lodging place for most bankers, businessmen, lawyers, politicians, civil servants, diplomats, journalists, artists and academics, whatever their social roots. But it is the nature of the beast that no label sticks to its fuzzy mass.

All of that said, the upper class still matters, even if it no longer enjoys unquestioned control of the system. When I once asked an English friend about class in Britain, he answered in a doggerel: 'When Adam delved and Eve span, Who was then the Gentleman?' This is an old English riddle, he explained, recited in the days of Wat Tyler's insurrection but surely more venerable than that. The question of class, my friend sighed, is as old as the country. When God invented the Gentleman, he also invented class.

The Gentleman, I would guess, is the most stereotypical image of the Englishman. For centuries all sorts of people have mingled on this marshy social ground. Some were knights. Some were well-to-do squires who may have owned land but didn't have the lineage or luck to be titled. And some were merchants who possessed neither title nor land. Some professionals were Gentlemen and some were not. One friend told me his great-uncle had a certificate which said 'Gentleman Plumber'. Gentlemancy was a pretty vague business. Unlike the aristocrat, a Gentleman seemed more in a state of becoming than a state of being.

A Gentleman never enjoyed any legal standing in British society. The designation was not conferred by any authority. It was purely social and carried with it no special rights or privileges. The only real requirement for a Gentleman, as for a duck, was that you act like one. A superior Gentleman knew how to conduct himself in society. He wore the right clothes and knew the right friends. Gentlemanliness was exuded.

More important, a Gentleman seemed not to depend on his own labour for his own support. Money was something that simply appeared. He was a *rentier* and lived on the income generated by a once-removed form of capital.* Liberated from manual toil, a Gentleman was free to pursue the more cultivated things of life. He was a man of leisure, possibly a dabbler in life's little amusements or possibly an intellectual of the highest refinement. Above all, gentlemanliness was about manners, style and form, and how to be an Englishman. If I had lived in the eighteenth century, a Gentleman is exactly what I would have wanted to be, and I would have tucked a handkerchief into the frilly cuff of my sleeve. But all this was happening in Britain when most Americans were wearing buckskin and eating possum.

The gentlemanly ideal was so infectious in England that even lesser sorts adopted gentlemanly ways. Just as Gentlemen imitated the manners of the aristocracy, people who fell below the line of squirearchy imitated squires, and so on down the food chain. Having to work might be an economic necessity for most, but at least you could emulate the proprieties of those who didn't. This could be absurd, and by Victorian times the social mimicry often rose to buttoned-up parody.

To help me understand the Gentleman, Bob Ayling, who runs British Airways, gave me a verse by W. S. Gilbert called 'Etiquette'. It relates the story of two middling merchants who end up stranded on the same desert island after a shipwreck. Because they have not been properly introduced, however, they refuse to speak to each other. 'For Peter Gray, and Somers too, though certainly in trade

---

* Early on in my British experience I learned never to ask a gentlemanly stranger the typical American question, 'What do you do?'

/Were properly particular about the friends they made/And somehow thus they settled it without a word of mouth/That Gray should take the northern half, while Somers took the south.' Later Mr Gray and Mr Somers discover quite by accident that they have a friend in common named Robinson, and this allows them to become friends themselves on their isolated island. Word subsequently arrives, however, that their mutual acquaintance has been convicted of fraud, thus causing each acute embarrassment.

> They laughed no more, for Somers thought he had been rather rash
> In knowing one whose friend had misappropriated cash;
> And Peter thought a foolish tack he must have gone upon,
> In making the acquaintance of a friend of Robinson.

> At first they didn't quarrel very openly, I've heard;
> They nodded when they met, and now and then exchanged a word;
> The word grew rare, and rarer still the nodding of the head,
> And when they meet each other now, they cut each other dead.

> To allocate the island they agreed by word of mouth,
> And Peter takes the north again, and Somers takes the south.

The idea of the Gentleman was very English because it established a generally accepted form of behaviour and accorded status without upsetting anyone else. The little distinctions among the species were big enough to make a difference but not so big as to give offence. A 'Mister', for example, was not as elevated as an 'Esquire'. But close enough. Even nowadays, an American is confused by the distinction that a doctor who is a general practitioner is called 'Doctor' while a surgeon is called 'Mister', recalling the time when surgeons were inferior and not received at Court because they worked with their hands. A friend from Scotland Yard once told me that, when he started out as a policeman, a Chief Constable in a county was considered a Gentleman, but a Chief Constable in a borough was considered 'in trade'. So when one gentlemanly Chief Constable wrote to another, the salutation was a brotherly 'Dear Smith'; but when he wrote to a borough Chief, the salutation was a more distant 'Dear Mr Smith'.

And still today, there seem to be little encrypted distinctions between, say, a scientist as opposed to an engineer, or a solicitor as opposed to a barrister, or a businessman as opposed to a banker.

It's a subtle game. The point, however, is that every Gentleman had a precise sense of how he related to everyone else. Like a social galaxy, the different pieces of the Gentlemen's class drifted through space in a poised and balanced pattern.

Many Americans continue to think the upper class in Britain is full of stuffed shirts, but I rarely came across this classic, blimpish type. One reason is that most of the Old Establishment is no longer idle. Taxes saw to that. And so did a more general sense that work and worth are connected. Still, in the higher altitudes of contemporary British life, I think it is true to say there remains a sense of apartness from the rest of society that continues to resemble the faded ethos of the gentlemanly past. Oak-panelled clubrooms and old-school ties still count. Courtesy, respect for tradition and knowing the rules are the norm. Conservative in its disposition, if not necessarily in its politics, the Old Establishment as a whole is non-sectarian, though Anglicans always enjoy the post position (I was nonetheless surprised one day to be told by a senior British diplomat that he always felt a little on the margins of the Foreign Office because he was a Catholic). The biggest sin is frightening the horses, but otherwise the upper class is forgiving of almost everything except treason and zeal. And it still sets a noticeable, elegant, gentlemanly tone in London.

The origins of the New Establishment, on the other hand, are more straightforward, or at least more recognizable to an American. They are diverse and largely post-imperial with little in the way of inherited status or wealth. If there is a unifying characteristic, it is the entrepreneurial urge.

Because Britain is no longer the exclusive playground of the upper class, the word 'elite' isn't a simple social judgment any more. This is principally because Britain today cannot afford to coast. Modern Britain, with no particular advantage over any other nation, needs all the talent it can get, and the change in the composition of Britain's decision-makers comes from the demand-side of life rather than the supply-side.

You see this today in almost any British boardroom – individual businessmen who have made it to the top on ability. You can see it in the shift of the City's weight from Billingsgate to Broadgate. You also see it in the political parties, where neither the Conservatives nor

Labour any longer derive their tone from their older social interests. In fact, the era of the Tory grandee and the Labour proletarian is a thing of the past. And you see it in the heady rise of the 'chattering classes' – primarily the media – which have probably done more than anything in modern Britain to break the choke-hold of the old system.

Most of this change reflects the burgeoning expansion of Britain's broad middle class and its progressive enrichment. So expectations have changed too. Jokes about Britain's food, for example, are a little out of date, a marked contrast to my first time here when most of the country's stick-to-your-ribs restaurants should have posted a health warning. You are as likely to find a good meal in London today as in any capital city in the world, and Delia Smith, Pru Leith and Terence Conran have done more for Britain's taste buds than anything since the discovery of mustard.

From an American point of view, British society has simply loosened up. Calculating protocol and tugging forelocks are more or less out of place these days. One incidental sign is that the British now use first names with each other more easily and frequently than in the past, and across a wider spectrum. The revolution in informality is hardly universal (I know one businessman who received a life peerage and immediately instructed his household help to address him as 'milord'), and when the new, call-me-Tony Prime Minister institutionalized first names in Cabinet sessions, there was some unmatey reaction in clubland.* But a lot of social stiffness has dropped out of British society, and the real point is that Britain is much less stuffy than it used to be.

When John Major became prime minister he expressed an ambition that Britain should have a 'classless society'. This produced many sniggers around the circuit, and he never mentioned the goal again. But his sentiment, in my view, was closer to the mark than the customary description of Britain in thrall to a 'class system'. Ironically, the Labour government of Tony Blair in many ways seems a validation of what Major had in mind. Britain's profile has been changing in a dynamic fashion which the country hasn't known for years, and the way Britain makes decisions about itself is

---

* Mercifully, the country still has a long way to go before reaching what the writer Christopher Buckley once called the 'precipitate familiarity' of the Americans.

different from what it was when I first lived here.

Part of the genius of British society is that it has always been able to replenish itself. Not 'mobile' in the American sense of the word, the social structure here nonetheless seems to know almost by instinct when one order has exhausted itself and something fresher is needed. Unlike the social constipation that long afflicted the Continent, British society has never been impermeable or impenetrable. And in the early 1990s, it seemed to me, this sort of dynamic metamorphosis was well under way, melding the old and the new into an uniquely British pluto-meritocracy.

The British are immensely skilled at holding on to the baby when throwing out the bathwater. So some characteristics from the past are entrenched in the new Decision-Making Zone and unlikely ever to change. One example is the simple, immutable fact of London.

More than ever, London is the omnipotent, all-knowing, unassailable hub of the nation, and today's DMZ* remains an intensely capital-city phenomenon. If London itself were not so dominant in the Kingdom, this convergence of decision-making wouldn't seem so conspicuous. As it is, however, the national apparatus is concentrated in a few streets that run along the north side of the Thames. Only Paris compares. The United States has nothing like it. To an American visitor, London is like Washington, New York and Los Angeles rolled into one.

London seems the centre of everything English except universities, sports and the shrinking manufacturing sector. Government, politics, finance, business, transportation and communications are all concentrated in the capital, and so are television, radio, newspapers and publishing. The great museums, the great operas, the great ballets are within a stone's throw of each other. Most visitors would naturally expect to find the Archbishop of Canterbury in Canterbury, but he is not. In a comfortable day's walk, you can circumnavigate an area of central London where virtually every important decision about the wellbeing of the nation is made. So London-centric is the locus of power and influence that city addresses are casual eponyms – Whitehall, Downing Street,

* In government lingo, DMZ means 'De-Militarized Zone', so it's not entirely inappropriate to use the same acronym about British society.

Westminster, Mayfair, Threadneedle Street, Harley Street, Islington, 'the City', the generic Fleet Street and so forth. Like a Monopoly board, you know where you are with each move.

As a close-in capital, London is not a city of secrets. Everybody bumps into everybody else, and interior communications are naturally well developed. Information and gossip pass along the metropolitan circuitry with cybernetic speed. I once gave a small luncheon at which Margaret Thatcher scolded a handful of British businessmen in her usual jack-hammer manner. It was not an exceptional performance on her part, but under the barrage the guests slumped closer and closer to their plates and any thought of genuine conversation was abandoned. By the evening, at dinner, each of my new companions had already heard the story of the luncheon débâcle. In the London syndrome, everyone knows what everyone else is up to.

No matter where you happen to be geographically, you always go 'up' to London. And, once arrived, no one ever seems to go away. The city is full of ex-chairmen, ex-ministers, ex-editors and ex-diplomats so that someone is always looking over your shoulder to offer the helpful or unhelpful comment. In the United States, by contrast, when a president leaves office or a corporate chief retires, he goes home, wherever home happens to be. All of Britain's former prime ministers hang around in London. You can easily become an ex-minister but rarely an ex-Londoner. To a degree unknown in America, power in London is literally just around the corner.

A second old-fashioned characteristic that remains alive in the DMZ is the Great Weekend Diaspora. London's leadership is still linked to the English countryside by a mystical umbilical cord, and the English weekend has stayed sacred and inviolable. It used to be that those who had land governed; now it seems that those who govern have land.

On Friday afternoons, London hangs a Do Not Disturb sign on the national door. Somewhere in the suburban environs of the capital runs a shadowy frontier beyond which lies the outer English sanctum. By Friday evening the roads leading out of the city are clogged by the exodus. No distance or frustration seems too great a barrier to the weekly rural quest.

The Prime Minister goes away to Chequers, the Foreign Secretary to Chevening, the Chancellor of the Exchequer to Dorneywood. In fact, everybody in government seems to go away on weekends.* Whitehall is more or less abandoned. Westminster on a weekend has the feel of a ghost town. The lonely resident clerk in the echoing halls of the Foreign Office is the only link between the English weekend and the rest of the diplomatic world. When I was at the embassy and needed to speak to someone at the FCO on a weekend, I would telephone the resident clerk, who usually sounded as if he were speaking from the bottom of a deep well.

Some country houses are baronial estates set in the green hills of Wiltshire or the flatlands of Norfolk, with all the grandeur and ambience of a pastoral patrimony. There are cows and sheep in the meadows, big oak logs in the fireplace, a stable or kennel behind the yew hedge, and all the gentrified atmosphere of an old-line family home except a row of ancestral portraits mounting the stairway. But, more often, the country retreat is a converted mill house or restored vicarage, with an orchard in the back garden or a herbaceous border beside the pathway that leads to the gate. Here there are rhododendrons to tend and wellingtons to wear and lanes to amble, and here, with an audible sigh, the urban refugee shuffles off the burdens of the metropolis and settles into an imagined, rural past like a warm bath. In the Saturday–Sunday countryside, successful Londoners regularly reconnect with a fancied, landed heritage. And on Sunday evening, revitalized by this quick fix of gentrification, everyone struggles back to town.

As it was for the Old Establishment, the countryside routine is an affair of the heart, a pre-Raphaelite embrace, where the weekend squirearchy can adopt the otiose airs of yesterday's Gentleman. The explanation may be no more complicated than the fact that rural England is peaceful and alluring. Some critics, however, are harsher in their judgments. Max Hastings, the editor of the *Evening Standard,* calls this weekend exercise 'the Old Rectory Syndrome'. He once sent me a disapproving article about it which he composed between shooting weekends. In England there do seem to be more old rectories than there ever were old rectors, but his point was that the siren of the countryside distracts the managers of the British

---

* Some Londoners regard their city house as a *pied-à-terre*, though the *pied* can often cover a lot of *terre*.

economy. And Professor Martin Wiener, in a long study called *English Culture and the Decline of the Industrial Spirit*, concluded that the thrusting, energetic, urban character of a Victorian entrepreneur evaporated in a miasma of pseudo-squirearchy as soon as success was achieved. The Victorian work ethic was left behind in London, and with his new wealth the *arriviste* Englishman slipped into his country tweeds and strode across the green tufts of his weekend abode on a damp Sunday morning as if he had been there for generations. The present imitated the past, and in some measure it still does.

All this may be a little severe for a simple weekend in the country, but the migratory patterns which characterize the DMZ are still pretty noticeable, especially to a foreigner. However you analyse the weekly diaspora, there is more to the English weekend than a couple of days off.

On the other hand, some telltale features of the modern DMZ suggest how different it is from earlier days. One of these is language. If there used to be a behavioural homogeneity about the old ruling class, it started with accent. One Gentleman sounded pretty much like the next.* For the British upper class, speech was largely de-regionalized, and even Scots who were put through the classic gentlemanizing process sounded English. This was different from America, where regional accents never gave away too much. While the plummy upper-class tonalities remain distinctive today, however, you can't be entirely certain what accent you will encounter when you walk through the door of a contemporary decision-maker.

Robert Alexander, now Lord Alexander of Weedon, was a friend when I was at the embassy, and he always impressed me as the refined epitome of the socially established Londoner. His background is unexceptional: middle-class roots planted in middle England. He went to boarding school, studied brilliantly at Cambridge, pursued a dazzling career at the bar and is now the chairman of the National Westminster Bank. He speaks the King's English. But Alexander says he started life pronouncing 'glass' and 'grass' in

---

* Clemenceau unkindly observed that, if you stood ten English nobs in a row, they all sounded alike, except one of them was smart.

the regional way that sounded American. This was beaten out of him as soon as he went away to school. When he was young, you had to talk upper-class proper if you wanted to move along. It was as simple as that.

Another London friend of mine was born in a cockney neigh-bourhood of London during the war and brought up in a council flat. He became a messenger in a big corporation when he was sixteen, and it took a while before he noticed that the people at the top of the company spoke one way and all the rest, including himself, spoke another. Ambitious to move up, he started to practise the toffy accent, mimicking the BBC's 'received pronunciation' while standing in front of a bathroom mirror every evening to rehearse the broadening of his *a*s and the rounding of his *o*s, a little like Eliza Doolittle.

By the time he was eighteen, my friend had to alternate between the two accents depending on his companions. But he now recalls with a laugh that, just when he had reached maximum fluency in his new tongue, Michael Caine became a big star and the cockney accent was suddenly fashionable. My friend ended up running a substantial advertising agency in London, and he now speaks with a kind of middle-distance accent. He would agree that much of the DMZ can still be defined by enunciation, but purity of speech is no longer a necessary credential for position.

In some quarters, usage is still a distinguishing mark. I remember when the editor of a grand newspaper gave me his opinion of the then Prime Minister, John Major: 'A decent enough chap,' he commented, 'but do you know what he says sometimes? He says, "Pardon my French"!' Loud guffaw.

In any event, the language barrier, though important to some, seems to me less and less relevant, and accent is no longer a reliable clue to power. A Tory Cabinet minister told me he had two sons. One spoke Etonian English and the other spoke Estuary. The DMZ has the same consistency.

The peculiarities of accent, however, reflect the biggest, continuing fault line running through today's Decision-Making Zone: education. It remains true, for example, that of all the predictable credentials for position, none is more significant than a degree from Oxford or Cambridge. The Ivy League in America used to be this way too, but the exceptional status of the ivy universities has long been overtaken. Stanford, MIT, Duke, Georgetown, Tufts, Chicago, not counting any number of state universities, are now top ranked and seen as such. In Britain, however, Oxford and Cambridge remain unto themselves. They may confer no automatic guarantees these days, but they do continue to distribute a disproportionate number of tickets to the power game.

This is not surprising in a country where, until recently, even the idea of a university education was synonymous with privilege, and Oxford and Cambridge were educational monopolies. I would guess that half the men I know in London were undergraduates at one university or the other.* A friend, who is deeply embedded in the higher slopes of the Old Establishment, once said to me that the only way to change the British class system would be to abolish Oxford and Cambridge. An Oxford graduate himself, he put forward this proposition with the complete confidence that it would never happen.

An undergraduate degree from Oxbridge is no longer a pre-requisite for entering the DMZ. But, without one, a lot of ground has to be made up in some other fashion. Anthony Sampson, in his meticulous 1982 study of *The Changing Anatomy of Britain*, concluded that the anatomy really wasn't changing much, at least not to judge by the two universities which spawn the preponderance of Britain's pluto-meritocracy. British newspapers, which themselves are products of the Oxbridge factory, periodically survey the boardrooms, financial houses, government departments and legal benches of London to demonstrate that the old Oxbridge brain machine remains largely intact. A glance at any former Conservative Cabinet makes the same point.†

Most of the students at Oxbridge today, however, have middle-class backgrounds, and more and more come from state schools rather than private ones (Americans, incidentally, are usually surprised to learn that these two elite universities are an expensive part

---

* In contrast to America, these old universities, until recently, were also overwhelmingly male in composition.

† John Major's distinction in his Cabinet was not so much his humble origins as the fact that he had no university education at all. Ted Heath and Margaret Thatcher both came from simple backgrounds, but both had Oxford degrees. Tony Blair is also an Oxonian, but his Labour Cabinet reflects a more varied educational background.

of the publicly funded system). And Britain's recent conversion to mass higher education is tantamount to a social revolution. When I first lived here, the statistic that most distinguished Britain from its industrialized partners was the minuscule proportion of young people who went on to any university instruction. The number of male and female students is now ballooning, however, and the quality of education in non-Oxbridge universities is rising. It will be eons before Oxford and Cambridge lose their advantage in decanting bright graduates into the influential echelons of British society, but in a single generation the evidence of lasting change in higher education is compelling.

Because Oxbridge is still such a crucial hinge in how Britain works, it also explains the continuing phenomenon of the English public school. It used to be that a private education before university was a more important qualification for status than an Oxbridge degree. This is no longer true. But private schools, which the British insist on calling public schools, remain the most reliable escalators into Oxbridge and therefore into the DMZ. And, in some cob-webbed corners of the land, it's still better to have a private secondary education and no degree than to have a double-first from Oxbridge without the background of a public school.

Public schools account for only about 7 per cent of secondary education in Britain but consistently outrank state schools in the charts of academic achievement. The Conservative governments of 1979–97 were responsible for running the state system, but few Tories thought of committing their children to it. The old-style grammar schools used to skim off the best in the state sector and gave their students a semi-even break. But someone is always tinkering with the educational system, and ever since I first came to Britain the two political parties have fought endless battles across this territory with rallying cries of 'comprehensivization', 'opt-out', 'assisted places', 'national curriculum', 'streaming' and so forth, each phrase fraught and heavily laden.*

---

* The social gap which schooling once represented has narrowed considerably in the last generation or so. Jack Weatherill, the former Speaker of the House, once told me that, when he was a boy, his family moved away from Sunningdale because the local school would not admit the son of someone 'in trade'. His father was a master tailor. (Lord Weatherill was also the first Conservative Party whip who had not been an officer in the military.)

The private system still remains the Great Divide in Britain's social watershed. Nothing flummoxes Americans more about Britain than the peculiarity of an important number of parents who despatch their bewildered children, especially their boys, at the tender age of seven or eight to forbidding brick institutions far away from home. Boarding schools in America are rare enough as it is, but you can hardly find any now that take pre-adolescent children (many British think American children are pampered and that the United States is the only country in the world where the parents obey the children).

Caroline and I have had innumerable conversations with British parents who have sent their children to boarding schools at unbearably young ages. The dialogue is almost always the same. The mother's eyes well up at the thought of such an early separation, but, she says, her husband insists it must be so. The father says how painful the same experience was for him as a boy – bullying and buggering and all that – and how much he hated it. But when the social clock sounds the hour, off the child goes.

The rationales for this juvenile rite of passage range from the habits of the Empire to the poor quality of state education to the institutional provision of character and spine. Much of this thinking seems *passé* now. But, in the end, a private school is the seal of approval from the old system and the surest way to make it through the portals of a decent university, especially Oxbridge. For some, a private school is to the Establishment what baptism is to Christianity.

The impression that the Decision-Making Zone to some degree imitates the old gentlemancy is reinforced by the semi-annual publication of the Honours List. Though John Major and Tony Blair have both tried to make meritorious service the sole criterion for titled recognition, the uniquely British Honours system still suggests a kind of national schizophrenia between social present and social past. It was always hard for me to reconcile this elaborate pastime with a society that so frequently bemoans the class system or claims that it no longer matters.

Everyone likes to have an official pat on the back, and Americans are particularly susceptible to awards, certificates, diplomas and citations to hang on office walls. Americans also grab hold of the few titles which our society makes available – Judge, Professor,

Doctor, General, Ambassador. But, compared with Britain, the American cupboard is pretty bare.

The Honours system is a spangled cornucopia of earthly delights. The Honours are unitary in concept and all members of society are theoretically eligible. There are orders of this and orders of that and a lot of awards that scramble the alphabet into a social code: OBE, KCMG, OM, CVO, MBE, CH and so forth. Most of the names are confined to the tiny print of the next day's newspapers, and the general point is to recognize the good works of good citizens. The dedicated charity worker or dutiful fireman receives a fleeting moment of deserved national gratitude. An occasional rock star, television celebrity or athlete usually leavens the modern list. Because the awards are distributed in the name of the Crown, not the government, even those in the anti-Establishment camp succumb to the blandishment of an Honour. Nothing in Britain is better calculated to melt the heart of a firebrand radical. Few say no.

The loss of imperial glory has not noticeably impaired the British vision of sashes and sunbursts, and it is up towards the top of the list, where the more rarefied titles appear in bold print, that the Honours system bestows the adornments of class. Like the angels, there are nine orders in the chivalric hierarchy, and distinctions among them and gradations within them are so intricate that only a handful of experts really understands the system, and certainly no outsider. The complexities enhance the aura of the Honours and the sense of ancient origins. The evocative use of the words 'lord' and 'knight' and 'empire' conjure up images of Arthurian castles in deep forests and genuflections on velvet cushions.

I never discovered how all this happens. Most of the semi-annual list is the result of nominations from the shires and careful screening in the Prime Minister's Appointments Office. But that applies only to the small-print recipients. The bold-print, top-of-the-page, entitled-for-life worthies just happen. The selection process inevitably encourages speculation about political patronage and social trade-offs, but there are no explanations.* A senior Tory once told me about a well-to-do party supporter who one day left behind a

---

* James I sold baronetcies and Lloyd George conducted what amounted to an annual auction of Honours for his political supporters, so the connection between money and titles is hardly new.

£2,000,000 cheque at Conservative Central Office. The cheque was signed only with the contributor's last name, which meant that it couldn't be cashed until the man was made a peer. So the reason why the lordly tap falls on one individual's shoulder and not another's, or why this prominent chap is beknighted but not that one, is left obscure. Some win and some lose, and all the decisions are made according to private conventions.

Recipients usually disparage the distinction of a 'gong'. The cliché for a knighthood is that 'it is only useful for getting a good table at a restaurant', and I suspect it's true that, once a knight, you're unlikely to be seated near the kitchen. A peerage, the newly elevated say, means you are never wanting for a good parking space in central London. But this off-hand modesty barely disguises the gratification. After all, an honour is the summit of public recognition in Britain, the pennant atop the social order. A new salutation that accompanies a title or a new name that accompanies a peerage requires the rest of society to reprogramme mentally before speaking to the new honouree. With every Honours List, address books all over Britain are rejigged and you have to note whether it is 'Lady So-and-So' or 'The Lady So-and-So'. Even the male children of life peers, who have nothing whatever to do with the matter, may assume the courtesy title of 'Honourable'. And everyone goes along.

What is clear is that the system confers the outward and visible status of inward and social grace. Like a temporal canonization, a knighthood or a peerage forever distinguishes the bearers from the rest of their own society. In conferring titled promotions, the honours system, for all its dignity, exaggerates the stratification of British society so that some people are demonstrably more equal than others. There is a continuing reaffirmation about the way society is ordered or should be, and that life is a hierarchy in which one rank defers to another. It is hard to square all this with the declassification of Britain.

As a hearty democrat from a revolutionary republic, I would like to say I disapprove of the Honours system. I don't. I think it's cool. But not much more than that.

Like a dowager's scent, many of the old attitudes of old England hang on in the rooms of Britain's Decision-Making Zone. A pluto-meritocracy is bound to be confusing, especially to an outsider. But none of this should disguise the fact that a new kind of Establishment runs Britain today. The system is not nearly so impacted or stylized as it used to be. Social flux is more characteristic of Britain now than social stasis, and the Grand Compromise between the old upper class and the new middle class has transformed the dynamics of British society and undermined the sense of predictable system. The present may resemble the past, but after all, when the British make an omelette, they break as few eggs as possible.

Chalk and Cheese

The British workingman was once a character of mythic proportions who earned a brawny reputation in the long-ago days when Britain turned out most of the world's manufactured goods. Before I was a teenager, I knew the words of a song called 'Gor Blimey' without ever knowing what 'gor blimey' meant. The song, I suppose, was brought back to the United States by the American army after the Second World War. I can recall only fragments of the verse now, but its message was forthright: if you know what's good for you, don't muck around with a British workingman.

Long after the country's industrial apogee, 'the working class' is still a social distinction in Britain with vivid anthropological origins. As a description of a particular segment of society, the phrase conveys something much more than people with jobs and wage packets. Income wasn't any more a measure of the old working class than it was of the old upper class. 'Working class' is a social phrase, not an economic one. It is a theory of social relativity. It is a harsh phrase, too, because it suggests there is still a class in Britain which works and, by definition, another one which doesn't, and therein lies the tale.

Just like the rest of Britain, the working class is possessed by its own strong sense of the past, rural as well as industrial, with a direct line stretching as far back as the time when Adam delved and Eve span. The working class is intensely national, with deep roots in England, Scotland and Wales, and it is intensely nationalist. But, most important, working class, in the end, means belonging to something. It means fitting into the scheme of things, having a sure footing in society and knowing who your friends are. It is solidarity and fraternity with the lads who share the deep-seated belief that, in Britain, my class is as good as yours.

I always thought one of the most salient social facts in Britain's modern history was its rapid urbanization, far faster and more sudden than in any other nation. Britain became metropolitan when the balance in other countries was still decidedly agrarian. By Queen Victoria's death, more than half the British people lived in cities. There were more servants in London than farmers in Britain, and more than four million people worked in manufacturing.

The Dickensian dereliction that accompanied this massive domestic migration was meticulously chronicled by the Victorians, who seemed to measure everything. The social squalor of the lower orders, existing side by side with the social comfort of the upper class, inspired Marx and Engels. Charles Darwin provided the rationalization for a higher species and a lower species as the way of nature. This stark disparity moved Disraeli to proclaim famously that there were Two Nations, 'between whom there is no intercourse and no sympathy; who are as ignorant of each other's habits, thoughts and feelings, as if they were dwellers in different zones, or inhabitants of different planets'. Disraeli's words supplied the basic theme of British politics, British economics and British society from the end of the nineteenth century all the way through the twentieth.

In our conversations, Neil Kinnock often recollected the two-nation world of his youth. His early radicalism emerged naturally in South Wales. He recalls the impoverishment of Tredegar, where he grew up, as well as the community solidarity that came along with it. 'Tredegar', he once related, 'was as thoroughly working class and socialist as any place you could find in the United Kingdom. During the General Strike, before I was born, Tredegar was run by a "soviet", and when the Labour Party formed an alliance in the district council, it was with the communists.' The town was so collectivized, Kinnock said, that every worker, no matter how poor, gave threepence a week for the running of the Miners Hall and the Medical Aid Society. On weekends, faith was divided between church and rugby. On Saturday nights all the working-class families of Tredegar would gather at the Hall for a variety of entertainment. And, this being Wales, everyone sang. People stuck together.

When Kinnock tells these stories, his eyes glisten. The recollections seem to pull him between pride and bitterness. He managed to escape his future in Tredegar because he was a clever boy and he succeeded in his eleven-plus examination, going on to a grammar school and then university. Grammar school was the only exit from the working-class corral. The other children of Tredegar were, for the most part, locked into their futures. Kinnock's years as leader of the Labour Party tempered a lot of his reformist zeal, but at heart he remained a boy of the barricades. It was no accident that Wales produced such rhetorical flame-throwers as Lloyd George, Aneurin Bevan and Neil Kinnock, and it will be some time before the collective memory of the British working class forgets the grainy images of its early years.

The working class in Britain is not synonymous with the trade union movement, and never has been. But it is a natural mistake for an outsider to confuse the two. At their zenith, the unions included half of Britain's workers, a much higher proportion than in the United States. British workers were also more rooted in their geography and more radical in their language than anything you were likely to come across in America. In the romantic vocabulary of British unionism – 'the comrades', 'the proletariat', 'the struggle' – there was the fervour of a Second Coming, a sense of impending upheaval and an expectation that the red flag would one day flutter over the rubble of Britain's class system.

America's occasional flirtations with socialism were aberrations in our political history, and in any case America was simply too big and too loose for the kind of class-conscious regimentation that effective unionism requires. Americans also had other calls on their after-hours loyalties, especially their ethnic identifications. And the ambitions of American workers were different because they were not ideological and did not aim to overhaul the broader social order. After all, white American workers won the right to vote in the 1830s, whereas the British worker was disenfranchised for most of that century.

The words 'socialism', 'communism' and 'marxism' were considered almost interchangeable by Americans, and always nefarious. The language of British unionism, on the other hand, could sometimes be startling for a visitor from the other side of the ocean. When I first came to Britain, I had to adjust my thinking leftwards to take account of a social experience for which the United States had no real equivalent.*

The American distinction between 'blue collar' and 'white collar' never caught on in Britain. I think this is because in America a job describes the kind of work you happen to do at the time and not necessarily your assigned rung on the social ladder. Job mobility, at least for your offspring if not for yourself, is part of the American legend. So most American workers identify themselves socially and even economically as 'middle class'. With their own houses and their own cars and their own lawn mowers, American workers, even if union members, usually place themselves on this wide, middle ground in the social landscape of the country.

The reverse still seems to be the case in Britain. The material circumstances of the working class have changed dramatically in the last few decades, but the spiritual attitudes persist. Two-thirds of the British workforce describe themselves as 'working class'. A union friend of mine recalled his first visit to the United States, perhaps twenty years ago or so, where he encountered many people who performed the same kind of unionized factory work as workers in Britain. But the Americans called themselves 'middle class', and they seemed to resent the suggestion that in Britain they would be called 'working class'. The distinction is that a British worker isn't defined merely by his job or even by his mortgage. In Britain, he is defined by his accent, his education, his newspaper and his memory. And it is loyalty to all of these that makes the British working class as conservative as the upper class, despite the militant edge.

I lived in Britain when the miners' strike of 1984–5 was in full

* Still, except for the military, the affinity between the TUC and the AFL–CIO is probably the warmest of all organizational relationships across the Atlantic.

flow. And I learned something important about the difference between the British worker and his American cousin.

The strike was an epic struggle. At the time it seemed a fateful Gettysburg, a desperate high-water mark for British unionism. In fact, the unions had already peaked a few years before, during the strike-happy Winter of Discontent in 1978–9, when they went on a reckless binge of rolling call-outs, secondary pickets and general disruption. The unions then seemed to knock over everything that got in their way, including eventually the Labour government. But the miners' strike of the mid-1980s had all the character, drama and tension of a national passion play, and the long confrontation was acted out on the television screens, sometimes with violence and always with emotion.

For all the historical radicalism of the miners, they had always been viewed sympathetically by the British public. There was a grimy, sweaty romance about the coal pits, so long as you didn't have to work in one. No Labour politician's office was complete without a miner's lantern on the bookshelf or the window sill.

The men who worked at the coalfaces of England, Scotland and Wales established tight communities around the dark, dangerous holes that dotted the country, and for decades they reached deep into the earth and brought up the black deposits which fuelled the machinery of the nation. The miners were a sort of aristocracy of the working class, and if the real aristocracy had once bound together the different regions of Britain in a single cultural class, so did the miners glue together the working class on a broad, national scale. Every year, in July, miners from all around the British Isles – and all the top union leaders as well – gathered at the Durham Miners' Gala, where they displayed their colourful banners and where their brass bands played. The miners were also fighters. When duty called, the Durham miners became the Durham Light Infantry, throwing down their picks and going off to war for king and country. The miners were the true grit of the British working class. And by 1984 they were a condemned breed.

During the strike there was plenty of rough intimidation on the picket lines. Mounted police charged across open fields and into the taunting crowds of strikers. It looked like the 1930s. The British people were stunned, and, as an outsider, so was I. Arthur Scargill, the rabble-rousing leader of the National Union of Mineworkers, strutted before the cameras with all the swagger and bile of a tinpot dictator. Ian MacGregor, an Americanized Scot, represented management with all the political and social sympathy of a barroom bouncer, and I recall cringing whenever he appeared on television. The Tory government, under the severe glare of Margaret Thatcher, treated the strike like a siege. The language on both sides was bitter and the atmosphere volatile. The national mood swung back and forth. The strike seemed to be an old-fashioned, setpiece battle in the long campaign of British class conflict, and it took me a while to figure out that, in the British way, its purpose was not to overthrow an old order but to preserve one.

While the strike reeled along its course, I had lunch (which is what diplomats do in times of crisis) with a union friend, Bill Jordan. Jordan is anything but radical. He was then a tough-minded, tightly coiled figure on the rise among his brethren in the engineers' union. He had a deep sense of what British unionism stood for and the imperatives of sticking together. His personal support for Arthur Scargill you could measure in a thimble, but his support for the miners was devoted. I looked at British mining as an economic anachronism and thought that, if the industry was to survive at all, it had to modernize, as painful as that process might be. I was too naive to recognize that much more was involved. Jordan proceeded to set me straight.

Jordan agreed that British mining was overmanned and inefficient. But the strike was not about market forces and competitiveness. The markets had already killed off the steel workers and the shipbuilders, he said, so we know what 'the market' does. The miners' strike was certainly about jobs, but it was just as much about community and a way of life. For the miners, Jordan said, jobs are like property. But the Tory government refuses to support the miners so they can keep what belongs to them. Maybe that would be okay if everyone in Britain got the same treatment. But the government doesn't think twice about subsidizing the farmers. If you left things to Thatcher's 'free market', there wouldn't be any farmers left in England. But the farmers and the landlords get their government pay-offs because they vote Tory and because the Tories want to preserve their class and their way of life. The miners deserve equal treatment. The grandfathers of these strikers used to work in the mines. And their fathers did too. And now these men work in the mines, and they have every right to pass on their jobs to their sons. Their jobs are the only property they have to bequeath. After all, this is what the upper class does. The upper class passes on its property to its sons, and this is bloody well what the miners have a right to do too.

By the time Jordan had finished, he was halfway across the table and shaking me by the lapels. This was more than an argument about conditions of employment or pay levels or the right to work. It had nothing to do with economics or the effects of technology or all the folderol about modernizing Britain. It was a concept of jobs as community property to be preserved for their own sake and passed on from one generation to another. And in that sense it was a separate-but-equal argument about class. There is one class on this side of the social divide and one class on the other side. So be it. But what is sauce for the goose is sauce for the gander, and the government's treatment of the two classes ought to be the same.

As I thought about all this, I recalled John L. Lewis, the leader of the United Mine Workers of America. When I was young, Lewis, with his bulky frame and bushy eyebrows, was often in the news. He seemed always to be calling out his miners from the pits of West Virginia or Kentucky or Pennsylvania. Conditions there were just as harsh as in Britain, and the realities of the economy pressed down on the American miners in the same relentless way, perhaps more so. But there was a crucial difference. John L. Lewis wanted better conditions for his union members, and better pay; and he wanted their jobs protected too. But he explained his goals by saying that his miners toiled hard in the pits and laboured long in the earth so that their sons would not have to. The coal pit was a place for the next generation to get out of, not stay in. There's the difference.

The miners' strike ultimately collapsed, and there are today only a score of pits still in production. Arthur Scargill was right, at least about that. And so was Bill Jordan about the destruction of the miners' communities. The last banner of the Durham Miners now hangs in the transept of Durham Cathedral like a funeral relic, and there are no mines left in that county at all. But the logic of Jordan's diatribe, and his view of British society as separate structures, existing in parallel and rooted in class, stayed with me for a long time. And in the end, it seemed, the working class was every bit as preservationist as the upper class, and, just as with the upper class, it was the attitudes and values of the working class that persisted in British society well after they had been overtaken by economic realities.

This theory of Britain as two sides of the same sociological coin used to be supported more obviously than it is today. The nation was neatly bifurcated, with each part a mirror of the other. People did the same things but the form depended on the class. Like Royal Ascot, where there still is a barrier separating the toffy side from the touty side, each British class gathered in its own way for the same national occasion.

There was, for example, a division between those who went to clubs and those who went to pubs; but, wherever they went, everyone had a drink, even if one side drank a pint of bitter and the other side drank a Pimm's cup. There were those who went on holiday to Barbados and those who went on holiday to Blackpool. One class read the quality press and the other read the tabloids. Some bet at Goodwood and some at Ladbroke's. One class worked in a credit economy and the other in a cash economy. Film was for the uppers and television for the lowers. In the army, there were officers and Tommies, and the line was never crossed. One side of the coin voted Tory and the other side voted Labour. There were those who grew flowers in the window boxes of their terraced houses and those who grew flowers in the walled gardens of their country houses. And so on. British lives ran in tandem, each reflecting the other. Society was like a big train, with a first-class carriage and a second-class carriage, both pulled together along the same rail line.

A lot of these observations seem frayed now, even though you don't have to look too hard to find traces. Social things in Britain are not the chalk and cheese they used to be. In the last generation, the working class in Britain has transformed itself beyond recognition. The change started with the welfare state of the Attlee government, and, whatever the economic merits of this new framework, the material profile of the working class improved, in part because of socialist legislation and in part despite it. The pace accelerated in the 1980s. The good things of life – quantified as refrigerators, washing machines, cars, telephones and videos –

became everyday necessities. And, on the whole, the working class gradually became middle class by any objective measure.

In the process of material change, the old industrial base of Britain started to dissolve and so did the old solidarity of the working class. The union voice is much weaker now and the Labour Party has found a new, middle-class footing. Time has softened the bitterness and the memories. Suspicions remain, and you can still hear the slogans of proletarian radicalism from people who wouldn't know a pick from a shovel. But the working class has largely lost its heart. And, in a way, that's a melancholy thing.

Most of Britain acquiesced in the old arrangement of class and seemed content with it. I'm-all-right-Jack at one end of the social scale was matched by I'm-all-right-Nigel at the other end. In the British class system, you knew your place, and knowing your place brought predictability and security. In the days of class, social relationships in Britain were more or less reliable, and so long as the codes were not transgressed you were safe if not necessarily satisfied. There were plenty of skirmishes along the front lines of class, but these were about the margins of wealth, not the acquisition of status. Each class had its own sub-sets which passed in and out of each other's ambits in a finely tuned social universe. In fact, for all the faults of the social system, my impression is that the British over the generations developed a strong sense of human community, divided perhaps, but real. There was a tranquillity about British society, and there still is, which is unfamiliar to an American accustomed to a frenetic hurly-burly where the emphasis is less on getting along than getting ahead.

But one thing is sure: there are no longer Two Nations in Britain today. The political *cognoscenti* now talk in terms of A, B, C-1, C-2, C-3 and other slices of the demographic profile. The large majority of the British population isn't part of the Old Establishment or the old working class or anything. 'Middle class' hardly captures the variety. The majority worries about mortgage payments and where the children go to school and how to build a pension, the commonplace concerns of commonplace lives, just as in America. In fact, the social alignment between the United Kingdom and the United States is probably closer today than it has ever been. This may distress some in Britain. But not many.

Instead of Two Nations in Britain, it is truer to say there are twenty or thirty, maybe more. Other barriers in British society today are more obvious than class and perhaps more important. The contrast between the North of England and the South is an example, and Scots believe the issue of class is largely an English problem that has little to do with their more egalitarian society. Class was always described in male terms, but today this doesn't make much sense either, especially now that women make up half the workforce. And a more intractable line runs between those who are part of the private economy in Britain and those who rely on the state, or between those with a solid education and those without. The non-class of Britain – those hardcore unemployed who live in the dreary stretches of rundown council estates, or the alienated ethnic minorities in the bleak blocks of Britain's inner cities – will probably have more significance for Britain's social future than the classic forms of British class. This all sounds familiar to an American.

The Harvard philosopher William James often came to England to visit his brother Henry, and at the turn of the century he concluded that the British 'lead arranged lives'. Depending on the layer of society into which you were born, your life was laid out ahead of you. Your relationship to those around you was predetermined, and so were your habits and patterns. Your star was fixed.

This is no longer true. But the roots of class run so deep in Britain that some of the system and many of the attitudes persist long after the historic rationales have collapsed. It may be that after all the grumbling and socio-psychoanalysis, the British feel comfortable with class, not because it is equitable, but because they are fond of form and too preoccupied by belonging to let it go completely.

And so class hangs on in British society like a dull headache. By the time I had finished my embassy years, I still didn't know what to think about it. Sometimes class seemed like an indelible stain that couldn't be washed out of the national fabric. Sometimes it seemed irrelevant. But, either way, class today isn't the duck it used to be.

PART THREE

A Scratch Behind the Ear

Cats and Dogs

The British, I think, are still a rural society, at least in temperament, and this must be one reason why they have so many animals. The country is a huge national menagerie. There is a kind of pantheism about the British affection for their creatures and, if I ever wondered whether animals have souls, I can at least feel pretty certain that British animals do. I once came across a notice in Ely Cathedral announcing there would be a Blessing of the Animals the next Sunday, and I pictured all the pets from miles around crammed into the pews, eyes closed and heads bowed, as they entered that solemn state of British grace.

Animals are as much a part of British fantasy as they are of everyday life. There haven't been many lions in United Kingdom since the Ice Age, and there hasn't been a unicorn sighted for an even longer time. But the lion and the unicorn are joined together in a fanciful national symbol as if they were perfectly natural companions and perfectly at home in Britain, which I guess they are. As an emblem of a nation, these two creatures capture much of the British ethos and its balance between reality and imagination.

The Loch Ness Monster and the Beast of Bodmin also lie somewhere in this fantasy zone, and so do the thousands of gargoyles that peer down from ancient English churches. In fact,

Britain sometimes seems to be a fantastic bestiary.

Many British animals are fairytale creatures, cavorting in the margins of the Lindisfarne Gospels and the pages of Beatrix Potter. Paddington Bear lives near the railroad station in London and Winnie the Pooh resides in Kent. Toad lives at Toad Hall. In the nave of St Mary's Church in Beverley I have seen the small stone carving reputed to be the inspiration for the White Rabbit in Alice's Wonderland. In Hyde Park there is a bronze fountain made of two hugging bears, and, not far from the small pet cemetery on the Bayswater side, the statue of Peter Pan stands atop a plinth festooned with scampering creatures of enchantment.*

Oddly enough, the political parties in Britain have not used animals as symbols of their political virtues. In America there's a donkey for the Democrats and an elephant for the Republicans. But in Britain parties are identified by their true colours. Maybe if each party adopted an animal – say, a tortoise for the Tories and a hare for Labour, or perhaps the other way around – the voters might warm to them more.†

In the real world, or more real world, the British are especially batty about horses. Red circles are drawn on the equine calendar for the Horse Trials at Badminton, the Horse Show at Windsor and the racing meets at Newmarket, Goodwood, Epsom, Aintree or any of the scores of places where horses gather for a good run. There is no London scene more arresting than a rider galloping through the morning mist in Hyde Park like a messenger from the gods. And in the countryside you can always count on coming across a rider in jodhpurs and muddy boots trotting along a country lane or cantering across the distant downs.

At Winfield House, not long after dawn, I often heard the jangle and snorting of horses clip-clopping around the Outer Circle, taking

* Much of America's animal world has been taken over by Walt Disney, but the British somehow make sure none of their animals, real or imagined, simper.

† Choosing an animal as a political symbol runs some risks. In the 1997 general election, the Labour Party briefly tried to revive the British bulldog, but this squat, jowly, slobbering creature failed to capture the sleek image Labour sought to portray. And I recall standing in the East Room of the White House during President Carter's administration when Robert Mugabe, the President of Zimbabwe, explained the significance of the rooster as ZANU's emblem. 'All my success', he announced, 'is because of my big cock.' The room was quiet.

their morning exercise from the barracks in Albany Street, and I think something important in British life would disappear for ever if the dwindling troop of the Household Cavalry no longer clattered down Constitution Hill to meet the Queen.

Only a fraction of the British population actually knows how to get up on top of a horse, but the nation as a whole likes to feel it's in the saddle. The horse holds a special place that suggests older glories and simpler times. So the British have a love affair with horses, and, according to the tabloid press, whips and riding crops turn up in the most unexpected places.

Horses may be the aristocrats of Britain's animal hierarchy, but there are plenty of other important orders. Counting sheep in Britain is near to a hopeless task. The United Kingdom is the home of more sheep per capita than any country in Europe, which is an unusual statistic for a race which is not notably sheepish. At lambing time, there are about forty million sheep in the national flock. That's a lot of pullovers. Once, in the Lake District, Caroline and I came across a real shepherd, scruffy and bearded, with a slouch hat and a shepherd's crook and a shepherd's dog, and looking so Thomas-Hardy that we wondered whether he was employed by the English Tourist Board.

Cows, too, are an essential part of Britain's pastoral idyll. No rural picture in Britain is complete without a herd of Friesians grazing in a grassy meadow or a few Angus sheltering under a broad oak before the rain. After seeing the cosseted Charolais of the Duke and Duchess of Devonshire, Caroline concluded that, if she ever came back to earth as a cow, she would want to chew her transcendental cud in the bovine dreamworld of Chatsworth (the Duchess was pleased and said Caroline would be welcome in any circumstances).

Her Majesty keeps her own royal dairy at Windsor to produce the royal butter for the royal slice of bread, and the British as a race gorge themselves on milk, butter, cheese and a bewildering variety of creams. A thick slab of roast beef is still the national dish. The British, like the Masai, seem to have a symbiotic relationship with their cows, and, after the scare about BSE, cows have become the Kingdom's foremost Euro-sceptics.

The British admire animals and protect them like wards of the state. The deer park was a British invention. The RSPCA was founded by William Wilberforce in 1824, and London opened the world's first zoo in 1828. In this century, James Herriot became the spokesman for all creatures great and small, at least those who live in Yorkshire, and Sir David Attenborough is the modern voice of the natural world. In the 1960s, Desmond Morris popularized the thought that the human race doesn't have much of a leg up on the society of animals, and perhaps the best known political satire in literature is *Animal Farm*. For the British, you can tell a lot about life from the animals you know.

The British can be uncharacteristically passionate on this subject. It isn't hard to organize a demonstration against the wearing of natural fur, and a visitor swathed in a mink coat or decked out in a sable stole is always in danger of ambush in a British street. Citizens who wouldn't dream of carrying a placard of political protest will put aside their needlepoint or account ledgers and lie down in front of a two-ton lorry containing crates of calves for export. A leaflet stuffed into your hand outside a tube station is as likely to be about whales or badgers as about nuclear testing. And the Anti-Vivisection League and the Animal Liberation Front are probably the most violent domestic organizations operating in the British Isles save the Irish Republican Army.

But it is on the issue of fox hunting that British passions for tradition, social status, conservation, politics, morality and mission-ary zeal converge. The objective of the hunt does not seem entirely in keeping with the British compassion for animals. But fox hunting is variously defended as pastoral romance, pest control, cavalry practice (sic) and a rural way of life that is essentially classless because everyone joins in. One friend claimed that the foxes themselves enjoy the sport, though I had a hard time following his reasoning. Opponents of the hunt, on the other hand, see only barbarism and snobbery. They say the hunt not only violates the sanctity of animal rights – a proposition with which most foxes would almost surely agree – but also perpetuates the pretensions of Britain's social past.

Over no other British issue are righteousness and hypocrisy so in heat. Every autumn the mounted hunters gather on the rolling estates of England, and every autumn the saboteurs fan out across the same territory. Autumn becomes a season of flaring nostrils and flaring tempers, and there is always a story of a red-clad, red-faced hunter beating a protester over the head with his riding crop, or a protester somewhere wrenching a hunter from the saddle.

It takes an American a while to figure out what all the fuss is about. There are hunts in America too, but the dogs are trained not to attack their prey. So an American hunt, unlike a British hunt, is bloodless. You would think the reverse would be the case.

Over the last decade, the House of Commons has been circling around the issue of fox hunting like a wolf around a fold. Both main parties have tried to duck the issue because there is no consensus on either side. The Blair government may blow the final horn, but up to now there's been a lot of parliamentary manoeuvring and bluster in the Commons while the House of Lords looks on aghast. One thing is sure: when it's a question of animals in Britain, the gloves are off.

Most of all in Britain, however, it's a dog's life. Cat-owners would object to this statement, I know. Cats, after all, are in the ascendancy, and when thinking about Britain you should more properly imagine a cat slinking across a soft eiderdown in a little urban bed-sit rather than a dog flopping down by the hearth in a cosy country cottage.

After all, the cats are taking over, at least demographically: 7.1 million felines against 6.6 million canines (this reversal of canine fortune is true in the United States as well and in about the same proportion: 63 million cats versus 57 million dogs). Nowadays, you can detect a trace of self-satisfied triumphalism at the annual Cat Fancy. During my time at the embassy, Humphrey the cat ruled in Downing Street, and in my last year the transatlantic relationship turned wholly feline when Socks the cat displaced Millie the dog in the White House.

But, still, there is something unique about the British infatuation with dogs. Some say the British are such a reserved race that dogs fill the role of companionship in a way that two-footed British creatures cannot. A recent survey concluded that 60 per cent of dog-owners in Britain preferred the company of their dog to that of their spouse. I suspect the same poll in the United States would produce the same result. In fact, research at a New York university showed that in almost any stressful situation an American's blood pressure and heart rate are lower and steadier in the company of a dog than in the company of a spouse. So it does seem true, at least in the Anglo-American world, that if you want a friend, get a dog.

Another school of thought says that British dogs are simply an anthropomorphic extension of British society as a whole. The canine world and the human world are two sides of the same coin, and when it comes to dogs the British re-create themselves. The Queen, for example, walks around in a cloud of corgis, and the feature I remember most about the Queen Mother's home at Clarence House is the water bowl sitting in the hallway just before you step into the elegant drawing room. The annual Crufts dog show brings together the upper crust of Britain's canine society, and Scruffts is the show for dogs who didn't have a private education. The merchant classes are represented by an Old English sheepdog selling paint on television or a Labrador puppy flogging toilet tissue, and the annual border-collie trials display the no-nonsense skills of the working class.

Unlike American dogs, British dogs require no licence. There are powerful societies in Britain such as the Kennel Club or the Canine Defence League which look after the genealogical integrity and everyday welfare of dogs. The Battersea Dogs' Home takes care of some 10,000 strays every year, and there are many other shelters all over the country. Some hotels in Britain offer weekend specials for clients and their dogs, and I've met a man named Ron who sweeps the streets around Knightsbridge and carries a pocketful of biscuits for whatever hounds happen to trot by.

One sure sign that things were out of joint when I returned to Britain in 1991 was the Dangerous Dogs Act. At the time this was the principal matter before Her Majesty's Government, and it seemed to have very little to do with Britain's adjustment to the post-Cold War world.* When I went to see the Home Secretary, Kenneth Baker, he looked and acted as much like a Cheshire cat as serious politics would allow. At first I suspected feline plotting in high places, but when I asked him whether Britain had gone haywire, Baker admitted that the legislation was a dog's breakfast. A less jack-booted version of the bill finally passed.

* The main culprit in the dangerous dogs debate was the pit bull terrier. As the arguments developed, I noticed the name evolved into 'American pit bull terrier', as if this modification explained why a breed could turn nasty, even in Britain.

On the other hand, the good news for dogs – and cats as well – is that the six-month quarantine law may be on its last legs. Like any island race, I suppose, the British are suspicious of furry things from foreign parts, and, to be fair, once rabies is loose on an island, it is exceptionally difficult to eradicate. But nowadays quarantine is so unnecessary it seems quirky at best and cruel at worst. There hasn't been a death from rabies in Western Europe since 1928, and foaming at the mouth occurs in the United States almost entirely for political reasons. Moreover, there is now an effective vaccine against the disease and animals who have been immunized and microchipped can be properly traced. The last recorded case of a rabid dog in Britain occurred in Surrey in 1969, and the circumstances of that incident were cloudy. The last instance of a human with rabies happened in 1902. The British hang on to many unnecessary things but not many unnecessary things which are also unkind.*

This is not to say that those who administer the quarantine law are unkind. When Caroline and I came here in 1984, we had our young dog Topsy but also an old cat named Roger. From Washington, I telephoned ahead to make arrangements with a government-licensed kennel in Berkshire. The woman at the other end of the line enquired, 'How old is your dog?' 'She's three,' I said. 'All right,' the woman answered, filling out a biographical form. 'And how old is your cat?' 'Fourteen,' I replied. 'Oh, I'm so sorry,' she said, and she did sound sorry. 'You're not permitted to bring in cats over ten.' I thought about this for a moment. 'Okay,' I answered, 'he's ten.' There was another pause. 'That'll be fine,' she said.

There are now more and more British citizens who travel abroad for work or holiday and who want to take their animals with them and bring them back. The House of Commons Select Committee on Agriculture has recommended reform of the quarantine regime, and the Labour government has set up a blue-ribboned panel to review the scientific evidence. An organization called Passports for Pets, which is led by the redoubtable Mary Fretwell – a liberating

* Since 1972, more than 160,000 dogs and cats have been funnelled through the quarantine stalags of Britain, and, of these, about 2,500 have died. And over that same time quarantine has yielded just two possible cases of rabies. Neither animal had been vaccinated.

Boadicea for cats and dogs alike – lobbies hard for a more sensible system. Most veterinarians agree it's time for a change. But for the moment this most pragmatic Kingdom remains a dog in the manger.

Still, one of the things I like most about the British is this: the set face of the typical pedestrian dissolves when someone with a dog passes by. In a Pavlovian response, he or she will drop everything and bend over to offer a scratch behind the ear and a cooing word.

For whatever reason, there is something special about the British and all their animals, especially their dogs. 'Love me, love my dog' is a good rule to keep in mind if you live here. A stranger in Britain is a stranger. But a stranger with a dog is a soulmate.

Lessons and Carols

When I was growing up in America, there was always an Englishness about our family Christmases, most of which I remember like luminous pearls strung together on a long, white string. I didn't recognize this Anglicization at the time, and I'm not sure I would have cared much if I had. Christmas was such an exciting occasion that the origins of our family habits didn't matter one way or the other.

But I should have smelled a rat. All those plum puddings, mince pies and fruit cakes could not possibly have been invented in America. They tasted so unAmerican, and to this day I make a point of avoiding them, the same way, I suppose, most British will make a detour around a Christmas bowl of American eggnog. Still, my parents tied a big Victorian bow around our Christmases, and only later did I discover that much of this was British, or at least British-processed.

Mercifully, my family never went so far as Christmas crackers and the indignity of paper hats. In fact, when I first came to Britain, I didn't know what a Christmas cracker was. I knew about Georgia crackers, and Graham crackers, and when I heard about Christmas crackers I assumed they were something to eat. On my first Christmas in Britain, I spent ten minutes in the biscuit section of the local Tesco looking for something orangey-chocolatey called 'Christmas crackers' before a puzzled assistant pointed me in another direction.

In the Christmas season, when Caroline and I lived in Winfield House, I was always derelict in my diplomatic duties and far more likely to be suspending sprigs of mistletoe from a chandelier at home than attending to messages from Washington. We would spend many hours in mid-December decorating our Christmas tree, which in the voluminous drawing room at Winfield House stood at least twenty feet tall. With loops of white fairy lights and scores of angels, seraphim and cherubs, the big tree was heavenly.

We also decorated a smaller tree with a clutter of shiny childhood detritus and this one was suitably gay and gaudy. We hung evergreen sprays on bannisters and ribboned garlands from architraves. Winfield House was the first place we had ever lived where we could literally deck the halls with boughs of holly. We tied bright bows around our assortment of upholstered cougars, racoons, reindeer and teddy bears. Caroline baked gingerbread men and spent many of her waking hours wrapping gifts to such perfection that opening them was always a little sinful. And everywhere in the house there were candles. Winfield House at Christmas time had a magical glow and we invited many friends there to take in the glimmering light of the season.

But, of all my Christmases past, I remember most the crystalline sound of English carols. I do not normally associate the British with music. Music is what the Germans and French and Italians do. But Christmas for me is incomplete without the sound of an English choir, and from mid-December onwards the familiar carols played at Winfield House from morning to night, as they had when I was young.

One Christmas Eve, we went to Cambridge to hear the choir in the chapel of King's College. There, the pure voices soar straight up to the lacey, stone vaults and right back down your spine. On that night, when we emerged from the chapel, the ground was covered with a crunchy white frost, the kind of still-frost that clings to tree branches and spider webs, and when I glanced around at the dark silhouette of the chapel, broken by the light of its stained-glass windows, it looked like a magnificent Christmas ship floating away on a Christmas sea. In Britain, at Christmas, it always seems like Christmas is supposed to be.

There is another reason why Christmas in Britain seems to me just right. The British take their time to celebrate the occasion. The country closes down and everything unwinds into a kind of Christmasy dream world. You can almost hear a collective national sigh as Christmas approaches. Many Londoners decamp at this time of year and steal away to familiar family places. For those who remain behind, London at Christmas has an archaeological feel to it, as if a great and ancient metropolis has been abandoned by its inhabitants. Streets are empty. Stores are shut. Markets are closed. You have to lay in supplies in advance, and even the noisy British press is mute for a moment. At Christmas in London, everything outside seems to fall away. The city hunkers down, goes all quiet in a mellow, fluffy, year-end, wintertime muffle.

All of this is possible because the British have contrived to cluster three public holidays in one week, and the real mark of British genius at Christmas is the invention of Boxing Day. Nowadays people forget about the origins of Boxing Day, when the lower orders were invited to receive their Christmas boxes from the grand masters. Downstairs came upstairs for a little while, and tenants assembled at the back door of great manors. But that was a long time ago. The origins of Boxing Day don't matter much any more, and there is already too much sociology in Britain as it is.

Boxing Day in modern times is a civilized concept: everyone gets an extra day right after Christmas to recover from all the devotional and familial ardours. There are no special religious or social expectations on Boxing Day. It is a slumbering, flop-around day. People can use the extra time to try on a new pullover, pick up a new book, test a new toy or assemble some new electronic gizmo. And there is time to eat up all the left-overs from the Christmas groaning board. Boxing Day is a time of contentment, a day of broad digestion. If I were ever elected President of the United States, I would, as my first act in office, proclaim Boxing Day a national holiday.

So, around Christmas, the British organize their public holidays to maximum effect. This is perhaps unremarkable in a country which is so earnest about personal holidays as well, especially summer holidays. In fact, as soon as the calendar is flipped over to the new year, the British start the feverish business of planning their summer 'hols'.

Beginning in January, booklets and pamphlets pour through the letter box in a flood of promotions and promises. Every other advertisement on television seems to be from Thomas Cook or Lunn Poly or any of a number of travel agents who thrive on the annual British holiday bonanza. The travel sections of newspapers fill up with reports on holiday bargains. On offer are package tours to faraway places or coach tours just around the corner. There are countless pictures of rentable villas in Tuscany and two-week cottages in Cornwall. You can go hiking in the Himalayas or the Lake District. There are safaris in Africa and pony treks in Wales. We never met a taxi driver who hadn't been to Disney World. In a pinch for holidays, Brighton and Blackpool will still do, and a few days of frolic at a Butlin's resort or camped at a coastal caravan site or chugging along in a canal boat remain perfectly acceptable domestic alternatives to more exotic and adventuresome journeys.

No one in Britain ever asks whether you're going away for a summer holiday, only where you're going. The British adore their hols. The point is to take a holiday whether you like it or not.

One reason the British are devoted to personal holidays is because they are so stingy about national holidays. There are only seven of them, fewer than any other European country except Holland. The Germans have a dozen national holidays. The Americans have ten. The Scots, sensible as they always are, take a couple more days off than the English, and each community in Northern Ireland naturally insists on its own day of sectarian commemoration in order to provoke the other. So, when it comes to public holidays, the English for once rank at the bottom of the national charts. But, even counting the regional variations, the British as a whole do not spoil themselves with public holidays.

British public holidays, few as they are, also seem to arrive during the year in a needlessly helter-skelter fashion, as if they were dropped into the calendar by accident. Three holidays are lumped together around May when two would do perfectly well, and there is another one in August which isn't needed at all. But then, from the end of August to the end of December, the weeks stretch out in the diary like an endless desert without a holiday oasis in sight. Autumn in Britain is a season bereft.

The principal problem with British national holidays, however, is that they do not really celebrate anything. Except for Christmastime, Britain's public holidays are bland and, for an American, downright boring. They are called 'bank holidays', the legacy of Sir John Lubbock who coaxed the Bank Holiday Act through Parliament in 1871. Lubbock was a reformer, and when he secured a secular day off for the nation on the first Monday in August, it was originally known in the grateful streets as 'St Lubbock's Day'.

It is hard to imagine anything more uninspiring than a 'bank holiday'. The Germans celebrate Unity. The French celebrate Revolution. The Americans celebrate Independence. And the British note the fact that the Bank of England is closed for the day. This hardly sends a shiver down the national spine.

There are a lot of shortcomings to the United States, but most observers would admit that Americans have put together their national holidays reasonably well. Technically, there is no such thing as a national holiday in America because the United States is a federal system and each state has jurisdiction over its own days-off. The President and Congress can only designate legal holidays for federal employees and the federal enclave of the District of Columbia. But as a practical matter the individual states have fallen in to line with the federal calendar.

More important, and most unlike the British, each American public holiday is designed to commemorate something, and the holidays are evenly spread over the year. In the middle of January, for example, comes the anniversary of Martin Luther King's birth, and in February, when the mid-winter is bleakest, there is George Washington's Birthday, or Presidents' Day as it is sometimes called. In May comes Memorial Day to remember the dead of past wars.

The pyrotechnic patriotism of the Fourth of July celebrates freedom from the crushing yoke of British despotism. Effigies of the English King are no longer hung from streetlamps in American cities, but when the Glorious Fourth rolls around, it is always a good idea for British residents to stay indoors. The United States is an exceptionally capitalist country, but on the first Monday in September Americans salute the labour movement. Labor Day is treated as the last barbecue of summer, a day to put away summer things and cast a serious eye down the remainder of the year. And, for children, Labor Day is the bogeyman that lurks at the end of the long summer break because traditionally it is the day before the schools open.

Columbus Day falls in October and celebrates the discovery of America in 1492.* In some politically correct places, the holiday is now called, with a straight face, Indigenous Peoples' Day. There is more saluting on Veterans Day – the old Armistice Day – which comes at the beginning of November. It is a time for parades, of which Americans are very fond.

In the United States, the fourth Thursday in November is the best American holiday of all: Thanksgiving, an all-embracing, non-sectarian, wholly national celebration of good and blessed things. For an American living in Britain, Thanksgiving is just another day, but it is probably the day when Americans most miss home. And in America, when Thanksgiving is over, it is a short and easy ride to Christmas when the holiday cycle starts all over again.

If the British decided to have another public holiday, I would like to believe they have so many things to celebrate that they might not be able to decide which one merits a day off. But the British are such a cantankerous race that the decision would probably divide the country more than uniting it. The flat neutralism of a 'bank holiday' at least spares the nation the debate about what to celebrate.

In 1978, for example, the Labour government introduced May Day as a bank holiday, and the Conservatives have wanted to get rid of it ever since. May Day was sneaked into the calendar as a surreptitious recognition of the international socialist brotherhood, but the Callaghan government disguised the holiday by recalling the more traditional rites of spring such as the maypole and the May Fair and the dreaded Morris dancing. Once a public holiday is granted, it's politically risky to try to take it back, and the Tories never made much progress.†

* Oscar Wilde said that America had been discovered many times before but it was hushed up.

† The Conservatives did manage to move the bank holiday from 1 May to the first Monday in the month.

But this does not mean the British are undeserving of another holiday, preferably in the autumn. A day off when the leaves have turned and the winter darkness approaches would be healthy for the national psyche. Still, it might be hard to find something to celebrate that is both national and uncontroversial.

Guy Fawkes Day, with all its firecrackers and bonfires, would be a candidate. But there might be too much popular sympathy nowadays for a man who wanted to blow up the House of Commons. Trafalgar Day falls conveniently on 21 October, but, in an era of European harmony, the French and Spanish, who were on the losing side, would surely take offence. In fact, it's hard to think of a European country that Britain hasn't tangled with at one time or another in its military past. (That's the problem with history – you end up annoying so many people along the way.) A Trafalgar Day might degenerate into patriotic jingoism, a kind of national bash of hope-and-glory hooliganism that wouldn't sit very well with the neighbours. And surely some would argue that the last thing Britain needs is a public holiday that looks backwards.

What I think the British really need is a national day of thanksgiving, a holiday to think that maybe things aren't so bad after all, a day off from the customary British blues. A friend of mine said the British are too cynical to have a day of thanksgiving, too jaded. But I doubt this is true. It doesn't take more than a glance at the international headlines to see that Britain is doing okay. Compared to most other places, Britain is honest and safe, and the basic freedoms and rights are, for the most part, secure in this land. On top of everything else, Britain is such a beautiful country that the heart sometimes aches. And for a nation which prides itself on good manners, a day of thanks is the courteous thing to do.

In the United States – and in Canada too – Thanksgiving is built around a great family feast of traditional foods such as turkey and yams and pumpkin pie. It is a harvest holiday, a time to think of what has been sown and what has been reaped. In Britain, it might be difficult to persuade the nation to sit down and tuck into a meal of jellied eels and toad-in-the-hole, but I'm sure it wouldn't be too hard to come up with some traditional substitutes.

As things are, however, I doubt the proposal for a British Thanksgiving is likely to prosper. The Bank of England wouldn't like it and it probably sounds too American to swallow. Autumn in the United Kingdom will remain long and dreary, uninterrupted and unrelieved. But I suppose this barren season is made bearable by the Christmas light at the end of the tunnel.

Gentlemen and
Players

At Lord's cricket ground, in the Pavilion dressing room of the England team, I once noticed an American baseball glove poking through the zipper top of a player's kitbag. I was told by my host from the Marylebone Cricket Club that the leather mitt was used by English players during warm-up before a match. To discover this token of Americana in the hallowed English sanctum of Lord's was a little like coming across an alligator in St James's Park, so out of place did it seem.

History has kindly spared our two countries the heavy burden of playing the same national game. This was not always so. In the early part of the nineteenth century, cricket was played in America almost as much as in Britain, even though the puritan ethic of the young nation generally frowned on such dalliance. The St George's Cricket Club was formed in New York in 1846, and the first international cricket match is reputed to have been played between Canada and the United States in the same year. But, once baseball took the Yankee fancy, American cricket faded into sporting oblivion.

In Britain, cricket has easily seen off baseball's occasional thrusts across the ocean. An American team toured England in 1874 but failed to light a fire, and professional leagues in Yorkshire and

Lancashire made brief appearances before folding during the Second World War.*

Baseball doesn't seem to fit the English character. An American elementary school coach came to Britain in 1994 to teach English schoolchildren the intoxications of the American game. He put his finger on one of the critical differences between the two national sports when he described his experience. 'For baseball truly to succeed in Britain,' he said gravely, 'they need a lesson or two in how to hustle – on, off and around the field. The kids just don't run here. They walk on the field and they walk off the field. It's just not in their nature to hustle.' (This was a coach speaking, not an economist.) In baseball, as in America, you have to hustle. So, on the expansive playing fields of the Anglo-American relationship, baseball and cricket keep their distance.

Estrangement is not the case with other sports. Britain has given America and the rest of the world a remarkable number of games. The British are good makers of rules. Tennis, golf, running, boxing, rowing and so forth are common to our athletic repertoires. Horses and horse racing are as much a part of one sporting scene as the other, though there are different horses for different courses. The steeplechase, for example, is unknown in the United States nor can one easily find a rodeo in the United Kingdom. Some sports are played in both countries but with different accents. Pool, for example, is preferred in America and snooker in Britain, but the game is pretty much the same. (In pool, incidentally, when a ball is struck in such a way as to make it spin in reverse, it's called 'giving it some English'. This may be a compliment, but it's worth thinking through.) Baseball and cricket, however, are like secrets we have kept from each other.

History explains some of this alienation. America never had much of an empire, so there was no convenient way of transplanting the national game. This, I think, is just as well. It's bad enough that Canadians play baseball. The Japanese are also addicted to the game, though the United States has so far managed to avoid a national contest against the Japanese, with whom an encounter will one day

---

* Amateur baseball is still played in Wales. A friend of mine claims that the Welsh invented baseball and that Welsh miners took the game to Pennsylvania. This is implausible, but I wish it were true.

doubtless prove calamitous for our national ego. Some Central American republics have taken up the sport after unexpected visits from the US Marine Corps. But on the whole baseball is a home-grown occupation, even though the grand finale of the long season is called the 'World Series', as if the game were played on an interplanetary scale.

The British, on the other hand, ruled over a gargantuan empire. They exported democracy and cricket, the latter proving the more durable. The English now have to submit themselves to the ordeal of visiting teams from faraway former colonies who come to England to beat them at their own game. Every summer, when the Pakistanis or the Australians or the West Indians arrive, you feel as if the entire country has been strapped into a dentist's chair. The British have learned to accept these painful encounters with their customary stoicism and good manners, but at least there's no Test Series against the former colonies of North America.

If you search hard enough, you can find some cricket in America and a little baseball in Britain. Thanks to Hollywood, the British residents of Los Angeles have played their national game on Californian lawns since the 1930s, and the West Indian community in New York introduced the sport to a city that is ready to try anything once. On a summer afternoon in Washington DC, in the parklands that run beside the Potomac River, the cricket-playing community of expatriates sometimes practises the sport to the bemusement of passing spectators, myself occasionally included. And when American Major League baseball players went out on strike as the 1994 season approached its climax, cable television carried several cricket matches to see whether the English game could act as a kind of methadone for American fans suffering from withdrawal. But the experiment failed to stimulate much interest.

For baseball in Britain, you can go to Hyde Park, near the riding ring opposite the Horse Guards' Barracks. Bare smudges in the grass, like big thumbprints, show where the American colony in London has gathered over the years to play a little weekend baseball (or the gentler version of softball). Curious pedestrians pause a moment to watch and then stroll on. Two professional teams from the minor leagues in America came to London in the autumn of 1993. They played an exhibition game at the Oval, and along with Kate Hoey, the Labour MP for Lambeth, I was invited to throw out the first ball. The occasion was a courageous replica of an All-American afternoon, supercharged by hot dogs, a frenetic organ, a giant prancing chicken and all the razzamatazz of American sport. But the stands were sparsely populated, and the game generated the same kind of enthusiasm I would expect to find at a day of cricket in Yankee Stadium.

So, in both America and Britain, these respective national games are largely kept alive by loyal expatriates in a kind of subversive, over-the-shoulder souvenir of home.

Those British who think of baseball at all look at the game as a peculiar mutation of cricket, as if a laboratory experiment had gone horribly wrong.* Some baseball phrases such as 'ballpark figure', 'touch base', 'play hardball' and 'rain check' have crept into the British vocabulary ('rain check' is a particularly useful one). Baseball caps are now ubiquitous in Britain, and baseball bats seem to be the weapon of choice for British thugs. Otherwise, baseball has made little impression. After all, if a game that looks like cricket can be settled in an afternoon, it can't be all that serious.

On the other hand, even an American living in England usually finds it easier to become a practising Buddhist than a cricket fan. For an American, cricket seems more like a puzzle than a game. My own knowledge of the sport is pretty thin, though I believe one explanation for my appointment to the Court of St James's may have been the fact that I was the only living American diplomat who could tell the difference between a yorker and a googlie. But I still shake my head at the thought of a game so leisurely that it can last for days, with breaks for lunch and tea, and so patient and open-ended that the score can run into the hundreds without either side winning. Cricket is a game of long perspective, but for an American the perspective is sometimes so long that it disappears over the horizon.

There are exceptions. One American resident of Britain has become a kind of godfather of cricket. John Paul Getty, the California billionaire who has transplanted himself to Britain, heart

* If you try to describe baseball to an Englishman, he will suddenly interject, 'Oh, it sounds like rounders. That's a girls' game here.' Few put-downs are more finely calculated.

and reclusive soul, is devoted to the English game, which he learned at the unlikely knee of Mick Jagger. Getty helped build the Mound Stand at Lord's, and he rescued the bible of the game – *Wisden Cricketers' Almanack* – from financial collapse. So boundless is his enthusiasm for cricket that he has literally moved mountains at his country estate in Buckinghamshire. There, in a green bowl of the Chiltern Hills, Getty has constructed a manicured cricket pitch with a thatched-roof pavilion, and he has raised his own Getty Eleven to play the game in the languorous atmosphere of summer Sundays. Like a shire patron of an earlier era, Getty has attempted in this fantasy setting to distil the game to its essence. And with the pressing conviction of a convert, Getty insisted to me one day that cricket is to baseball as chess is to draughts.

Conversion, however, can be a two-way street. Michael Howard, who was Home Secretary during most of my time as ambassador, is still a rabid fan of the New York Mets. With dewy eye, he recalls slipping away from his temporary home in a Manhattan law firm in the 1960s and pushing his way through the turnstiles at Shea Stadium on a breezy summer afternoon. The Mets then were probably the worst team ever to play modern professional baseball, but their lacklustre performance only intensified Howard's devotion. Even at this distance, Howard follows the fortunes of the Mets, but this was a lonely interest to pursue in Whitehall.

Drawing parallels between cricket and baseball is a tricky business, but there are a few important similarities. Baseball and cricket, for example, are straightforward games of skill with no particular reference to brawn or height or even speed. Both are centred on the intrinsic formula of eye and ball. In both games there is an evolving strategy and a set of interior tactics which unfold in infinite permutations as a match progresses. Cricket and baseball are organized as one team playing against another, but within this collective context it is the performance of the individual which is on display. Concentration is critical in both sports. It must be sustained in cricket over long periods, which can lull the wits, whereas it comes in spurts in baseball as the tension rises and ebbs.

To a fair American eye, there is more skilful variation to bowling than to pitching. In baseball, the pitcher coils himself up on the mound and rifles the ball sixty feet to the target. The ball in flight curves or dips or slides, and the point is to trick the batter. In cricket, the objective is to ricochet the ball past the batsman, and there is also a lot of chicanery. The bowler runs to make his delivery, wheeling his arm to release the ball, and there is a wild intensity about bowling that you would think better suited to America. But in either game the allure is to see what a man can do with a ball.

The combination of defensive and offensive batting that is fundamental at the crease is only rarely seen at the plate. In baseball the batter can pick and choose what the pitcher has to offer, but, with a limited number of misses and a limited number of passes, the pitcher and batter have to get on with it. In cricket, on the other hand, the batsman parries what comes at him, and the cat and mouse between batsman and bowler, in which each waits for the other to make a fatal mistake, can theoretically go on until the sun sets off the Cornish coast.

Fielding in cricket, even if it is bare-handed, doesn't impress an American eye. It seems undemanding because the ball almost always stays on the ground. The ballet of baseball, however, is in the field, where the sprint of the player intersects with the trajectory of the ball. Still, the idea is the same.

In the end both games come down to the shared objective of scoring runs, and this was once eloquently expressed by the American baseball great, Wee Willie Keeler. When asked one day for a tip about baseball, he said, 'Hit 'em where they ain't.' So the pieces of the two games are alike, but the rhythm of play is different. You can probably say the same thing about the two countries.

Parallels are perhaps more obvious in the feeling of the games than in the playing of them. There is a sweet romance about both sports. In America, there is nothing quite so evocative as a dusty baseball diamond etched in the field behind a neighbourhood school. And in England, a green cricket pitch laid out on a village common, with the white batting screen parked at the edge, is a rural idyll. Cricket and baseball both luxuriate in their grassy origins. There is a haughtiness about both sports too, and they look with disdain on the bulky aggression of American football or the raw, rowdy, urban energy of English football. Baseball and cricket are gentle games that fathers pass on to sons in the back garden on Saturday afternoons, the swing of the bat and the grip of the ball.

Both games are the stuff of heroes, legends, old glories and endless statistics.

Both sports also have a natural, lackadaisical charm, and they both prize an easy grace. Unlike the hectic pace of most other games, cricket and baseball are not played against the clock. They are played despite the clock. They are, literally, timeless. Life is more impatient these days, and cricket and baseball have each invented gimmicks in recent years to quicken their tempo. But the ingredients of the games cannot stand too much manipulation. And certainly nothing should be rushed.

As with many things, America has developed in baseball something grand which reinforces its national experience and its sense of national exceptionalism. There is probably no more reliable measure of the shifting pattern of the American population, for example, than the changing locations of its Major League baseball teams. When I was growing up, there was only one Major League club located west of the Mississippi River (barely: in St Louis) and none at all in the states of the Old Confederacy. New York City had three. Now more than half the teams are in the West, and Atlanta, Tampa, Dallas, Houston, Miami and New Orleans all have teams. New York is down to two, and Washington hasn't seen a Major League baseball game in thirty years. Baseball, like America, is dynamic.

Cricket, like Britain, is more stolid in its ways. There has been only one new team admitted to the Championship play-offs in the last six decades. But cricket, like baseball, is a sport for the hinterlands, and the heart of the game lies in the counties and village clubs where its pastoral roots flourish. In fact, cricket is one of the few features of British life that isn't dominated by London.

In America, there is no sport so intensely democratic as baseball. Today the roster of any professional baseball team reflects the variety of America's ethnic composition. Baseball integrated black players and white players well before the Supreme Court pondered the issue of racial segregation in schools. And baseball was second only to the English language in the process of Americanization which millions of immigrants experienced.

I have heard it argued that cricket also has a strong democratic streak in its history. This is hard to square in a game which used to divide teams between 'gentlemen' and 'players', with a giant social gulf running right down the middle. Until the last Gentlemen versus Players match in 1962, the separation was seen as the perfectly natural order of things. The two sides dressed separately, ate separately, lodged separately and thought separately, and the twain met only at the wicket. Players played cricket for money, however little, which meant they were by definition of inferior social standing. Gentlemen did not play for money, at least not obviously, and cricket is often blamed for elevating the British cult of amateurism to a national ideal. But, within the strait-laced conventions of the traditional social system, cricket at least broke down some of the barriers. At informal games, the baronet did bat with the butler and the peer did bowl to the porter, and nowhere else in Britain were the classes more likely to come together on level ground.

Like most professional sports in America now, baseball suffers from too much exposure and too much money. Professional cricket seems to be going this way too. Major League baseball players, who earn an average of one million dollars a year, have gone out on strike eight times in little more than two decades, and the owner-tycoons, surrounded by lawyers and merchandisers, pick the plump fruits of their local monopolies. The media deal-making of the Test and County Cricket Board is beginning to look familiar to an American, and the endearing fogeyism of the once all-powerful Marylebone Cricket Club has been overtaken. But somehow these games retain the myth and magic of their essential characters. If this is an illusion, we don't want to know about it.

Professional baseball is an altogether coarser game than cricket. On the field, there is a great deal of tobacco-spitting and crotch-scratching. The organ blares in staccato bursts and the scoreboard nowadays flashes in pulsating electronic patterns. A coach will challenge the decision of an umpire in a nose-to-nose confrontation, and occasionally both teams will surge from their respective dugouts into a general dusty brawl. Baseball is a rousting, hustling blue-collar kind of game, just like America.

Without the rough edges of baseball, cricket strikes an American as a bit prim. The poise of the game seems a little self-conscious and the detachment of the fans a little studied. A player is admired as much for fair play and Victorian sportsmanship as for natural skill. Cricket, after all, is a game of manners. Foreigners might tamper with the ball, but certainly not an Englishman. Fans approve of rectitude, or at least pretend they do. In baseball, a runner is encouraged to steal a base if he can get away with it. Such shady goings-on wouldn't be condoned in the English game. It's just not cricket. Perhaps this undramatic restraint is why the British don't make movies about cricket the way Americans do about baseball.

At a baseball game, the stands bustle and the crowd hoots and hollers. The fans nibble Cracker Jacks and shell peanuts and shout insults. There is a party atmosphere about a baseball stadium. It is a family afternoon, and everyone is meant to have a good time. Cricket fans, on the other hand, do not go to a cricket match. They drift to it. They come late and leave early. It doesn't seem to matter. A cricket game is like a winding river with no discernible source and no discernible mouth. Like England, it is always there. Cricket fans glance at the Sunday newspapers or rummage around in their picnic baskets. Cricket is a day out. Occasionally during a game, a subdued moan rises from the crown in recognition of a particularly good play. Or a desultory applause accompanies a defeated batter as he ambles off the pitch insouciantly dragging his bat behind him. It will not do to be too demonstrative. Neither the player nor the spectator should seem to try too hard. The dignity of the game derives from this steady, unalarming continuity, the stately progress of a grand sailing ship catching the imperceptible shifts in the wind. Cricket is a most English game.

These respective national sports probably do reflect something about our respective national characters, although cricket and baseball are games, not social metaphysics. Nor are they as national as we like to pretend. Cricket belongs to the English, not the Welsh or the Scots, and for many Americans baseball is too dulcet when set beside the clamorous clashes of other professional sports.

There is little likelihood the sporting divide between cricket and baseball will ever be crossed. In 1991, when the Queen visited the United States, President Bush whisked her away to Memorial Stadium in Baltimore to watch a few innings of Orioles baseball. Her Majesty sat with her back erect and her crossed ankles tucked beneath her chair. The President spread out in his seat like a large giraffe, his arms dangling over the sides and his long legs stretched out in front of him. From time to time Bush would try to explain why the men on the green field below were running around, and the Queen would nod her head and give a pleasant, how-nice smile. I don't think transatlantic understanding advanced much that night, and when it comes to cricket and baseball I don't think it ever will.

Still, at Trent Bridge on an infinite English summertime afternoon, or at Fenway Park, under the lights when the heat of a July day has passed, there is in these games a mystic reconnection with something important in each nation's history, something we can't quite put our hands on these days, something we now seem to have misplaced. In these two games, it seems to me, we each remember the way we were – or the way we think we were. In America, baseball recalls an imagined innocence, and in England cricket stirs an imagined past.

Most Americans, I think, believe the world would be a better place if there were a little more baseball in it. If the politicians played centrefield and the economists played short-stop, and if the philosophers got an occasional turn at bat, things would probably work a little better. When Americans compare baseball and life, baseball comes off better.

The English are not so earth-bound. I suspect most Englishmen believe that, if there is a sport played in heaven, it is almost certainly cricket. Somewhere beyond the frothy rise of the clouds lies a celestial cricket pitch, the wicket neatly trimmed and the players clad in angelic white. The English may be right. After all, cricket comes as close as anything in sports to eternity.

Sound and Fury

If I had to instruct a stranger on the contrasts between the United States and the United Kingdom, I would start with some televised weather reports from the two countries.

In Britain the weather is presented in a mild, diffident, terribly-sorry-for-the-inconvenience manner. There's not much variety or excitement. The typical British weatherman appears in front of the camera with his head lowered, shoulders hunched, hands clasped and jacket buttoned. He speaks softly, almost meekly, as if telling a child's bedtime story. He points to curvy isobars that bend into the country from the sea. They all seem to mean the same thing. He might talk positively about 'sun showers' or 'sunny spells', but usually the day will be 'dull'. In Britain the weather is so lacking in spunk that it is reported apologetically.

In America, on the other hand, the weather is pitched with the verve customarily reserved for a used-car lot. American weathermen report the next day's outlook as if they were trying to sell it to you. There is always a lot to talk about and big things are happening out there. Most prognostications are delivered in a you're-not-going-to-believe-me tone of voice. There are heatwaves in one part of the country and blizzards in another. Hot fronts and cold fronts march across the map. A freeze oozes ominously down from the

Canadian wastes, and a tropical storm builds up in the Caribbean. American weather is raucous, and so are American weathermen.

American weather is also intimidating in a manner you hardly ever see in the equable British climate. Americans know their weather and they watch it warily. In Caroline's home town in South Carolina, for example, the heat comes early in the year, balmy and lulling at the start of spring. But by the summer high it spreads out across the land like a heavy duvet. You can almost cup the humidity in your hands, and it's impossible to take more than a few steps without breaking into a glistening sweat. There is no relief at night. The air buzzes with the electric sound of cicadas and the infinite insect life of fields and forests. And when it rains there, it rains biblically. The heat gathers itself up in a darkening sky, and by afternoon there is a still, humid anticipation that something from the Old Testament is about to burst. The trees rustle and the land goes quiet until a sudden split of lightning streaks across the black heaven and a cracking slap of thunder makes the clouds rumble. The earth shakes and the rain comes down as if the bottom of the sky had collapsed under its weight. It beats against the land in fat, hammering drops, filling the streets and creeks and gulleys with torrents.

As rainy as it is in Britain, it never rains this way. Here the sky looks like a grey veil. It often seems about to rain but it takes for ever to get on with it. And when the rain finally comes, it sprays down as if the sky had sprung a couple of small leaks, and you think more of nourishment than retribution.

The American climate can be so quixotic and so destructive that the federal government and the National Weather Service have established a network of 450 radio transmitters across the nation to beam warnings of impending hazards to unwary communities, and commercial radio stations are required to test their civil emergency systems at regular intervals. An American cable television channel offers twenty-four-hour coverage of the weather. The Federal Emergency Management Agency is geared to respond to the natural disasters that regularly afflict the nation, and a president or state governor runs major political risks if he fails to react swiftly enough to a civil calamity.

The moderation of British weather and the volatility of American weather fit naturally with the character of the two countries. The climate in Britain is hardly ever out of sorts. A wind storm or a drought are major aberrations. Except for the swings of daylight, it's sometimes difficult to tell one season from another, so subtle are the shifts in pattern. Britain is not a country for surprises.

American weather is the opposite. A meteorological study once concluded there were two places on earth which could boast the world's worst weather: the Gobi Desert and Amarillo, Texas. For extremes of heat, cold, wind, rain and so forth, it's hard to beat Amarillo. But what is true of the Texas panhandle is more or less true of the rest of the country as well. In 1913 the temperature in Death Valley, California reached 134 degrees Fahrenheit. In 1995, a heatwave incinerated the Midwest and East Coast with temperatures as high as 109 degrees reported daily for a week. In New Hampshire one year the wind reached 231 miles per hour before the aneometer broke. On average there are 106 complete days of fog in the appropriately named Cape Disappointment, Washington, and in nearby and inappropriately named Paradise 1,224 inches of snow fell in the winter of 1972. In 1979 a town in Texas recorded nineteen inches of rain in a single day. And in the winter of 1993, the wind-chill temperature in Devil's Lake, Wisconsin touched minus 92 degrees Fahrenheit.

Sometimes, when Americans say 'God bless America,' they're thinking about their insurance premiums. Every autumn Americans watch with a gambler's fascination as hurricanes pinwheel northwards from the equator and slam into the Gulf coast or the eastern seaboard at some random, unlucky location. In the spring scores of tornadoes wreak sudden devastation on communities throughout the South and Midwest. Earthquakes rip apart the ground in California, and the eruption of Mount St Helen's a decade ago blistered the land around for miles. Forest fires consume some two million acres of wilderness every year. And in the great floods of the summer of 1993, the Mississippi River, which burst its levees and inundated sixteen million acres of farmland, crested in St Louis, Missouri, at forty-seven feet above its normal high level with seven and a half million gallons of water rushing past the city every second.

Drizzle and sunny spells in Britain. The climate is moderate and restrained, with no extremes of anything, and so the isle is green and providential. Fire and ice in America. The climate is fearsome and doesn't work by half-measures, nor does it take much for an American soul to believe in the wrath of the gods.

Heaven and Earth

From the village of Porlock Weir in Somerset there is a narrow road that leads up the hillside to a latch-gate at the edge of the Exmoor forests. From here a footpath winds along the side of a steep incline. Through the slats of trees, you can see the Bristol Channel where it begins to open out to the sea.

After a mile or so the sound of a brook overtakes the wooded quiet, and the trail gradually leads down to a clearing. In this green coombe, over a small bridge and beyond a low stone wall, stands the church of St Culbone. The church leans into the hillside, and it's been there for a thousand years. St Culbone was probably built by mendicant missionaries who came across the channel from the wilds of Wales to try their luck with the Celtic heathen of the Somerset coast. Another story claims the church ministered to lepers who roamed the forests of Exmoor, and this explains its isolated situation. Whatever the origins, the church at Culbone is ancient, and it appears in the misty woods like the setting of a fairytale. If you were in Scotland, you would think you had discovered Brigadoon.

St Culbone is reputed to be the smallest parish church in England. From east to west it measures a little longer than eleven yards. Thirty-three people can squeeze into its old wooden pews. In the thick stone walls there are three crooked windows, one of which is surely Saxon. A miniature organ is crammed into the west end of the church and a wooden rood screen separates the nave from the tiny chancel. Suspended from the beam of the pitched roof, a kerosene lamp gives the only interior light. There is no electricity in the coombe.

When Caroline and I visited this church at the end of one September, we encountered two women who were preparing the sanctuary for the harvest festival. Bunches of beans, carrots, corn and cauliflower were clustered in the corners of the window sills and along the altar rail. On top of the altar, to the left side, sat a small basket of eggs, and one of the women said she would go into the baker at Porlock early the next morning to pick up a fresh cottage loaf to place on the right side. We had seen the autumn harvest celebrated the same way in many village churches around England, but there seemed to be a little magic at St Culbone.

An American coming across such an enchanted, tranquil nook, where an old stone church seems to grow out of the land around it, can understand that Britain is an ancient place long inhabited. This is an impression repeated over and over as you make your progress along the byways of Britain: the monoliths of Stonehenge brooding over Salisbury Plain; or the solemn line of Hadrian's wall marking the far reach of a vanished empire; or the ancient disc of stained glass in the church at Jarrow overlooking the North Sea. It seems that people have washed over the British land for year upon year, turning the earth and working the soil and leaving behind a deep sediment of history. English centuries dissolve into each other, and to an American the iridescent land of England seems layered and kind.

For the British, there is a divinity about their land which describes a lot of the English spirit. Stepping into a church built in the Perpendicular style, for instance, is like stepping under a stone canopy of tall, leafy trees, their branches reaching out across the vault of the nave. St George's Chapel at Windsor is like a stone forest, and so is the chapel at King's College in Cambridge.

For many years I have kept on a table in my office, wherever it happened to be, a stone replica of an English Green Man. It is a reproduction of a boss from Salisbury Cathedral. I was always intrigued by this old forest numen which English medievalism embraced. I have come across the Green Man peering from the dark corner of a church porch or staring through the stone foliage of a capital. Vines grow out of his mouth or roots spring from the crown of his head. The Green Man, I think, represents the English link to English nature. There is a little bit of pagan in every Englishman.

As old as it is, the land in Britain never seems to wear out. Even in the spare, grey winter, the countryside is moist and vibrant. In the early spring, there are sudden crocuses and yellow daffodils in the parks and gardens, and splashes of yellow rapeseed against the green fields. With the nudge of summer, the English land opens up in billowing, white life. There are flowering white orchards and blossoming trees of chestnut, cherry and almond. Long white arms of spiraea and elder and hawthorn reach out to the roadside. Queen Anne's Lace and Old Man's Beard tumble out of hedges. Pale roses ramble over brick walls. The English landscape is so lyrical to behold you can sometimes hear the cadences of Wordsworth or Betjeman and see the pictures of Constable and Turner. The British cherish their land and seem to court it like an ardent suitor.

For an American, or at least for me, there is a carefree, blowsy romance about the English countryside. How theatrically British, I thought, when I learned that eighteenth-century English travellers carried tinted 'Claude mirrors' into the countryside so they could admire the reflections as perfectly framed pictures of natural rural beauty. I suppose the effect was not so very different from today's caressing, gauzy focus of a Merchant–Ivory lens. After all, landscape painting has always been a particularly British genre, and, unlike the formalism of the continent, nature in Britain had to be natural to be appreciated, even it meant you built new hills and moved old lakes to do it. Humphrey Repton and Capability Brown were masters of the art of earth, and they rearranged a lot of the English countryside in pursuit of the natural. Great country houses were set in little arcadias where English demi-gods played in English fields.

All this naturally carried into the English garden. Everyone knows the English are a race of gardeners, born with green thumbs and green fingers. Gardening is surely Britain's most distinctive contribution to civilization, and only the English would name a war after roses. 'Our England is a garden,' said Kipling, and every corner of Britain is planted and pruned, snipped and clipped. When Thomas Jefferson toured the Home Counties in 1787, he didn't think much of the British people – a rude lot, he reported – but he was enchanted by the English garden. Jefferson was ideologically committed to the geometric parterres and intersecting *allées* of the French. But he found the English garden irresistible, and against his better political judgment he brought the English ideas back with him to Virginia.

For half the year, Britain is awash in flowers. Before I came here, I don't think I paid much attention to flowers. But when I'm in the United States now I notice their absence. In America, flowers do not spill out at you the way they do in Britain. Americans are devoted to their lawns and care for them with a national passion, and growing vegetables is a national pastime too. But the odd flowerbed seems a token in most places. I don't know why this is so. Perhaps the American soil doesn't enjoy quite the same delicate disposition.

But in Britain flowers tumble out of window boxes and crawl up stone walls. Flowerbeds line the smallest houses and crowd the shortest pavements. Blossoms trail from hanging baskets on shop fronts and lamp posts. Every neighbourhood seems to have its corner flower stand. Television and radio give you *Gardeners' World* and *Gardeners' Question Time*. Flowers bloom on traffic roundabouts and beside canal locks. Kew Gardens is a shrine for horticulturalists, and every year the crowds flock to the Chelsea Flower Show.

Some say the English grow their flowers because the climate of the island is so temperate and gentle. Others say they grow their flowers because it is a private escape from a strapped society, a kind of aromatherapy. Maybe these observations are true. But I think the British grow their beautiful flowers because they love their land.

The relationship between the British and their land is balanced, relaxed and intimate. Occasionally things get testy when the government proposes a new bypass road or a company wants to build a suburban shopping centre. But, for the most part, the British treat their island as if it were a sanctuary. The land is nurtured as a joint heritage, a common posterity. There are 'greenfields' and 'green belts'. The National Trust, which is perfectly named, is the guardian of thousands of scenic acres and is the largest charity in the United Kingdom.

This is not to say the land belongs to everyone – in fact, so far as I can tell, it belongs to a very few – but it is there for everyone. Trespass laws in Britain suggest that private ownership is an incomplete idea. The right of access is protected, and there are scores of organizations devoted to its preservation. One hundred and twenty thousand miles of public footpaths criss-cross private property all over the country, many of them lined by Britain's treasured hedgerows. The country is full of walkers, ramblers, climbers and hikers. The Scots go 'munro-bagging' and fiercely guard their 'right to roam'. The bosky parks of Britain's cities* and the thousands of village commons preserve this social right to enjoy the land. And country sports such as fox hunting, shooting and angling have an almost mystical air in Britain, so devout are their practitioners. In Britain, everyone seems to be a Shropshire Lad.

In America the relationship with the land is much more argumentative and rambunctious. Americans wrestle with the majestic ferocity of their land. The bounty of the continent – the waves of amber grain, from sea to shining sea – is by God's grace, which can be pretty capricious, and if the New World was once seen by Europeans as a New Eden, Americans found it to be a severe and unforgiving paradise. American authors – Melville, Emerson, Thoreau, Longfellow, Whitman and Faulkner – wrote about the awesomeness of the primitive land and its transcendental purity. John Locke, from his British distance, said, 'In the beginning . . . all the world was America' – vast, untouched and powerful. America is not a garden, like Britain, but a wilderness, and to stand today at the edge of one of America's great, jagged canyons or by the bank of one of its broad, swift rivers is like standing in a primeval place before history. British land is Psalms; American land is Genesis.

For all the roughshod taming of the last century, America's raw geography still conveys this sense of muscular immensity. The forests of the north seem boundless. Not so long ago, a squirrel could leap from branch to branch all the way from the Atlantic Ocean to the Mississippi River without once touching the ground.

---

* There are 387 parks in London alone. Many have signs which say something like: 'No food, no games, no noise, no dogs, no children, no foreigners, no fun.'

The endless Western plains roll away to the sky on a scale so great that it can make you dizzy with space. Rivers that would have spawned civilizations in Europe flow silently through silent land. There are thousands of coastal miles edging in and out of the oceans on either side of the continent, and the mountains and deserts and marshes are together splendid and forbidding. There are still huge tracts of land in America where it is easy to imagine no man has ever gone. When I travel around the country, I feel that America's grip on the land is still tenuous. Beyond the confident, hustle-bustle of America's cities, the land is captious and moody and can toss aside the brilliance of an engineering feat with a swipe of a hand.

Even the things that live in America's wilderness have a sharpness that is unknown in Britain. There are bears, cougars, civets, coyotes and wolves in the forests and mountains. Alligators lie in the swamps and sharks swim in the seas. The land is full of mosquitoes and gnats; horse flies, deer flies, sand flies and yellow flies; chiggers and ticks; hornets and wasps and bees; tarantulas and scorpions; rattlers, copperheads, diamondbacks, water moccasins and cotton-mouths. The American countryside has bite.

Naturally, the land has shaped much of the social geography of the United States and the United Kingdom. I suppose we are where we live. In Britain there is so little land and in America so much. Until the last generation, the British couldn't grow enough food to feed themselves; Americans have never known what to do with all their food. The British built their houses in solid stone and the Americans in wood. The British conquered an empire, in part to find more land; Americans found an empire in their own backyard. The British emigrated from their country in search of more open spaces, but Americans just moved from one valley to the next to get a new start. New arrivals in Britain have always had a hard time fitting in; the infinite American country absorbed millions and millions of immigrants. The pattern of people and land in one nation has always seemed to be the reverse of the other.

An American has to remember that the roots of the British social system were planted in the soil a long time ago, and that the British developed a special twist to landownership. Unlike the rest of Europe, the custom of primogeniture assured that the great estates remained intact one generation after another. This might not have made for congenial family life, but the primacy of the long-straw son kept the land together. Landowners in Britain consolidated property and married property, so that by the nineteenth century, when Britain emerged as a full unitary state, three-quarters of the land was in the hands of not more than 5,000 families. Even today, a tenth of the population owns 85 per cent of the land, and British farms are, on average, the largest in Europe – about four times the size of the average French or German farm. Land consolidation in Scotland is even more striking. Today five families own 750,000 acres, and fewer than 600 people own half the land.

Primogeniture is a very British notion. The bond with the undivided land makes sense only by counting generations. The interests of one generation were subordinated to the next. Preservation was a duty. Old estates were not really owned but occupied, like a territorial stewardship. Aristocrats seemed like tenants on their own property, which is pretty much what everyone else was. Landowners were charged to bequeath exactly what they had received, or more, not merely for the benefit of the family but for the order and stability of the nation. This created a long-lasting tenancy culture in Britain with a feudal flavour.

Country ways were also brought to the city, and little was lost in the transfer. When Buckingham House first went up at the end of the Mall, the motto 'Ars in urbis' was carved over the stone archway. Like an oligarchy, major property owners in London, such as the Westminsters or Portlands or Bedfords, conserved their urban estates and let out the buildings on them. An Englishman's home might have been his castle, but it was probably a leased castle.* And in this century the government has also become a great urban landlord. I was told in the 1970s that Scotland had more government-owned housing than any communist country in Eastern Europe.

There has never been a thoroughgoing land reform in the United Kingdom, unless you count the Enclosure Acts in England and the break-up of the clans in Scotland, which together probably constitute the most bitter social experience in Britain's modern history. Until

---

* Much of this is changing now; two-thirds of the population in Britain own their homes today, while only half did a couple of decades ago.

the last century, Parliament was almost entirely in the hands of the landed interests.

I was impressed when the Duke of Buccleuch, who is today the largest private landowner in Europe, wrote an article in the *Spectator* in 1993 lamenting the deterioration of the old system which had bestowed on Britain 'the historic structure of the countryside'. The special quality of the nation's sylvan environment, he argued, stemmed from the attitudes of the great landowners, each of whom possessed 'a strong sense of duty based on an inherited belief that he is merely a link in a long chain of continuity with responsibility for a comprehensively managed rural community'. All the ideas of the British ethos are revealed in his words: continuity, heritage, community, duty and the love of the land. Each is connected to the other.

American colonials rejected primogeniture well before Independence. That should have been an early sign of trouble brewing. The South did for a while emulate the ambience of great estates and family seats, and, even after slavery ended, sharecropping and tenant farming were still common. But for most of the new country there was such an abundance of land that primogeniture did not make much sense. The eldest son might or might not take over the farm of his father, but more likely, he and his siblings headed west to claim some land for themselves. In an era when land in Britain was good as gold, America had struck it rich.

Alexis de Tocqueville, the shrewd observer of America's character, noted early in the national evolution that the absence of primogeniture meant Americans developed only passing attachments to the land. There was little sense of territorial patrimony. From the start, America was a restless country whose people were always ready to move on. They drifted across the land like the shadow of a summer cloud. Something better must lie just over the next hill or just around the next bend. Land lured the land-starved: the British came because land at home was unavailable except for the chosen few; the Germans came because their land was so subdivided and fought over that it could no longer be sensibly managed; the Irish came because they were dispossessed. America turned into a huge, continuing land rush.

This process of settlement could not have lasted indefinitely except for the extraordinary territorial aggrandizement of the new United States. By seizure, war, suppression, purchase, expropriation, negotiation, chicanery, good deals, broken promises and dumb luck, the United States, from 1803 to 1867, staked out an enormous continent from one ocean to another. It was Manifest Destiny, and by the middle of the nineteenth century the territorial cornucopia of America fairly overflowed.

The federal government assumed jurisdiction over all this newly acquired land. There was no aristocracy to give it to. Washington became a land bank, the repository of more than a billion acres lying on the far side of the Appalachian Mountains that was twice the size of Western Europe. The government systematically surveyed the land, partitioned it into meticulous sections, and put it up for auction. The end result was a delineated grid of territorial squares that looked like a giant trellis. America became a nation of straight lines and right angles, and if you travel today in the United States, especially in the West, the state borders run straight, the roads run straight and the fences run straight.

This grid also turned America into a gigantic public marketplace of land, divided into shares to be freely traded, sold and resold more or less according to the peculiar economic imperative of infinite supply and infinite demand. The United States still doesn't know what to do with all its land.* If land in Britain was treated as a permanent, limited, unalterable asset, land in America was treated as an over-the-counter commodity.

This distribution of the wide open spaces was also an experiment in social engineering. The government gave ideological priority to the citizen–yeoman farmer. It aimed to mould the national character into the tangible shape of Jeffersonian and Jacksonian ideals and prevent the formation of a landowning class. In 1862, at the start of the Civil War, the Congress passed the Homestead Act, which literally gave away the land to anyone who would take it and develop it on a small scale. As it turned out, a lot of people got pushed around in the process, especially the Indians. As often as not, the cattle barons, speculators, mine-owners and railroad magnates won out. Nonetheless, by 1930 there were almost seven million independent small farmers in America, and though the number has

---

* More than 135 million acres in America remain in the old grid system.

gradually declined, enough of the social objective was implemented to enrich the national lore and create much of the way Americans see themselves.

In 1893 the American historian Frederick Jackson Turner delivered a lecture in Wisconsin entitled 'The Closing of the American Frontier'. When Turner was born, Wisconsin itself was the frontier, but by the time of his address the line had long since crossed the Mississippi. Turner concluded that for the first time in American history there was no longer an identifiable frontier. The fluid lines of settlement, moving towards the centre of the country from both east and west, had finally converged. Years of pioneering were at an end. America's greatest natural resource, the limitless land, had run out, but not before America's expansive political and social culture had been planted.

Of all the contrasts between the United States and the United Kingdom, none is so stark as the land – how we each regard it and how it in turn has shaped us. The perspectives we each have about ourselves, about each other and about the world around us are conditioned by our geographies, and these attitudes are as likely to change as the geography that spawned them. The apparent elasticity of the American land channelled American history along its special course, just the way the confinement of land moulded Britain's.

In America, for example, the thirteen original colonies were alone so big that their rebellion could not be suppressed by a British force logistically confined to the coast. Nor would slavery have been a viable proposition were it not for the land-intensive plantation economy in the South. Organizing the new Western territories upset the balance of the federal system and precipitated the Civil War. The settlement of America's frontier also generated many of our most durable political themes: popular sovereignty, rugged individualism, states' rights, public domain and so forth. American politicians drank at this well of frontier culture and its cult of pioneers and cowboys. Lincoln was the 'rail-splitter', Teddy Roosevelt the 'rough rider', John Kennedy invoked the 'New Frontier' and Ronald Reagan arrived in Washington 'standing tall'. The Cold War was *High Noon*. Americans were pioneers, set in a divinely mandated struggle with nature where government promised land and God promised redemption, and if you could not find these in one place, you could pack up and move on to another.

The constraints of land in Britain, on the other hand, imposed an order on the country which produced a society of intricate, stratified relationships. The land was fixed and there wasn't enough of it. The geography of England was carefully catalogued in the Domesday Book, like a warehouse inventory, and much of British politics, from the Civil War to the Corn Laws, has been driven by the owners of property and the non-owners. The British quest for land produced the Empire. It also produced the Irish dilemma. Without much land, Britain became a trading nation. Above all, the British became a nation of conservers, a race of guardians, who have always treasured their ancient, flowering earth.

Ebb and Flow

The ocean is another matter. The United States and the United Kingdom may be opposites when it comes to land, but they have always been up to their necks in the same body of water.

Though America has two oceans, you are much more aware of the sea in Britain – you're never more than a few miles away from salt water, and a gull looping over any British city is an unremarkable sight. British history is so pelagic that, at almost any point on the map, you can stand on the national deck and breathe in this bracing, spumey past.

If the British land is benign, the British sea is treacherous. Like many people, I always feel a little barometric foreboding when I hear the hypnotic monotone of *The Shipping Report* on radio. I think of swinging lanterns, oilskins and broken spars. In fact, I never really understand these bulletins – 'southwesterly seven, becoming gale nine; Faeroes falling', or something like that – but, whatever the code means, I know the sea around the Kingdom is a fateful zone.

Emerson said, 'Europe ends at the Alleghenies; America lies beyond.' This is true. Many of the states on America's eastern seaboard are named after British potentates, but, once across the mountains, the names are mostly native and enchanting, and there is little whiff of salt air. Still, the old houses on the Atlantic coast have widow's walks on the roofs, and the briny outer banks are strewn with old wrecks from old adventures.

It is equally true that the ocean continues to bind Britain and America more than it separates them.

Both countries are islands, more or less. Calling the United States an island may be stretching a point, but the oceans on either side of the continent do have an insulating effect. As for the British, the English Channel sometimes seems as wide as the Atlantic. The sea has always acted as a protective barrier for both countries, making it difficult for any other nation to interpose itself between the two. In the Atlantic, Britain and America are each other's principal landfall, and for most of our histories we have each been relaxed if not entirely comfortable when the other has dominated the sea lanes.

Both countries early on in the relationship recognized a common interest in the freedom of the seas. And free trade, while not quite an economic catechism in either country, is nonetheless endorsed with a kind of conviction rare among most non-island peoples. We have also shared the same concept of naval power, with all the flexibility and reach which that implies, and we both have a tendency to neglect our peacetime armies because of the lulling effect of the sea. More recently, nuclear co-operation between the two has been primarily sea-based.

Bickering and outright hostility often characterized transatlantic relations in the past, but the underlying geopolitics were always inescapable. Foreign Secretary Canning proposed an Anglo-American partnership in 1823, and the same idea was fashionable in transatlantic circles at the turn of the century. Canning's premature approach led to two well-known quotes in the annals of Anglo-American relations. With his customary arrogance, Canning explained his proposal by saying, 'I called the New World into existence to redress the balance of the Old.' And with the pugnacity that can only come from distance, James Monroe rejected the overture by saying, 'America will not be a dinghy in the wake of a British man-o-war.'* Both countries have naturally been wary of

* The end result of all this was the Monroe Doctrine. In the 1820s, Americans were more suspicious of the British ambitions in the western hemisphere than confident of their good intentions.

expansionism on the European continent or from it (French, Spanish, German, Russian and anyone else), so the implied partnership was always there. But it was not explicit until more recently.

In the second half of the twentieth century, Britain became America's strategic forward post, and America became Britain's strategic hinterland. In its isolated struggle against the Nazis, Britain turned to the New World as the only possible source of supply, and the United States came to understand that America's security would be jeopardized if Britain failed. As in the First World War, the sea lanes across the North Atlantic pulled Washington closer and closer to the conflict. Pearl Harbor finally pushed America into the war, but I'm sure the risks President Roosevelt was already running in the Atlantic would have eventually produced the same result. Once the United States entered the war, the ocean routes from the Gulf and East Coast ports of America to the west coast ports of Britain became an Atlantic boulevard for American troops and *matériel*.* By 1943, Britain was a huge Anglo-American depot as well as a launching pad for the great Cross-Channel assault against the continent.

This geographic synergy remained the strategic linchpin between the two countries during the Cold War. In the event of another conflict, the Anglo-American bases were designed to empty quickly on to the continent and then immediately receive a huge surge of reinforcements from North America. The military infrastructure in Britain was founded on the simple geographic realities of the sea, and this has been the most tangible strategic link between the two countries in this century. And I do believe that, because the two countries were so well prepared to fight another war in Europe, there wasn't one.

With the end of the Cold War, a lot of the energy has seeped out of the strategic partnership. But the British Isles remain the geographic hinge for Anglo-American security in Europe, hollow though a continental threat may seem today.

---

* Many empty Liberty ships departing Bristol carried bomb rubble as ballast for the return journey, and when they put in to New York harbour the rubble was dumped along the edge of Manhattan island and formed the foundation for the East Side Drive.

Both nations have also developed their political unions to the natural boundaries of the water's edge. This has allowed each country an exceptional degree of political coherence and stability, and there is little prospect their geographic composition will change any time soon.

America's territorial expansion came to an end in the nineteenth century, and the brief flirtation with overseas empire following the Spanish–American War proved fickle. Detached from the continental mass of America, Alaska and Hawaii are condemned to insets in a corner of the map, but since 1952 they have been full states within the Union. The Commonwealth of Puerto Rico exists in its own political limbo, and so does the District of Columbia. One is a stepchild and the other a juvenile delinquent, but their situations are unlikely to change much in the foreseeable future.* For the Union as a whole, there hasn't been much talk of secession since Appomatox.

The only real geographic uncertainty that now hangs over America is the possible dissolution of Canada. For the last thirty years or so, Canada has been out of kilter, but, for all the talk about break-up, Canadians have so far stopped short of the destination. If dissolution did eventually happen, however, it would be a tumultuous development of great consequence for the United States. Some Canadian provinces would probably go their own way, alone or in combination, but others would almost surely consider accession to the American Union. America's geographic neighbourhood, however, is otherwise benign. The United States feels no real sense of menace from any quarter in its hemisphere, the lone exception in this century being our neuralgic relationship with Cuba.

The geographic integrity of the United Kingdom is also intact, at least over the near term. Great Britain is territorially a little less tidy than the United States. There are some peculiar bits and pieces of land which seem to float around in a constitutional twilight zone. Guernsey and Jersey off the Brittany coast are examples, or the Isle of Man in the Irish Sea, all of which appear to be vaguely illicit centres for off-shore banking. The seigneurial Isle of Sark sounds

---

* If Puerto Rico and Washington DC became states, they would probably add four Democratic seats to the Senate, and it will be a cold day in San Juan before the Republican Party would willingly let that happen.

like a location in a Dr Seuss book. But I don't suppose you can expect the British to have everything in order.

There is some possibility that Scotland will go its own way, and sooner or later Ulster will probably leave the Union or the Union will leave it. But these are both questions for another century. And with the exception of a few left-overs strewn about the globe, the sun has pretty much set on the British Empire.

The point is that both the United States and the United Kingdom are just what they say they are: united. And they are united on territory largely defined by their natural island geography. Because of the sea, the frontiers are more or less fixed. We take this for granted and there isn't much we could do about it anyway. But this natural territorial coherence has given both countries a strong sense of impregnability and security.

There is hardly a country in Europe, on the other hand, that wouldn't rearrange its own frontiers if it had the risk-free chance to do so. But neither Britain nor America nurses any territorial grievance nor harbours any expansionist ambition, nor are we the objects of anyone else's serious designs. Freedom from the preoccupation or fear of irredentism is a rare geographic luxury which has allowed each country to maintain a particular detachment from the customary woes of the world. This attitude is sometimes described as 'isolationist' in America and 'Little Englander' in Britain. But, whatever you call it, it comes from the sea, and in order to understand the two countries and the relationship between them, you first have to get your feet wet.

Chapter and Verse

One winter evening Caroline and I went to dinner with Stephen and Natasha Spender in their simple house, with a crooked gatepost, in St John's Wood, not far from Regent's Park. Sir Stephen, who died in 1996, was one of the great figures of twentieth-century British poetry, a person whose name and work many Americans have known for many years. He was a tall, handsome man with bewitching blue eyes and a flowing white mane to match his status as the last lion of English letters. His face always seemed on the verge of laughter, which isn't normally the case with poets, but he always seemed a little unkempt as well, as poets should.

For Spender, poetry was a special window through which you could see an artistic whole. The eulogist at his memorial service, Richard Wollheim, told the story of visiting the cathedral at Autun one day with Spender. Spender looked around the great church for a while and studied the tympanum. He then walked across the square to a small café where he wrote three postcards: one to Stravinsky, one to Auden and one to Henry Moore. These were all his friends, and as far as he was concerned they all together did the same thing.

Spender had been part of that unusual British literary movement which flourished between the wars. Britain doesn't seem to have literary movements any more. Perhaps this is just a sign of the times or perhaps it is part of a general fatigue. There are plenty of good writers these days, but there doesn't seem to be much of a national voice any longer. Spender knew a different creative era whose writers left a lasting mark in literature, and when he talked about the past you sensed the Indian summer of English letters. He summoned up the haunting Bloomsbury names of Lytton and Clive and Virginia and Vita, and he told of his chats with the American interloper, Tom Eliot.

At dinner, we sat around a small table in the dining room. One of the other guests was Peter Ackroyd, whom Caroline and I had known and admired for several years. Ackroyd is an inventive, voluble man with a round, ruddy face and a flat, greying moustache. He is a geyser of words. He writes them and speaks them as if he thought he might run out of paper or time. He seems in a hurry even when standing still.

Naturally enough, Spender in his gentle, bemused manner and Ackroyd in his rapid-fire fashion carried the evening's conversation. It was one of those occasions when a voice in the back of your mind suggests you would contribute more to the discussion if you kept your mouth shut. Spender the poet and Ackroyd the novelist conjured up characters and incidents from the past and present, and with the greatest delight they scampered down conversational alleyways which were dark and obscure for me. Their talk was part gossip and part literary criticism, and these were virtually indistinguishable. But I noticed that, whenever Spender spoke, the garrulous Ackroyd immediately fell silent and listened.

What I remember most about that evening was the feeling that I was witnessing a kind of literary rite which an English-speaker is only likely to find in London. Here in Spender was one of the great chieftains of British literature, a man for whom almost all the twentieth century had been first-hand, and in his random anecdotes and tales he was passing on literary lore to Ackroyd, as if the novelist were an excitable young warrior primed to hear of earlier tribal exploits. The grand patriarch told stories about demi-gods and what it was like to know them. And the younger man listened.

Spender, I suppose, when he was young and ungainly, also sat at a different, older knee and heard similar stories about Forster and Shaw and the other important figures of British letters who had preceded him by a generation or so. And if Ackroyd ripens to an old age, he'll tell his stories too, and repeat the ones he has heard. I exaggerate this, I know, but I nonetheless felt that evening that I was listening to an oral tradition conveyed by one literary generation to the next, a process which I suppose has gone on in London's clubs and salons and little dining rooms for centuries.

This transmission of knowledge from grand master to skilled apprentice takes place in all crafts. But, when it comes to words and the writing or speaking of them, the British are passing on the most precious aspect of their national heritage. There is nothing unusual in the observation that novelists and poets love words. But what is naturally true of British artists is equally true of Britain as a whole. The British adore words. They are a race of talkers and writers, and words are probably Britain's greatest natural resource. If you are a foreigner, and if you speak English, and if you like an extravagantly verbal society, there is no place like Britain. Britain is not a land for the taciturn or tongue-tied.

This ebullient use of language is a characteristic which binds the United Kingdom together like no other. Words, and how you pronounce them, define where you fit into British society, and perhaps this linguistic security is in part responsible for the linguistic excess. Certainly the Welsh, the Scots, the Irish and the English all delight in language – not other people's languages, but their own language. And in Britain, it seems, nothing goes without saying.

The Irish, whether Catholic or Protestant, are perhaps the most extreme. I am told there is a special chemistry in the marriage of Gaelic syntax and English words, but, whatever the explanation, the Irish treat language like an infinite medley of music.

I once gave a speech in Belfast. My carefully prepared address lasted twenty-five minutes. The chairman's introduction, however, ran for half an hour. The vote of thanks took another half-hour and the words of gratitude on behalf of the guests lasted almost forty-five minutes. And each of the three Irish speakers, without a note in sight, was fluent and funny from start to finish, and I suspect any member of the Irish audience that night could have stood up and turned in a similarly entertaining performance. I wasn't too surprised. I have always thought the troubled politics of

Northern Ireland might eventually be resolved if and when the Irish had finally talked the subject to death, though this could take a long time.

What is true of the Irish is true of the others almost in equal measure. The fiery Welsh, the deliberative Scots, the mellifluous English are all talkers. The copious use of words is their sustenance. Real food matters less for the British because they are linguistic gourmands who far prefer to savour the flavours of their language than whatever might be sitting on their plates. Conversation is meant to be as much diverting as informative, and no one is more esteemed than the accomplished port-and-cigars raconteur with his stock of amusing tales. I used to marvel at English friends such as John Julius Norwich or Tony Quinton who, at a moment's notice, could stand up in a room full of strangers and speak for whatever amount of time was required, wittily or gravely as the occasion demanded, fresh and lucid as if their point had just occurred to them, and without misplacing a comma.

In December 1993 I was invited to speak to a London group called the Saints and Sinners, a prestigious dining club devoted solely to amusing discourse. This time I was to be introduced by the young captain of the Hampshire cricket team, Mark Nicholas, and I expected something brief and guttural in the fashion of most athletes. But not so. He spoke for twenty minutes in a non-stop monologue with one funny story after another tripping off his sharp tongue as if stand-up comedy were his profession. I then took my place in front of an audience almost exhausted by laughter. I felt like a cop who had come to bust up the party.

Polonius asked Hamlet what he was reading. 'Words, words, words,' replied Hamlet. Shakespeare knew a thing or two about the British. Samuel Johnson was so enamoured of words that he listed them alphabetically and gave each one a definition, the better to use them. The British pretty much invented the modern novel and turned the essay into a form of art. At school, I studied history, but when I read Gibbon or Macaulay or Taylor I was never sure whether it was history or literature, because it was both. Appropriately enough, Winston Churchill is still the only person ever to have won a Nobel Prize for talking.

Words are all around you in this wonderfully prolix nation.

Television, the bane of modern American conversation, is banned from most British pubs. Public houses in Britain are places where people meet to converse, and, leaving aside the lager and ale, this is why pubs remain national institutions. British opinion-makers, broadly defined, are called 'the chattering classes'. And talking is the purpose of all those clubs and all those dinners with all those toasts and all those speeches.

The British prize linguistic inventiveness and the little twists and turns that words can take. This is a nation of Scrabble players and anagram addicts and crossword aficionados and code-breakers. The British enjoy disaggregating their language and putting it back together again. And there doesn't seem to be a newspaper editor in the land who can resist an excruciating pun in a headline.

Britain surely has the wordiest politics in the world. Macaulay wrote that 'parliamentary government is government by speaking', and you don't have to spend much time in Westminster to get the point. The House of Commons is called the 'talking shop', and the person in charge of the proceedings is called 'the Speaker'. A British politician is judged by his or her ability to speak, not in order to rouse the nation, but in order to impress other politicians. The repartee of parliamentary debate can establish or destroy a politician's reputation, quite apart from any other skills he or she may possess. The British discovered 'soundbites' long before the Americans even thought of them. Denis Healey once proclaimed that being attacked by Geoffrey Howe was like being 'savaged by a dead sheep'. I never thought this was a particularly witty remark, but the timing was right and Howe has to live with it for the remainder of his parliamentary life. And when John Moore, a shooting star in the mid-1980s Cabinet of Margaret Thatcher, literally lost his voice, it was the equivalent of parliamentary castration.

It is not the force of logic or reason that necessarily carries the day when speaking in the House of Commons. It is the manner and skill of expression that counts. The clever use of words as weapons – the put-down, the cut, the *bon mot* – are what is prized in British politics, and if you are not prepared for it, you had better stay away. Old timers say the oratorical quality of the House of Commons has deteriorated over the last generation. This is probably true. But for an outsider the verbal acrobatics on the floor of the

Commons remain one of the best shows in town.

The British are taught to talk in school. In fact, the end-of-year ceremony at a British school is called 'Speech Day', a term I came to understand only after attending a few of them. The verbal training is relentless and disciplined, starting with Latin, which remains the armature of a good British education. In America, it is hard to find a school which still offers Latin, and except for one brief and infelicitous encounter I managed to escape its torments. But in Britain Latin until recently was an unavoidable part of the curriculum, especially in private schools. And as the students mastered the cadences of declensions, they learned the liturgy of their own English language. As a consequence, the British still enjoy inserting Latin phrases or quotes into the texts of articles and books without the courtesy of a translation, which in their view is *ne plus ultra*.

The tutorial system at Oxbridge is mainly built around the idea of instruction through dialogue. The point is to learn to talk convincingly. I recall a group of students at the Oxford Union describing for me one day the difference between a British debating team and its American counterpart. The Americans will research their brief like lawyers, organizing the facts, marshalling the statistics and citing the precedents in a well-ordered exposition. The Americans want to score points and win the argument on the factual merits. Not so the British debaters. They are the light cavalry on the field of linguistic combat. They aim to expose the contradictions of an opposing proposition, probe for the weak spots and cleverly turn the flanks. The British do not search for the most reasoned presentation of a case but for the most original, and the argument is given special texture by a well-turned phrase. In British debate, substance and style are separable. And in the political Unions of the various universities in the United Kingdom, the objective, really, is to talk well.

British radio is naturally full of words. The BBC, like a warm-hearted auntie, tells morning stories and afternoon stories to its listeners, and bedtime stories as well. Word games are a feature of daily programming on Radio Four with wordy names like *Wordly Wise* and *Working Words*. Nicholas Parsons hosts a show called *Just a Minute* in which the object of the game is for the agile panellists to talk non-stop for one minute with 'no hesitation, repetition or deviation', so the rules say. Just talk cleverly. And keep talking. In America, the programme would be off the air before it reached the first commercial. In Britain, however, talking is a sport.

London, especially, is a talking town. Speakers' Corner at Marble Arch is only an exaggerated version of a common, daily phenomenon. The whole of London is a speakers' corner. In the City, the motto says, 'My word is my bond.' This is a little old-fashioned now – and a little risky – but words in London have always suggested value. Only the British could sustain the private London Library, a sacred monument to the use of words, where on any given day you will discover another author or two scribbling away at one of the writing tables, adding to the national wealth. In London's stylish courtrooms, 'silk' refers as much to the manner of speech as to the manner of dress. At the Garrick Club, like many other clubs, there is a long table running down the centre of the dining room, and if you are alone you are expected to sit there and chat with whoever else has dropped by – silent solitude is frowned on.

On any London weekday, there is bound to be a lecture or a speech in one West End hall or another, and lecture series, such as the Reith Lectures or the Dimbleby Lectures, remain annual fixtures in the metropolitan calendar. Every evening the theatres from Soho to the suburbs resonate with words. And with all the smooth talk, it's no wonder that London is the international capital of advertising.

In Britain, language is nationality and civility and manners, the stuff of daily intercourse, social identification and intellectual attainment. For Americans, words are more like tools, practical and necessary instruments for getting the job done. For American heroes, the fewer words the better. Gary Cooper and John Wayne portrayed laconic Hollywood frontiersmen of little talk and much action, and their more modern equivalents, such as Bruce Willis or Sylvester Stallone, seem incapable of any speech at all. It is hard to imagine any of them as Lear or Macbeth or any genuine British hero. The British hero says just the right thing at just the right time. The strong and silent types are admired in Britain, but they are not natural heroes in British eyes, or ears.

This national logophilia is not just idle talk. The British are also tradesmen and purveyors of the written word. This is especially noteworthy in their diplomacy. On a wall in the Ambassadors' Waiting Room, across from the Foreign Secretary's office in Whitehall, there is a painting of the Tower of Babel. The Foreign Office is nothing if not ironic. But British diplomats know that clear words count in a cacophonous world. Early in my career, I learned you could almost always count on the British to circulate the first draft at an international negotiation. These were invariably well crafted and micro-processed. The British, clever as they are at words, try to tie down international decision-making by capturing the choices on paper. And it's rare to have a meeting with a British minister without a scribe at his side.

Words also pour off the nation's printing presses in a floodtide of ink. The national newspapers alone produce at least two million words every day. If all the column inches from a single morning of publication were laid end to end, they would stretch from Land's End to John o'Groats and back.

There are more hardback books published annually in Britain – some 70,000 titles – than in the United States. Another 150,000 softbacks come out each year. The writers of good fiction have no problem finding their way into print. Today, Julian Barnes, Penelope Lively, Martin Amis, Anita Brookner and so on keep up a steady flow of imaginative novels, always with something to say. Literary prizes are awarded throughout the year, the Booker and the Whitbread being the most prestigious and snippiest. Agatha Christie, P. D. James and Ruth Rendell long ago set the international standard for literary crime, as did John le Carré for literary espionage. Ken Follett, Joanna Trollope, Frederick Forsyth and even Jeffrey Archer deserve the praise that comes their way for the voluminous production of words and good yarns.

This being Britain, the past is never left unremarked, which may explain the British fascination with books of biography. And old letters, diaries and journals are also edited and published for the public to share. History is constantly folded into the present, and the present is carefully readied for resurrection. Douglas Hurd, when he was Foreign Secretary, somehow managed to write in his diary every night, no matter where events had taken him. Nigel Nicolson keeps a daily diary too, and at the end of each year he puts the annual journal on his shelf at Sissinghurst and never looks at it again. But, in one way or another, the British like to say what they think, even if they say it to themselves, or to those not yet born.

Bookstores are a particular British landmark, the perfect commercial expression of the national culture, though the American trend to franchise chains has caught on here too. But there remains a special charm about browsing for a book in Britain, and the British are never so helpful as in a bookstore. Americans go to Heywood Hill and Hatchards just to be there. I first learned about Blackwell's in Oxford when I lived in Nairobi, and I discovered that Blackwell's would be pleased to deliver a book to the top of Mount Kenya if that was where I wanted to read.

Even the apocalyptic termination of the Net Book Agreement has so far failed to squelch the old sort of independent literary shop for which Britain is revered – tranquil, intimate havens where you have all the time in the world. Caroline and I are devoted clients at John Sandoe's off the King's Road, where the books exude a delectable, leathery odour and cats lurk in the corners. The managers seem to have read everything in the store, and a subterranean network will eventually produce whatever book you may request.

In Britain, books are a national currency. There are book fairs across the land. Bookstalls spring up in small markets and on street corners. The country is a huge bazaar of second-hand books, and the musty, helter-skelter business of trading rare books goes on every day. Cheltenham hosts a festival of books and Hay-on-Wye is a village of books.

The transmission of the written word in Britain is also a matter of supreme national importance. This remains a nation of letter-writers. British newspapers invented the daily forum of letters-to-the-editor, and British radio regularly programmes letters from here and letters from there (the most famous of which is the missive is delivered on Sunday mornings from the one-man institution of Anglo-American relations, Alistair Cooke). And the British write massively to each other, preserving their words in a way the telephone cannot.

In fact, since the inauguration of the penny post in 1840, nothing in Britain has moved faster than the mail. An American here is almost stunned to discover that a letter despatched one day is sure to be received the next. So confident is the Royal Mail of its sophisticated system of postal codes, as well as its ability to decipher the execrable handwriting of the citizenry, that return addresses are not required on envelopes.

With a stern and steady eye, the British Post Office handles about sixteen billion pieces of mail a year, with another half-billion items going overseas. Christmas alone produces a white blizzard of two billion greeting cards, and they all get to where they're supposed to. The Royal Mail is so good that it regularly turns a profit, and it is so esteemed by the public that the government in 1994 was forced to abandon its plans for privatization. In Britain, words are valued, so they are handled with care and efficiency. And, after all, William Makepeace Thackeray and Anthony Trollope both worked for the Royal Mail, and so did Bertrand Russell. They were true men of letters.

This respect for the post was a revelation for me. In America now you can claim you never received someone's letter or notice, and this is a perfectly credible excuse. You can't get away with that in Britain. There is much more mail in the United States – ten times as much – though only about 4 per cent is made up of letters. And years ago America's postal service proudly bound together the sprawling, rural nation. One of the little visual features of Americana which a visitor notices today is the ubiquitous metal letterbox mounted on a wood post at the end of most American driveways, sometimes with the little flag turned up to signal to the postman that there is mail to be collected even if there is none to be delivered (a benefit not offered by the Royal Mail). But the quality of America's postal service has deteriorated over the years. Etched boldly above the frieze of the imposing General Post Office building in New York City is a free translation from Herodotus which long served as the inspirational motto of the American postal service: 'Neither snow nor rain nor heat nor gloom of night shall stay these couriers from the swift completion of their appointed rounds.' But bureaucracy shall.

For most Americans these days, the extraordinary verbal quality of British life is probably best known through the theatre. Sometimes the country seems like a large repertory company, and mystery plays, music halls, pantomimes, interludes and masques are all part of the nation's history of performance. Americans still come to Britain on theatre tours, spending a week or so in London prowling the latest productions in the West End or on the South Bank, or undertaking a pilgrimage to Stratford-upon-Avon.

An American would be hard pressed to name more than one or two living playwrights who regularly make a mark in American theatre, and Broadway nowadays often seems more like live television. But in London theatre is as vibrant and challenging as it has always been, even if the occasional dry spells seem a little longer than they used to be. Alan Ayckbourn, Simon Gray, Tom Stoppard, David Hare, Harold Pinter and so forth maintain a theatrical balance between dramatic supply and dramatic demand. And somewhere in London the Shakespearean clock is always ticking, and Restoration theatre is regularly restored. The Shavian legend is periodically recounted and warmed-up Wilde is often on offer. On any given night, there are usually some peculiar goings-on at the Royal Court Theatre, and whatever the critics may sniff about Andrew Lloyd Webber, he has brought an originality and vitality to the musical stage, which for the last decade or so has beaten the Americans at their own game.

For all the good writing and production, however, it's British acting that stands out. The British seem to be masters of illusion and disguise and they adore dressing up in costumes, uniforms and drag. But it is their use of words which is legendary, and there seems to be more acting talent jammed on to the British Isles than any place on earth. Sometimes a foreigner wonders whether everybody in Britain is an actor.

In fact, the British presence in the American mind these days comes largely through its actors. A well-informed American could not confidently identify a single member of the British Cabinet, but he could reel off a string of British performers. This is largely due to the cinema, and it's worth noting that British film-making didn't really take off until the 1930s, after the arrival of the 'talkies'. For the British, a movie without words was like tea without milk. And year after year, British actors appear in the middle of America's big screen.

Most of these skilled performers are 'switch-hitters', able to play convincingly in either accent. And an American who lives in Britain comes quickly to appreciate that the scores of famous names, from

Alec Guinness to Vanessa Redgrave, constitute only the tip of the acting iceberg. Many of Britain's finest talents rarely make an appearance in America – I think of Ian McKellen or Judi Dench or Derek Jacobi or Alan Bates – and just behind this phalanx of national names there are legions more. Acting comes so naturally to this country that the depth is virtually bottomless.

I once asked Edward Fox how he would describe the difference between British actors and American actors. He said there were two main distinctions. The first is that almost all British actors pass through a Shakespearean apprenticeship where they study the ancient secrets of the stage and learn to suppress their individual personalities within the characters they portray. American actors, by contrast, come up through a variety of acting backgrounds, and the goal is to be 'a star'. The second is that British actors rarely confine themselves to a single medium because they enjoy the versatility of theatre, cinema, television and radio, each of which requires a different emphasis of talent. American actors, as good as they may be, do not often stray from the one dramatic dimension they have adopted.

Answering the same question, Ian Richardson gave a third difference. Americans rely on action, he said, while the British rely on words. Bingo.

All of this may be a long way from a dining-room table in St John's Wood and an eloquent old poet swapping stories with an eager, younger novelist. But that evening, as Spender and Ackroyd talked, I thought there really was something unique about the British and their words, something much more than a good conversation over a sherry or a pint and much more than a stirring monologue across the footlights. Ronald Harwood, the playwright, says this British verbalism descends mainly from the Reformation and the turbulent times of the seventeenth century. The Reformation and what followed was a kind of cultural revolution that destroyed the graven images of the visual arts and caused the British to fall back on the colloquial colour and vigour of language.

That may be so. It perhaps explains the intensity of language in Britain. But I concluded that British wordfulness is genetic, something bred in the British bone, and that, whatever the explanation, one of the great pleasures of life in Britain is the daily, dappled flow of words and the Kingdom's swooning, exuberant romance with the English language.

Jot and Tittle

When I'm in the United States, there are two things I especially miss about Britain: McVitie's digestives and the BBC. Almost every one of my mornings in the United Kingdom has started with a hot cup of black coffee, a crisp, dark-chocolate McVitie's and at least one hour of Radio Four's *Today* programme. In America I can find the coffee and a respectable alternative to the cookie. But there is no substitute for *Today*. On either side of the Atlantic, this BBC production is the best example I know of the Fourth Estate at work and play.

The British used to be confident they knew how to get things just about right – certainly righter than any foreigners, especially Americans, were likely to get them. And the British Broadcasting Corporation was always one of those things that led foreigners, especially Americans, to think the British might just have a point. With its bureaucratic undercarriage and the peculiarities of its Royal Charter, the grandly autonomous public service of the BBC can sometimes seem cumbersome and hard for an American to figure out. Americans, after all, are instinctively hostile to public funding of the media. But somehow Auntie has concocted a balanced formula between the zippy agitation of commercial journalism and the plodding pace of state broadcasting. The

BBC surely enjoys the most respected brand name in the world.

When I lived in Africa, my short-wave radio was usually tuned to the sonorous World Service, and though I sometimes felt a twinge of disloyalty in ignoring the flat tones of the Voice of America, there was something reassuring and sturdy and delectably clandestine about those five pips and a bleat from far away. They signalled that all was well with the world, or at least with the BBC. So it was natural for me, when I came to live in Britain, to set my dial to the Beeb.

When I first heard the *Today* programme, in the great days of Brian Redhead, I was a little put off by the prosecutorial style of questioning in which every political guest in the dock was presumed guilty until proven so. American journalists are more conversational when they put an interview on the record, and most British newspaper reporters I found almost too polite and deferential. But British broadcast journalists are as tough as old boots and as tenacious as terriers, and they are proud of their adversarial, balloon-pricking style, pioneered on television by Robin Day and emulated by Brian Walden, Jonathan Dimbleby, Jeremy Paxman and so forth. For British broadcasters, interviews are confrontations. And on radio the *Today* programme is kung-fu journalism.

Like a live morning newspaper, *Today* decides what is important to know for the next twenty-four hours and elaborates how to think about it. It is a national tom-tom for the elite. Because politicians and experts are so readily available for a morning grilling, the programme is about as authoritative as you can get. The presenters not only convey news but make it too. They set out the daily agenda and send out the warning notices to the Establishment, and before launching yourself into the wide world you had better know what transpired that morning in the cramped BBC studio at Broadcasting House. About two million people listen in – shaving in front of their mirrors, crunching on their cornflakes, driving into work or wondering whether to have a second McVitie's.*

When I was ambassador I was occasionally asked to come on the programme to explain what the US government was up to. The

---

* At about 7.50 the programme features 'Thought for the Day', a semi-religious, not-too-sanctimonious little homily, usually delivered by a priest, rabbi or minister. At this moment, I imagined, the water pressure all over London suddenly dropped as listeners stepped into their showers.

invitation was a little like receiving a summons from the bailiff. I never went to the BBC studio because the BBC would send a radio car to Winfield House. At first this was an old London taxi fitted out with all the necessary electronic gear. Once I was confused about the time of the interview and hastily climbed into the back seat with a raincoat over my pyjamas. Later the BBC went all posh and equipped a roomy mini-van.

Before an interview I would make myself sit alone for a moment in the big Gold Room on the ground floor of the house and silently ask what was the one thought, the one message, I wanted to get across. Stick to it, I said. And I would try to guess which interviewer I would draw – John Humphrys or Anna Ford? Or maybe Sue MacGregor or Jim Naughtie? It was a little like Russian roulette. But it didn't really matter. They were all smart, contrary and jugular. When my time came, I swallowed hard and stepped outside.

American radio these days is largely the preserve of rock'n'roll, Bible thumping and, more recently, the snide, snappy, opinionated political talkshows whose primary purpose is to demonstrate how quick-witted and folksy the host is (a particular challenge in the case of Oliver North, for example) and whose primary victim is objectivity. But radio in America is largely a commuter's medium – background noise – and it's almost impossible to compare the American and British versions.* I became so enamoured of British radio, or at least Radio Four, that I found myself worried what that cad Simon Pemberton would do next on *The Archers*.

It used to be that, unlike radio, you could compare American and British television journalism and feel you were in an interesting contest. Sad to say, this is no longer the case. The news departments in America's top three networks (CBS, NBC and ABC) were once first-class pace setters. Driven by a public-service ethos and intensely professional, they were generously subsidized from the corporate profits of their owners. News was the prestigious flagship of each channel, and the commercial competitiveness among the three networks gave their news departments the feeling of late-breaking edge. This was especially true in the 1960s and 1970s, and when I

* There are some 10,000 stations in the United States.

first lived in the United Kingdom I found the British equivalent of television news tepid, stuffy and provincial.

Things are different now. I remember sitting in a Boston hotel room in 1995 and turning on the *CBS Evening News*. The United States (and other allies) had just started enforcing the No-Fly Zone in Bosnia. This story led the broadcast. But the screen showed some old file footage of combat jets taking off from an aircraft carrier and a few seconds of those grainy, day-glo, Gulf War images of smart bombs zeroing in on someone's front door. There was a brief gee-whiz voice-over, but no explanation of the significance or context of what was happening in Bosnia, and no thought that American pilots might be killing people on the ground in a distant land. No one was interviewed. As another jet roared into the sky, I felt I was riffling through a Captain Marvel comic book.

After this vapid minute, the presenter, Dan Rather, switched to the O. J. Simpson trial in Los Angeles and the programme went on about O. J.'s tribulations for another fifteen minutes or so, including an analysis of what O. J.'s prosecutor, Marcia Clark, was wearing that day. This, obviously, was the good stuff. Welcome home, I thought.

The other American networks aren't any better these days. The presenter at NBC, Tom Brokaw, now occasionally stands up from his news desk to deliver a brow-furrowing 'in depth' report on some heart-rending subject such as a group of Sunday Schoolers in Indiana who are trying to make a kidney dialysis machine out of discarded Coca-Cola cans. At ABC Peter Jennings casually offers up titbits of news as if he were sitting on the next bar stool. The problem today is not merely that domestic news pushes out foreign news for air time but that 'human interest' wins out over 'public interest'.*

The decline of American television journalism has occurred, I think, for three reasons: the end of the Cold War, which has distanced America from the customary concerns about international order; the tightening of corporate budgets at network headquarters, which has converted editors into accountants; and the emergence

---

* Even the occasional international stories are measured for their emotional clout. The tacky network coverage of Princess Diana's death scraped new depths of soppy bathos.

of the multi-channel universe, which is good for people who treat choice as avoidance. There is perhaps a fourth reason. The Americans more than the British are disposed to prefer image over content, and television is the ultimate medium of image.

Whatever the explanation, fewer and fewer Americans take their news from the networks, so the networks scramble for a dwindling share of a fragmented market. Competition used to force network television news up-market. Now the momentum is in the opposite direction. The pressure is on Dan, Tom and Peter to be entertaining and cuddly, like celebrity emcees in a variety show.

If you want serious television news in the United States, you have to join the underground at the Public Broadcasting Service. But PBS, whose stingy federal grants are shrinking, struggles to survive on the donations of its small band of loyal viewers. Except for the staccato bulletins at CNN, there isn't much alternative. And after night-time settles across the great American expanse, prime-time television becomes an information wasteland.

So the television shoe is now on the other foot. For an American interested in the outside world, the contrast with BBC and ITN is almost alarming. The arrival of ITN in the 1950s provided just enough competition to jolt BBC television out of its narcoleptic frumpiness. Today these two outfits, in my opinion, are the best electronic news organizations in the world by almost any comparison.* British politicians from time to time grumble about bias in the news rooms, but the British produce superior news programmes, both technologically and journalistically. Government licensing requires this public service, but that only half explains the quality.

An American television executive would have an apoplectic fit if someone proposed putting on a fifty-minute, prime-time news show, as Channel 4 offers under the prodding hand of Jon Snow, and the idea of a ten o'clock bulletin on commercial television, as Trevor McDonald presents with consummate ease on ITV, would provoke rollicking laughter at any New York network headquarters. Cable and satellite are bound to put the squeeze on the audience for television news, but so far BBC and ITN have held their own

---

* You can say the same thing about British photo-journalism. American channels these days rely heavily on the London-based services of VisNews and WTN.

without much compromise in standards. For an American, it's impressive.

Moreover, the investigative or documentary programmes that you find so effortlessly on British television – the durable *Panorama*, for example, or *World in Action* – couldn't find a slot on American television at two o'clock in the morning. Sometimes British television overdoes it. A leaden half-hour on Birmingham's sewer system isn't necessarily what you're looking for in the middle of the evening. But then that's why God invented the remote control. In any event, I'll take British television news over its American counterpart any day.

When it comes to the printed press, the game is a little more mixed. The playing field seems level because newspapers in both countries are commercial enterprises. But the contexts are different.

Journalism in America is a holy vocation. You wouldn't necessarily notice this from the practitioners, but, like monks and nuns in the Middle Ages, reporters should be appreciated for what they say and not for what they do. Journalism enjoys a special status in the United States because it is the only profession specifically protected by the constitution. Free speech and a free press are enshrined in the first amendment of the Bill of Rights, and together they have inoculated journalism against the normal constraints of society. When the Supreme Court upheld the right of the *New York Times* and the *Washington Post* to publish the super-classified Pentagon Papers in 1971, the constitutional immunization of the press seemed complete. The United States has also developed a refined body of privacy and libel laws (the 'right to be let alone', as Justice Brennan called it), but, because a plaintiff who is a 'public figure' must prove premeditated malice as well as inaccuracy, these laws rarely trip up the American press.

In Britain, on the other hand, you're always aware of the government coughing quietly in the background. This is true of all the media. The Official Secrets Act and D-Notices have been around a long time, and when I was ambassador the media were required to gag the voices of Sinn Fein spokesmen (actors were substituted, so what Sinn Fein had to say sounded more convincing). My only serious brush with British law occurred in 1987 when a friend from America brought me a contraband copy of *Spycatcher* at a time when the *Independent* was banned from printing extracts. Though I've never seen one, I know there are Ton-Ton Macoute characters out there patrolling the streets to catch anyone who hasn't paid his television licence fee to the BBC. Every movie in Britain begins with the seal of the official censor, and even a local council can axe a film at a neighbourhood cinema. This is hardly *Brave New World*, but if push comes to shove, the brawn is usually on the government's side.

Libel laws also make life dodgy for the British press because it is the publisher who carries the burden of proof in a court case. John Major holed the *New Statesman* below the legal water line when it ran a trumped-up story about his supposed affair with a Whitehall caterer. And Jeffrey Archer won a notorious case against the *News of the World* in which the court apparently agreed that a £2,000 payment to a prostitute did not necessarily prove he had engaged her professional services. The British press seem to be able to intrude at will – in this most private country, privacy laws remain undeveloped – but what it comes up with better be accurate. I was in the House of Commons the day David Mellor – an old friend whose libido had fallen victim to Britain's unusual brand of gotcha-journalism – colourfully warned the press that it was 'drinking in the Last Chance Saloon'.

Like most sanctions, government discipline of the press is more effective as a threat than a reality. It would be a foolish government that really went after the newspapers. But the fact that politicians can even suggest penalizing the press is a discovery for a constitutional American. As a practical matter, the British press is uninhibited and not easily intimidated, but it usually plays the game by the government's rules. In the anonymous snuggery of the lobby system, reporters and politicians schmooze about news in the long shadows of government (nowadays both Washington and London have the same problem distinguishing between 'briefing' and 'leaking'; the rule of thumb is that a 'leak' is when someone else does it). Like most things British, gathering information is a matter of convention, not right, and while the press operates with liberty it doesn't exactly operate with freedom.

The curious paradox of American and British journalism is that they seem to produce behaviour which is the opposite of what you would expect. America is a country of sensationalist dimensions, but the press is staid and restrained; Britain, by contrast, is a country of staid disposition, but the press is carefree and sensationalist. Somebody got it backwards.

One reason for this peculiar inversion is that print journalism is the only area of economic life I can think of where the competition is more ferocious in Britain than in America. Britain's dozen principal newspapers are all published in London, naturally, but they are national in distribution. By six o'clock in the morning you can buy the same newspaper in almost any corner of the land. And there are so many to choose from. An outsider hardly knows where to begin. At Winfield House I started by subscribing to fourteen tabloids and broadsheets, including the international editions of the *Herald Tribune* and the *Wall Street Journal*. I eliminated one per week until I whittled the morning take down to five, and I couldn't even manage these.

All the British papers are after the same readers and the same advertisers in the same market. The price war between *The Times* and the *Telegraph* has been going on for almost as long as the First World War. It's a rough business whose main preoccupation seems to be less in presenting news than in hyping it. So reporters are often slipshod, editorials are often boisterous and a compromising photograph is pure gold.

In the United States, all papers, like all politics, are local. No American newspaper can be called 'national' in the British sense. There are around 1,500 American dailies but only four enjoy a circulation above one million: the *New York Times*, the *Wall Street Journal*, the *Los Angeles Times* and *USA Today*.* The first two of these, along with the American edition of the *Financial Times*, are now distributed nationally on the day of publication, so for the first time in American history there are a few 'national' newspapers, at least for the boardroom decision-makers. But the usual focus is local. The *Washington Post* even publishes daily supplements tailored to the immediate interests of subscribers in the Virginia and Maryland suburbs.

Not more than a handful of American papers face hometown competition. In fact, there are only a couple of dozen cities in the

* In Britain, the *Daily Telegraph* reaches more than a million and the *Sun* more than four million.

United States which can still boast as many as two dailies. Everywhere else the metropolitan newspaper is a virtual monopoly in its own local market, and over the years this has dulled the sharp end of American journalism.

Because American newspapers are as untroubled by competitors as they are prickly about their constitutional privilege, they have developed a more professional if puffier attitude to journalism than their British counterparts. In a respectable American news room, the rules are strict: separate fact from opinion; track down at least two corroborating sources on every story; always give the subject of an article the opportunity to comment; respect the ground rules of off-the-record, background, not-for-attribution and so forth.* It's hard to land a job with an American newspaper unless you have a graduate degree in journalism. Without much competition, American newspapers find that taking the high road isn't such an arduous trip, whereas British papers are usually on the lookout for a short cut.

Professionalism is not the first word that comes to mind when describing British journalism, though it seems that every other student at a British university is pursuing 'media studies'. The broadsheets are still self-conscious about propriety, but even here I often came across reporters whom I guessed the managing editor had hired after a couple of drinks at a nearby pub. The recipe of fact and opinion is a spicy mix in British journalism, and I was frequently surprised to see how easily speculation was published as hard news. I can count at least four times during my tenure when stories about the Anglo-American relationship read more like obituaries than news reports. And I recall one occasion when a reporter pressed me repeatedly about who might be appointed to a senior government position. I said I hadn't the foggiest idea, which I didn't, but in the end I stupidly said, 'I dunno – maybe So-'n'-So.' The next day the headline read, 'So-'n'-So Tipped for Top Job'. This was not unusual.

In the 1992 election, most British papers were so slanted they seemed like political pamphlets for one party or the other. And when I was minister at the embassy during the 1987 election, I set

---

* George Shultz, who is a savvy Washington navigator, followed his own rule: '*Anything* you say in Washington is *always* on the record.'

up a kind of 'hot line' with Neil Kinnock's chief of staff, Charles Clarke, because we both knew the British press would serve up confections about the 'official' American view of the Labour Party. We weren't disappointed. I suppose you can argue, as British editors do, that what the papers lack in professionalism they make up for in liveliness. I guess so.

For an outsider a lot of preconceptions about the British evaporate on learning that Britain's most popular daily newspaper is the *Sun*. This kind of long-lens, grunting, mammary journalism is almost unknown in the United States, not because Americans are more puritanical than the British but because tabloids in America simply aren't regarded as newspapers. In fact, most American tabloids are so down-market they are only sold in supermarkets or drugstores, and they normally concentrate on circus stories such as the last, verified sighting of Elvis Presley or the incredible love-life of a fat dwarf. Only 5 per cent of the American population reads these sheets (though in the last few years exposés in the *National Enquirer* and the *Star* have managed to scalp two prominent political figures). If American tabloids have any stylistic influence, it is more on television news than printed news.

The influence of the tabloids in Britain, on the other hand, is rampant. When Princess Diana died, their quick-step transformation from pernicious voyeurism to pious hagiography should have embarrassed the most cynical hack. The active symbiosis between the princess and the press, especially the tabloids, presaged a tragic outcome (Maureen Dowd, the *New York Times* columnist, called this relationship 'riding the Nikon tiger'), and the capacity of these papers to create superficial images, to trivialize important events and to manipulate the national mood is breathtaking.

For all their vapidness, however, the tabloids often break stories which the broadsheets can't ignore, and together the tabloids reach more readers than all the others combined. A familiar lament I often heard from the British Establishment was the apparent decline of *The Times* as the dignified organ of the nation (in Britain, 'decline' and 'change' are often confused), and this reflected the marauding agenda of the tabloids. Others noted sadly that the top papers no longer carried verbatim texts of parliamentary debates (though this may be more a comment on the House of Commons than on Fleet Street). And substantial foreign ownership of the British press

suggested to some an international conspiracy to undermine the
sanctity of Britishness by playing to the low-brow and prurient.

There has always been a jostling rivalry between the two sides of
the Atlantic when it comes to journalism. Tetchy transatlantic
scribblers regard each other as not quite up to the mark.* British
journalists call American newspapers boring and parochial, a haughty
view perhaps, but one more politely echoed by many other British
visitors as well. International news is indeed hard to find in even
the best of American papers. And the trend is downwards. Stories
about Britain are few and far between and as often as not centre
on the royal family, the charms of the Cotswolds or some distinctive
British eccentricity. British journalists suspect American editors
believe the earth is flat.

Some American journalists think of British newspapers as big,
flashy fish floundering around in a small, shallow pond. The British
coverage of America is indisputably extensive, especially the gaudy
and lurid events which America serves up in such generous portions,
and when reading these you can often detect a trace of British
schadenfreude. But while the British press may be more cosmopolitan
in breadth, it's hard to name a columnist (outside the *Financial
Times*) who regularly writes about anything other than British
domestic preoccupations, turning over the same soil until it is
dust. This self-absorption is one reason why many American
correspondents in London find the British beat a big snore and
hanker to return to the action back home.

America compensates for some of its journalistic parochialism
by a healthy production of national magazines. *Time, Newsweek* and
US News & World Report are obvious examples, though nowadays
they seem to be following the same entertainment format of
television news. Behind these three, however, is a deep rank of
intelligent, sophisticated journals such as the *Atlantic Monthly*, the

* This goes back a long way. Henry Morton Stanley was an American correspondent
for the *New York Herald* when in 1871 he pulled off the scoop of the century by
finding Dr Livingstone in darkest Africa. When he reported his discovery of Livingstone
(who hadn't realized he was lost), the London newspapers didn't believe him and
instead ridiculed Stanley's claim as well as his ill-chosen words of introduction on the
shores of Lake Tanganyika. And it was American publications in the 1930s which
rudely penetrated Britain's *cordon sanitaire* to report that the heir apparent was romping
around the world with an American divorcee.

New Yorker, the *National Review*, *Foreign Affairs*, the *New Republic* and many more which have no real British equivalents. The *Economist* (which idiosyncratically still calls itself a newspaper) can be counted in the same class, though it has more readers in America than in all of Europe including the United Kingdom. The *Spectator* trails somewhere in the distance. But that's all.

Many British names appear on the mastheads of these American publications, so I used to wonder at the paucity of good British magazines. Perhaps the abundance of national newspapers has simply supplanted serious magazines, I thought. Or possibly the British have run out of interesting ideas to debate in print – this may be closer to the mark. Or maybe there are more magazines in America because there are more doctors' waiting rooms.

After years of following the news media on both sides of the Atlantic, I have arrived at the following comparative conclusions. For radio and television, the British win hands down, and the gap is widening. Newspapers come out a draw – if I were an honest castaway, I think I would prefer to have the *Telegraph* or *The Times* delivered to my sandy shore than any American daily, though if I really wanted to know what was happening out there, I would ask for the *Herald Tribune*. But it's a close call. As for magazines, the British lose by forfeit.

Putting aside the comparisons, however, journalism seems to play a role in American and British societies which is almost unique in the world. American journalism sees itself as the semi-official, whistle-blowing, spade-is-a-spade guardian of the nation's constitutional integrity, but its range these days is increasingly narrow, especially in radio and television. In America today there is a phenomenon known as the 'CNN Curve', which means that history begins with the arrival of the first CNN crew. Like a tree falling in the forest, if CNN isn't there, it hasn't happened. Even the quality papers devote less and less space to international events, and by the end of my term as ambassador I began to worry that a veil of ignorance was once again descending over the American republic. American news organizations used to be part of the solution to whatever troubled the nation. Now they are part of the problem.

In the British garden of the Fourth Estate, there are plenty of shady spots as well. British electronic journalism may be incomparable, but commercial pressures will make the standards and audience share harder and harder to sustain. The BBC is already showing the strain. British newspapers are more obviously political than Americans think proper, and they are also more flippant in tone and more casual with the facts. But, because all political power is concentrated in the government of the day, the British press is one of the few independent sources of genuine and effective opposition.

It is probably true that modern Anglo-American journalism has become too glamorized and wields too much arbitrary power. The political process in both countries has been distorted along the way. I rarely had a conversation with John Major that didn't end with some bitter expression about the press, and it's hard to think of a post-war American president who didn't blame at least half his woes on the media. Cynicism, paranoia and manipulation seem to be the common language between politicians and journalists on both sides of the ocean, and there is no obvious method of self-correction.

But I would make one last point: there is something about the iconoclastic irreverence of American and British journalists – their sheer pizzazz – that makes them the best possible company, right down to the last McVitie in the packet.

PART FOUR

A Day Late and a
Dollar Short

Toil and Trouble

When I first lived in Britain, in the 1970s, it was hard to find anyone who had a good thing to say about the place. Or at least a good economic thing. In a country once notorious for self-confidence, self-deprecation had become the common trait. The nation sat with its head in its hands bemoaning its fate, once so grand and now so grim. Britain then was a hangdog nation.

The decade of the 1970s seemed to prove that Britain really was in irreversible decline, a clapped-out, ungovernable basket case of shabby appearance and bleak prospects. Everything had been tried on but nothing fit. The only optimistic observation seemed to be that things could be worse. Some suggested that since Britain was the world's first industrial society so it would also be the world's first post-industrial society, and in that respect at least Britain was ahead of the pack. Otherwise, a wizened and wheezing Britain was ready to check into an economic retirement home to see out its twilight years with gentility and grace and one last snifter of brandy.

I also learned another thing: for all its problems with productivity, the British economy was the world's largest producer of metaphors.

All economies suffer the gyrations of boom and bust, but the old British economy, after one of its elliptical swings, always ended up a little further behind the others. Rather than simple cycles, Britain spiralled downwards. And with each new turn, the industrial and manufacturing base of the country contracted. When a shipyard closed, when an automobile factory shut its gates, when a steel furnace fired for the last time, it seemed as if another large chunk of masonry had fallen off the economic edifice. Imports to Britain usually outstripped exports and wages usually outstripped growth. The result was inflation followed by higher interest rates which suppressed investment which stifled growth, and the dog chased after its tail.

Periodically along this perilous way sterling would lose credibility in the financial markets, and the government of the day would be forced to devalue. Variations on this monetary theme stalked successive British governments for half a century. The pound was devalued in 1949 and 1967. It floated into another embarrassing crisis in 1976. Sterling lost almost half its value in the 1980s, and it tumbled out of the Exchange Rate Mechanism in 1992. Britain always seemed to be the country to order one more drink just before the bar closed, and once the British economy was sobered by some drastic financial crisis, it picked itself up and headed straight back through the saloon doors.

For the British, this entropic pattern was painful. British economic nerves, I think, are especially sensitive to economic news because Britain is an economically literate place, far more so than the United States. Economic items always appear further up the agenda on the evening news than you find in America or most anywhere else. The great universities treat politics and economics as indivisible. From Adam Smith to John Maynard Keynes the British have played with economic theories and produced many of them. Even Karl Marx did his work in the British Library. The statistics of economics, such as interest rates or trade balances, form part of polite, everyday conversation, and the flight path of the pound is tracked like a duck in shooting season. Standing at the front door of Number 11 Downing Street, the Chancellor of the Exchequer poses with his scarlet budget box held aloft in an annual photographic fixture of which the nation never seems to tire. And only Britain could produce a weekly magazine so drearily called the *Economist* or a daily paper so formidably entitled the *Financial Times*. The attention to the economy and the economic sophistication of the average

Briton made the decline in national fortunes an acute national experience.

Everyone seems to have a list of explanations for Britain's decline, and if the order is often different, the theories are usually the same. Near the top of my list is the simple observation that the shock of the twentieth century left Great Britain stunned, like a champion prizefighter suddenly floored in the third round.

There was a period not so long ago when Britain was the greatest wealth-producing country in the world. The inventiveness of the British and their early industrialization gave them a near-monopoly position in the making and selling of goods. Well before 'globalization' became the economic fashion, British ships crowded the ports of the Chinese coast and every jungle clearing in Africa had a Barclay's branch. American railroads and Australian mines were backed by British financiers. The Victorian zenith seemed effortless, and the world then was an Anglicized oyster. At the turn of the century, the word 'English' was synonymous with quality, and English products were envied and emulated to such an extent that they set the international cultural and economic standard, especially in the United States. People tried to do things the English way with English things. It has been plain hard for a nation to reconcile this supremacy of the past, which was so complete that it must have seemed divinely ordained, with the sense of failure in the present. The reversal of fortune has been so extreme in this century that the nation could scarcely believe what had happened.

A second explanation for the British decline blames the Empire. For most of its existence, the theory goes, the Empire dulled the commercial instinct of the British by fostering a mercantilist system of protected markets. The economy may have looked competitive but it really wasn't. In fact, the Empire permitted the British to set the parameters of economic order and to restrict competition.* Imperial Preference was a controlled system directed by the state. If you lived anywhere in the colonies and you wanted to buy a piece of cloth, it was sure to come from Lancashire. And wherever you happened to want a cup of tea, the sugar passed through

* This was not uniformly true. At the turn of the century, Britain led the world in free trade until it hurt.

London. Without much competition from outside, the British metropole grew self-satisfied and flabby. The Empire was an easy, ready market, grossly protected, and once it fell away the British found themselves in a rough-and-tumble world for which they were ill prepared and ill suited.

A third common explanation for Britain's decline, at least for the acceleration of economic misfortune, is that the British spent their money unwisely. Britain's welfare state was long in coming but fulsome in arrival. For a country unaccustomed to radical change, the remarkable outburst of never-again legislation that followed the exhausting world war was close to revolutionary. I doubt whether the National Health Service, for example, would have been possible without the powerful social consensus which underpinned the victory.

Britain created a plethora of national benefit programmes which were socially admirable and economically unsustainable. Her Majesty's Government became a spendthrift National Nanny. By the 1970s, nearly half the adult population in Britain received its primary income, in one form or another, from the state. And over the same period the capacity of the nation to earn wealth, rather than taxing it, turned in on itself. Instead of investing capital in its own industrial base and infrastructure, Britain spent its money on an increasingly impacted, conscience-stricken welfare system which it could not afford. In order to spend money you have to make money. The British spent before they earned, and the more they spent, the less they earned.*

All of these theories – and many more – have become the familiar, noisy playground for British economic historians. There is truth in all of them. But the most common explanation for the British decline is the belief that what is wrong with the British economy is not, at heart, economic but social. The problem with the British economy, the British say, is the British.

I once asked two accomplished British businessmen what was wrong with the British economy. 'Complacency,' said the first.

---

* My conversations with Tony Blair often centred on this British classic. From Blair's comments you could tell he was a different kind of Labour politician, but he said he couldn't do anything about spending over earning until he changed the Labour Party itself. This he proceeded to do.

'Incompetence,' said the second. If you asked the same question of an American businessman about the American economy, the answer would most probably be the 'national debt' or the 'savings ratio', or some such economic critique. But in Britain economic questions have social answers. The enemy is us, the story goes, and this self-flagellating theory is inevitably more painful and troubling than any other analysis. And it has several facets.

One European businessman, a Swiss who worked in London, concluded his review of the British economy by stating simply, 'The British are lazy. The managers go home when the workers do. They all shave time from the end of the day. That's the one thing they have in common.' It is a harsh judgment to say the British, particularly the English, just don't work hard enough, or that the layabout economy only manages to produce four days of work from a five-day week. And it seems especially unkind these days when the British are spending more hours at work than their continental counterparts.

Nonetheless, the compulsiveness about work and career that often characterizes the American ethic is, as a general rule, absent from British life. When an American chief executive I know showed up for work on his first morning with a British corporation, he found the building so empty he wondered if it was a national holiday. The word 'ambition', which is admired in America, has an unsavoury implication in the British vocabulary. Initiative does not seem to be much prized either. All the motivational books and seminars which are so popular in America receive little attention here (for better or worse). British visitors returning from the United States like to talk about the 'can-do' attitude of Americans, and many British who go to America stay there precisely because they enjoy the invigorating sense of economic liberation. It used to be said of the British that those with 'get-up-and-go' usually got up and went, which by the way is exactly what my Swiss friend did.

I doubt whether indolence is a wholly adequate explanation for the old waywardness of the British economy. But I do think it is true that the British are inclined to apportion their time less compulsively than Americans. This is one of the reasons why Americans find Britain so appealing, even if we are sometimes impatient with its economy. Americans may believe the sanctity of the British weekend is an indulgence, just as the British believe the

American working breakfast is a barbarity, but it is hard to live here without being seduced by the more refined British balance between work and leisure. For the British, enough is enough; for Americans, enough is a beginning.

The British seem to have a fuller appreciation that life is short and there are many pleasures. Work has its place but the place is unlikely to reveal anything metaphysical. And I would guess that in Britain one is more likely than anywhere else to come across a businessman given to quoting poetry or a machinist ready to discuss horticulture.* One thing is sure: Britain will not become a Switzerland, and this may be a relief.

Another trait of national character which is meant to explain economic underperformance is that the British are not by nature complainers. They may lament, which is broad and passive, but they don't complain, which is specific and active. Americans are enthusiastic complainers, a characteristic which brings a frown of disapproval to the stoic British brow.

I've never understood why the British are reluctant to complain when they seem so ready to scold. Perhaps it is that scolding enforces order whereas complaining upsets it. And making a fuss, after all, draws embarrassing attention to yourself and is discourteous. In any event, in Britain there is a higher value placed on the orderliness of the queue than on the quality of whatever is at the end of it. A willingness to tolerate, a kind of pride in putting up with the unacceptable and a patience in the face of inconvenience apparently demonstrate an inner fibre. And therefore the approximate is okay. Whatever is on offer 'will do'. This kind of stiff-upper-lip stoicism is admirable if the Luftwaffe is dropping bombs on your country every night, but it's unlikely to produce good service in peace time.

Another theory says the British never really liked the sudden grit and grime of the Industrial Revolution. They simply faked their way through it. At the end of the nineteenth century, William Morris, Augustus Pugin and that special group of pre-Raphaelites captured a fundamental yearning in the British spirit for the

---

* At a dinner one night Caroline sat next to the former Governor of the Bank of England, Gordon Richardson. When she mentioned her favourite poem was 'Spring and Fall' by Gerard Manley Hopkins, he recited it for her.

nostalgic, garden soul of medieval England. Despite industrialization, Britain was never far away from its hand-made Gothic origins. And it is true that many Americans think living in the British economy is, on the whole, a pre-industrial experience, as if the Industrial Revolution had never really caught on, even in the country of its birth. Britain remains rich in the old-fashioned artisanship of restoration, preservation and reproduction, and there is a devotion to quality in this kind of craftsmanship that is hard to find in America.

So if you want something made or repaired that was common before the blight of smokestacks and mass production, Britain is the place to be. The British know how to gild silver, weld bronze, grind crystal, stain glass, thatch roofs, pleach hedges, cast bells and stitch needlepoint. Plaster is still moulded, furniture is waxed, hats are blocked, boots are stretched, books are bound, rings are set, pots are thrown, pewter is beaten, paper is engraved, linen is embroidered, metal is embossed, stone is carved, marble is polished, iron is wrought, wood is joined, cane is woven, paintings are cleaned, clocks are calibrated, barrels are blued, wool is worsted and leather is lasted. Behind the disguise of the twentieth century a pre-industrial, bespoke economy thrives where care and detail are the standards and time is anything but the essence. Much of the British economy is an accumulation of the past. Nothing is allowed to slip away and this has made for a culture which is counter-industrial.

Some also argue that the British are not by nature competitive. For a long time the British economy was a neatly arranged affair, like a tidy medicine cabinet, and every High Street had its baker and butcher, its banker and chemist, its newsagent and ironmonger. In this structured, miniaturized, immobile society, restraint was the motto. Competition existed, but Britain was an up-to-a-point society. This is one reason why the British appear very well organized but not very efficient.

When I first came to London, I was told that the biggest difference between the American economy and the British economy was that Americans believed the economic pie expanded in the cooking whereas the British believed it stayed the same size. In America, everyone could take a bigger and bigger slice without diminishing anyone else's. In Britain, if your slice was bigger, someone else's was smaller. Like the land, there was only so much wealth to go around. Unbridled competition therefore was aggressive and threatening.

Americans, by contrast, believe that competition is the special ingredient that sharpens an economy. The British invented the capitalist marketplace, but American-style competition is seen as too selfish in its pursuit of profit, too careless in its consumption of gain, and too callous in its disregard of wider social responsibility. The sharp edginess of 'looking out for Number One' is not a phrase you're likely to hear in the United Kingdom. For the British, excessive competition, like complaining, is self-centred and anti-social. And it's not fair play.*

Finally, however, it is the faithful, reliable, dogged, ever-present, all-pervading, never-say-die British class system which takes the brunt of social analysis about the British economy. In Britain all the economic rivers and tributaries are traced back to this familiar source. The managers blame the unions for what went wrong in the twentieth century and the unions blame the managers. And analysts blame both.

For example, Michael Heseltine, who in 1993 was in charge of the Department of Trade and Industry, told me one day that Britain seemed incapable of transferring the effective management of its professional military into its industrial economy. 'In the army,' he said, 'communication goes up and down the line. The colonel and the corporal know each other, talk to each other and trust each other. But, when the military days are over, the colonel goes into the boardroom and the corporal goes on to the shopfloor and they never communicate with each other again.' I mentioned this exchange the next day to John Edmonds, the General Secretary of the Boilermakers Union, to which he responded, 'Well, of course. The difference is that in the army there is regular training. But there is no training in the work place, so there is no communication. The army is an exception because the possibility of getting killed is the one effective way of breaking down the class system.' Even in 1993,

---

* An Egyptian friend of mine once commented that he had never understood the British sense of fair play. 'The British', he explained with a puzzled look, 'insist that you should never kick a man when he's down. But when, may I ask, is there a better time to kick a man?'

the British economy was still analyzed through the social prism of class.

As Heseltine suggested, British management does not have a distinguished history. Countless commentaries describe a system which has fostered a kind of rampant amateurism at the top, otherwise known as the Cricket Theory of British economics. Because manual work has been traditionally disdained, managers have gone to the office to dabble. They would be ashamed if they were caught working too hard. After all, in a *rentier* culture, the cleaner your hands the higher your status. For the upper class the profit motive was regarded with suspicion. The thrusting business-man was seen as crass or, worse, American.* Profits were admired so long as they did not suggest greed or too much effort in their acquisition, but big profits were meretricious. In fact, the supreme social achievement in Britain was to have a lot of money without having worked for it at all.

The unions do not come off much better in these histories of blame. Unions were a just reaction to industrial exploitation, but they also became havens for Luddites for whom change and progress were threats to a self-satisfied status quo. Many unions were in the business of settling old scores. Economics was about resentment and getting your own, and this produced its own kind of shopfloor arrogance. Why try to advance yourself when you could get as much by standing still? Wage demands were unrelated to productivity, and the art of the fiddle was highly esteemed. If inflation and disinvestment followed, then devil take the hindmost.

The intensity of class naturally distorted everything else in the British economy. Education, for example, devalued technical, mech-anical and engineering disciplines in favour of the cultured if unpro-ductive mind. So the country ended up in the anomalous situation where the well-educated did not work and the ill-educated did.

So in the 1970s, when I caught my first glimpse of this economic portrait, Britain was in a pretty sorry state.

---

* The chairman of a British headhunting agency once told me that the biggest difference between a British executive and an American executive is that the Brit, after a certain level of income, is interested in the perks of the job, such as the size of the company car or the mahogany quotient of the office, whereas the American just wants the money.

When I think of then and now, the transformation of the United Kingdom has been little short of miraculous. Many of these old problems and characteristics remain, some more so than others. But the familiar economic excuses of imperial hang-over or social hang-up sound hollow these days. In fact, my own impression now is that the long, nagging saga of Britain's absolute decline is over. This is more a psychological observation than a statistical one, and such a statement requires many asterisks and footnotes. Perhaps it is better to say that the harrowing sense of British free-fall has finally come to an end.

Britain's relative decline will doubtless continue: in global rankings, the country continues to jump around the charts. But global competition is a problem which all advanced Western nations face. By most normal measures – output, income, employment, productivity, debt and so forth – Britain today is doing better than almost all its continental partners. You can argue that the continental partners are simply doing less well than before, and this makes Britain look as if it's doing better. British growth, for example, is not much different from what it was twenty years ago. But this conclusion would be a little churlish.

It is not just the economic measurements of the country which have changed, but its economic structure. Britain is more flexible, adaptable, educated and competitive now than when I first came here, and the economic strength is more than just a passing fancy. I never thought I would see the day when the United Kingdom was regarded as an economic model for Europe, but this is what has happened. Most critical analyses of the economics of the European Union must now be followed by the clause 'except in Britain'.

One reason is that Margaret Thatcher's years as prime minister snapped the British economy out of its stupor. When she arrived in Downing Street in 1979, it seemed the British themselves had had enough. In the decade that followed, the unions were disciplined and the tax burden eased. Privatization moved behemoth industries out of the public sector and back into the open market. Like an emergency blood transfusion, oil flowed into the economy from rigs which fortuitously appeared in the North Sea. Exchange controls were eliminated, credit was available for the asking, and the Big Bang in London's financial markets let loose an avalanche of equities and bonds. Homeowners and shareholders signed up in a new economic army of free enterprise, and for a brief and shining moment the national budget even produced a surplus.

The elections of 1983 and 1987 were political triumphs for a government which had finally located the country's economic pulse. The Labour Party then seemed to be offering answers to questions no one was asking any longer. By the end of it all, the phrase 'British management' no longer sounded like an oxymoron, and unions were negotiating contracts with no-strike clauses, unthinkable just a few years before. Deregulation, foreign competition and the discipline of the international financial markets sharpened corporate performance, and having led the world in the number of strike days, the strike record of British unionized labour became the lowest for the country in this century. Everything seemed to fall into place except a marching band.

Thatcher herself was so controversial in her leadership and so unBritish in her style that it will be a long time before an accurate appraisal of her achievements will emerge. She may be remembered more for what she undid than what she did. Detractors say that much of what happened during the Thatcher years would have happened anyway, or alternatively that, when the Thatcher dust had settled, Britain was the same old Britain. After all, the government was still responsible for more than 40 per cent of spending in the economy and, except for the top brackets, the tax burden was merely rearranged rather than reduced.

On top of this, the value of the pound continued to slide through the Thatcher decade. British companies still didn't invest enough capital in themselves and often seemed to take the money and run, and British research remained underfunded and lackadaisical. The change in union attitudes was more a matter of attrition than epiphany, and the arithmetic of productivity looked good only because large numbers of workers were laid off, many of them exiled to a gulag of permanent unemployment. And output figures looked good because – unlike the British – foreign investors, especially the Americans and Japanese, seemed able to extract high-quality performance from the British economy and the British workforce.

A lot of this is true. But even her most grudging opponents have conceded that Margaret Thatcher rewrote the economic agenda of the nation and broke up the old stereotypes. The Thatcher Effect is the single most important change I can identify over the years when Britain has been my periodic home.

With much less commotion and much worse luck, John Major's government managed to consolidate a lot of this important restructuring. When Major became prime minister, he inherited a serious economic recession and an unpopular poll tax. He reaped the whirlwind of the previous decade. For all the difficulties, however, the fundamentals of Britain's economic transformation became givens under Major's stewardship, and he got too little credit for this. Inflation was squeezed out of the system, Britain's fiscal house was put in rough order, and it is now easier for outsiders to do business in the United Kingdom than anywhere in Europe. Even unemployment, which for years seemed to be the harsh price of economic restructuring, finally turned around under Major. And for those with jobs, real take-home pay had increased by almost 50 per cent by the end of the Conservative era, while the average real wage in the United States, for example, remained stagnant. The evidence of transformation was so convincing that the Labour Party concluded it could not win office without realigning its policies and rhetoric to match Britain's new economic realities. Consolidation is not an exciting political banner, but John Major helped make economic change close to irreversible.

As a result the British economy has become much more complex and varied than it was even a scant generation ago. The adjustments have naturally been full of social stress and social disenchantment. Attitudes have not kept pace with the realities of economic change. The 'politics of envy', for example, continues to have a brittle edge, and when a chief executive of a big corporation receives a fat pay packet, the country still frets about the size of the pie and the manners of the diner. And old-style job security is a thing of the past.

The nation's education system, especially, seems trapped in endless wrangles about privilege and division. As in America, large segments of the population continue to be shut out of the wider economy, and the disturbing differential between the haves and have-nots is expanding like an accordion. Many of the old bogeymen still lurk in the shadows of the British economy, and it wouldn't take too much, I suppose, for the old woe-is-me gloom to descend again on the nation.

But I don't think it will. The problem with the British economy is not the British, or not any longer. Nostalgia and complacency don't seem quite the bedrock causes of British economic dysfunction as they once were, and it may finally be safe to say that Britain's grim days of industrial combat, as a kind of class war by other means, have largely vanished. The riddle for the British economy is less whether it is hopelessly old-fashioned, hide-bound and class-ridden and more what kind of future Britain can build for itself. There is plenty of room to quibble, but over the last few years, I think, Britain's adjustment to internal reform and external competition has meant that the nation enjoys better economic prospects today than it has known at any time since the war, and possibly in this century.

Milk and Honey

A principal cause of Britain's economic metamorphosis is that the international economy itself has changed in the last couple of decades, and most of the change plays in Britain's favour. Just when industrial Britain seemed to be going down the rusty tubes, along comes a spanking new economic era of English-speaking services and information which is tailor-made for the country. The British are a lucky race, and this has been the best of British luck.

When I was at the embassy, however, I was never certain whether Britain would summon its energy and talents to take born-again advantage of these new opportunities, or whether the country, in its hands-in-pockets, foot-dragging way, would arrive at this new economic destination a day late and a dollar short. As the British say, it's all to play for.

Britain's shift to services over the last generation is good news.* In fact, some economists say it's old news – that Britain has always been primarily a commercial nation, a nation which created its wealth

---

* Half of Britain's jobs in 1970 were in services; today, three-quarters are, and the trend continues (around 80 per cent of America's jobs are in services, but the change has been less sudden). About 70 per cent of Britain's GDP is based on services.

through commercial services. But Britain today fusses about this transformation, as if a service economy were somehow less respectable or less substantial than a manufacturing economy (which the British didn't much like in the first place anyway). The British seem to doubt whether a service economy can produce enough wealth to support the nation's obligations and expectations, and there is also a sneaky suspicion that Britain isn't very adept at services.

This last point may have some validity. Americans new to Britain run across lots of micro-economic evidence which suggests that British service is still a sometime thing. As trivial as these anecdotes may sound, the experience often supports the view that, in Britain's modern service economy, the service isn't very good. It is hardly as if twentieth-century service in France or Italy is notably better, but somehow one expects more from the crisper atmosphere of the United Kingdom.

I recall an encounter in a British tea shop not so long ago. The chalk-board menu offered ham sandwiches and cheese sandwiches. So I asked for a ham-and-cheese sandwich. 'We don't have ham-and-cheese sandwiches,' came the reply. 'But you have ham sandwiches and cheese sandwiches.' The woman nodded her head. 'So couldn't you put the ham and cheese together in one sandwich?' 'Well, I suppose so,' she said, looking nonplussed, 'but we only sell ham sandwiches and cheese sandwiches.' I thought for a moment. 'All right,' I persisted, 'could I have a ham sandwich and a cheese sandwich but only two slices of bread?' In Britain, if you ask for something out of the ordinary, you feel you should apologize for the imposition. This is service with a grimace.

Most Americans in Britain have a folio of little stories about local service: the repairman who leaves unexplained bits of metal on the kitchen floor; or the dry cleaner who can't seem to locate that missing skirt; or the truculent waiter who brings you salt and pepper as a favour. At my local bank, where even the most elementary transaction can sometimes seem like a first-time experience for the staff, I have often wanted to rap against the glass partition and ask, 'How do you people stay in business?' There is a three-to-one chance the neighbourhood hardware store will be out of whatever you're looking for, and at the local stationers a common item isn't restocked until the last one has been sold. As often as not in department stores, you have to drag information from a wary sales clerk as if you were a prosecuting attorney. Most American neophytes wonder how John Cleese can be in so many places at once.

A remarkable number of British visitors return from America extolling the service they usually find there, as if good service were a revelation. I've always liked the New York expression 'Yagodit,' meaning you've got the item the instant you ask for it. No sooner said than done, as in: 'Ham-and-cheese on pumpernickel, please.' 'Yagodit.'

The earnest, energetic American waitress who says, 'Hi, my name is Charlene and I'm your hostess today,' has become, for the British, an American cliché, but Charlene delivers the goods. There can be a gushing artificiality about this American eagerness to please the customer. And it is hardly found in every circumstance. But service in America is usually impressive because it is the competitive edge. In Britain, on the other hand, service has been seen as a social commentary, and the distinction between service and subservience has been blurred.

In Britain, too, how business is transacted seems to be as important as what is transacted. America is an urgent country, but few things in Britain ever seem urgent. The British on the whole deal with each other in a gentler, more patient way than one is likely to find in the brusquer pace of the United States.* One of the charms for Americans living in Britain is the effortless civility that seems to characterize the little negotiations of everyday life. To buy a stamp at the Post Office or a leg of lamb at the local butcher is likely to be an agreeable social experience. And when the proprietor of a shop tells you he is out of stock or when the electrician returns with his third excuse, they do so in the nicest possible way. Service and civility, however, are not the same thing.

Every generality about the United Kingdom has more than a few exceptions. An American, for example, would instantly trade all the taxis in the United States for London's roomy cabs with their gurgling diesel birdsong and their guild of knowledgeable drivers who offer a cheerful 'thank you' when accepting a small tip, as if

---

* The exception is the American South. When my wife goes into any store in her South Carolina hometown, it always takes fifteen minutes: three minutes for the transaction and twelve for the conversation.

they were startled by this unremarkable gesture. Supermarkets, too, have been transformed since the string-bag era I knew when I first came to Britain, though British supermarkets are still not entirely convincing to an American eye. On the whole, however, British service is a lottery.

Anecdotes usually don't mean much unless they are symptomatic of something a little more important. I recollect a discussion with a group of American businessmen one day at Winfield House. Some of the businessmen were new to Britain and some were well established. Each represented a different discipline ranging from investment banking to oil drilling. On doing business in Britain, the one point on which they could collectively agree was poor service. By this they did not mean ham-and-cheese sandwiches or supermarket check-outs. They meant the commercial failure to meet deadlines, the unresponsiveness to enquiries, the partial completion of tasks, the unanswered business phone, the tendency to capitulate if something proves too exacting, the inclination to lean away from a job rather than into it, the lack of creative options in solving problems, the aversion to risk in getting a job done. There was nothing whining about these statements, nor even critical. The American businessmen were simply putting forward a catalogue of observations, more cultural than economic, which required adjustments to their own way of doing things in Britain.

There are plenty of illustrations where Britain seems to fall behind the curve in economic services. Tourism, for example, has been around a long time. The British invented it, though tourism used to mean Britons travelling to someone else's country and bringing back souvenirs such as Renaissance triptychs or Greek statuary. Today, however, more than twenty million visitors every year wheel their carts through Heathrow or Gatwick or the other ports of entry around the country. Sometimes it's hard to hear an English word spoken in Oxford Street, and from early spring to late autumn heavy buses navigate the village lanes of the Wallops and the Slaughters.*

* Americans travel here in droves, between three and four million a year. Half of them have come to Britain at least once before; half come only to Britain, with no digressions to the continent; and half can trace some ancestral relationship to the British Isles.

Though much of it is taken for granted, tourism is a £10 billion business in Britain. Almost all this is services related, an accumulation of small-scale activity in hotels, restaurants, theatres and shops. But the British don't particularly like it. Tourism, after all, is intrusive, especially in a country where space is limited and privacy guarded (America, by contrast, is so huge that tourists simply disappear in it, sometimes literally). In Britain, there seems to be a niggling apprehension that the country might be turning itself into a nation of curators or a large repository for left luggage. Service is therefore unimaginative and the infrastructure uneven. Most British hotels still suffer from dribbling showers and 10-watt lamps; and the Euro-tunnel train whisks you from Paris to the Kentish coast in a matter of hours, but from the coast to London, it's faster to walk. The British think there is something light-weight about tourism which makes it hard for them to take it seriously, and so they don't.

Perhaps tourism is a little old hat when it comes to services. A more serious example is the up-to-date set of services which comes along with the information revolution, and here the story is a mixed bag too.

When I'm in the United States these days, I'm always impressed that the hardware, software and communications lingo of the Information Age has become so commonplace. Almost daily you read about some new development in our multi-media, interactive, channel-surfing, internetted, megabyting lives. And almost daily you read about one tycoon or another who, like the railroad magnates of the past, swashbuckle their way through the economy. Small companies toss up new products, new ideas, new programmes and new designs. Universities have rewired their campuses to make computer literacy as natural a part of daily academic life as the pencil. Hackers and techies beaver away in lofts, garrets, garages, attics and basements to come up with inventive new applications. Thirty per cent of American homes have personal computers, and the Internet already has thirty million subscribers. American enterprise uses more microchips in industry than any other country, and half the workforce in America is involved in knowledge-based production. In America these days, you can sense the fever of information services, and virtual reality is a virtual reality.

Britain doesn't have this same info-intensity, at least not yet. But the United Kingdom is a country with an immense reservoir of communications talent. The native gift for expression, the natural urge to develop and convey ideas, the predilection to educate and entertain make up a perfect British match for this new age. By all reckoning, the international market for information services – almost entirely in English – should play straight into Britain's hands.

And the British are doing all right, even technologically. They more or less invented the computer (though the country seemed unable to take any electronic advantage of its originality). The BBC, ITN and Reuters are global in scope and experience, and London has probably replaced New York as the world's news capital. British Telecom and Cable & Wireless were privatized when most other European countries regarded such ventures as economic heresy. SuperJanet connects British universities in an information network, and Cambridge is one of several islands of excellence in communications innovation. Britain is the world's second largest producer of CD-ROMs, and the British music industry holds on to 20 per cent of the global market.* About a quarter-million people already work in the audio-visual sector of the British economy, and a quarter of Europe's entire audio-visual business is British. This is a substantial record.

But, for the real content of the Information Age, I worry that the British may be falling behind. I found it curious that the Conservative government created a Cabinet post for National Heritage instead of something with a little more modern zing such as Telecommunications. I know the chairman of a now-successful British software company who tried to beg, borrow and steal from the cautious British markets to find the start-up funds he needed for his ideas. He finally found the cash in California.

The British are an inventive people, but their proportion of registrations in the international patent pool is diminishing. The World Wide Web was organized by a British genius, but he worked

---

* From the Beatles onwards, the British have produced a profusion of pop stars and continue to do so. Britain's cheeky, counter-cultural music business is world-class, and British bands are a startling contrast to the marshmallow music of the continent. In America, a teenager's room is incomplete without a poster of whoever is at the top of the charts in Britain. When it comes to pop music, Britain has gotten its stuff together.

overseas. Almost all the first cable companies in Britain were American. When it comes to innovative risk-taking in Britain's fragmented media market, it is the vilified outlander Rupert Murdoch who has made most of the running, and Britain has no first-rate media company that makes the world take in its breath.

The worst example, for me, is the movies. When the British go to the movies, it's usually to an American-owned cinema to see an American-financed, American-produced, American-marketed and American-distributed film. American movies, the good and the bad, nowadays command 90 per cent of the British market. In recent years, the great studios of Pinewood and Shepperton and Ealing have led perilous lives, and the Rank Organization, whose brawny, greased-up, politically incorrect flunkey used to gong us to attention in our seats, has taken a safe position on the sidelines of film production.

This is a national nonsense. Britain brims with movie-making talent. British actors, writers, directors, producers, cameramen, soundmen, editors, animators and technicians are among the most professional and creative in the world. The depth of the talent pool is one reason why Americans make so many movies here. But sooner or later, in the theatrical equivalent of the brain drain, these British artists find their way to Hollywood, as if they were hired guns or foreign mercenaries.* This has been true ever since the dawn of cinema. If Hollywood had made clocks, the Swiss would have come; but Hollywood made movies, so the British came. And every year, to the dismay of America's cinematographic establishment, British talent walks away with about a third of the Oscars.

There are many well-worn reasons why the alternative of making British movies in Britain barely exists. British investors, for example, are much too timid for the roulette of the movie game, so even when the British make a movie it's usually a one-off, niche-market event with someone else's money (and the someone else keeps the profits). Other critics claim British movie-making is too self-absorbed, wallowing in bonnets-and-breeches productions which drool over Britain's tinted past. And some say the Americans colonized the international network of film distribution while British distribution remained flat-footed, which it still is.

* About 20 per cent of BAFTA members live in California.

Another villain is Hollywood itself, which offends British sensibilities. The profligate studios, the narcissism of the star syndrome, the high-decibel hype, the gaudy and vacuous lotus-life of Los Angeles are all too much for the British to stomach (and a lot of Americans too). Many British believe the Tinseltown machine has overwhelmed the film business with noisy, violent blockbusters of no redeeming value while British cinema stands for purity if not profit. For these critics, a movie is meant to be more art than entertainment (though hardly anyone can sit through a Peter Greenaway film without medication), and Americans in their crass way have demeaned the form.

David Puttnam, who has seen the movie business from both sides of the ocean, preaches a message of resurrection from every pulpit in the land. He is the Jeremiah of British cinema. And in looking at the future, Puttnam also knows that in the Age of Information the same lessons which apply to British entertainment apply equally to British products in education, training, news, business service and so forth. The Labour MP Gerald Kaufman, who can recite the script of *Singing in the Rain* line by line, believes that a few changes in the tax code can resuscitate the British film industry, and the Blair government's first budget included some important new incentives. When Michael Grade was at Channel 4, he invested in low-budget movies one at a time, not so much to make a profit, he said, as to build up the collateral of a film library. And Kenneth Branagh in his whimsical way makes an occasional artistic stab in the same direction. They all know that the culture of Hollywood has too many sharp minds and too many sharp knives to find a comfortable home in the gentility of the British environment. None of them expects to see a British Babylon rise in Berkshire. But they all know that Britain is capable of much more than it is doing now.

There are signs of life. In 1986 there were only ten British-made films. A decade later there were more than a hundred (though only half with British money). There is a new studio in an old Rolls-Royce factory in Leavesden where business is booming. Maybe things are about to turn around. Maybe a new wave is swelling. But, so far, if British movies are an example of national possibilities in the Age of Information, the British may still be milling around the lobby after the show has started.

Perhaps the best good-news, bad-news example of the state of British services is the City of London, that square mile of international finance located on the north bank of the Thames, just above London Pool, where broad-beamed, tall-masted sailing ships once discharged their cargoes into the shoreline bustle of wharfs and warehouses, and where you can almost hear the banter from old coffee houses and the jingle of old coins. For all the troublesome liabilities that are customarily listed in the Great British Balance Sheet, the City today remains a weighty asset in the national ledger.

The City is legally and psychologically apart from London (a foreigner takes a while to get the hang of the generic term the-City-with-a-capital-C). The streets and lanes are a maze, and there seems to be a bank on every corner. The Square Mile surely enjoys the most efficient if encrusted local government in Britain. Gilded carriages take the Lord Mayor on his ceremonial duties and gold plate is laid before his guests. The City is also good for the soul. With so many little churches, I doubt there is any place on earth where things rendered unto Caesar and things rendered unto God are so richly concentrated, cheek by jowl. The City has made it convenient to pray for an upswing in the markets.

The British, it seems, are born bankers, and banking has long been the exception to the most baleful observations about the British economy. Coutts & Co., for example, is a very British bank. Like many things financial in Britain, including the Bank of England, Coutts was founded by a Scot (the Scots are notoriously shrewd with their money and other people's as well). Now owned by National Westminster, Coutts & Co. still exudes discretion and reliability, and it gives the impression that it has been in the banking business since the Romans first came to London, which it very nearly has. If you put your money at Coutts & Co., you feel it will be safely tucked away in a thick, steel vault where someone will count it every morning to be sure it's all there. When I visited the bank headquarters one day, I was greeted by the chairman in his black swallow-tail coat and striped trousers, and after a luncheon discussing the future of cutting-edge technology in Britain, I signed the visitors' book with a quill pen.

If Britain's imperial legacy has been a burden in the process of modernization, it has been a singular advantage for London's financial position. Nowhere has ever been too far away for a British bank to make a deal or run a risk. The City financed Britain's trade and Britain's wars, and everyone else's as well. It brought down governments and caught up kings. When I once visited Barings, I was given a folio of documents which told the story of how the bank financed the Louisiana Purchase, a transaction between France and the new United States at a time when Wall Street was still unpaved. Barings knew how to set up the complexities of such an international deal and the bank was wholly unruffled by the fact that Britain was between wars with both parties. London's financial prowess was so well established in the middle of the twentieth century that, when the flesh of Empire fell away, the skeleton of finance remained.

Today the City's financial services probably constitute the only sector of the British economy where it is true to say that if you want to be a global player, you have to be a player in London. Along with New York and Tokyo, London is one of the three hubs in the international money network. In part this is the fortune of geography, and in part the luck of language. London is the financial cusp between the dusk of America's markets and the dawn of Japan's, so that the pattern of world finance is carried on uninterrupted, twenty-four hours a day, in a great, revolving global continuity. And because London and New York together are the principal gateways to international capital, the chatter of finance is carried on in English. Location and language together make London's financial position unassailable.

Of the three financial centres, London is far and away the most cosmopolitan. The total value of transactions in London is less than Tokyo or New York, but the percentage that is genuinely international in character is far greater. The London Stock Exchange has a larger proportion of foreign company listings than any other financial market, and its turnover of foreign equities last year comfortably outstripped its New York and Tokyo counterparts.

One-third of all the world's foreign exchange trading goes on in London. British overseas holdings total more than one-half of America's, though the economy is only a tenth the size. The number of foreign banks in London has doubled in the last twenty years. There are now more than 500. I think it is still true that there are more American banks in London than there are in New York. So Britain remains the world's premier location for international banking and the premier source of long-term international funding. If the world had a single High Street, the most popular bank on the block would be Britain & Co.

The Big Bang of 1985 was the pivotal moment in Britain's modern financial history. The sudden-death liberalization of London's markets was a painful reform of the City's culture. But it has been a bonanza for Britain.* Big Bang restructured competition in the City and introduced rigorous disciplines to London's financial practices. The reforms wiped out most of the cosy, gentlemanly complacency that had characterized the operations of many British banks and British brokerages. The old-boy circuit, the chummy confidentiality, the tea trolleys, the furled umbrellas and the three-hour lunches vanished almost overnight, and so did a number of the City's oldest institutions that could not make the mark. For a while, it seemed as if Charles Darwin had become governor of the Bank of England. Only the fittest survived.

As a result, the City is a thriving concentration of markets where practically anything of financial value can be bought or sold by bankers, brokers, traders and fund managers. The Bank of England and the Securities Investment Board apply a light hand to the controls, just enough to assure probity but not so much as to gum up the works (in America the Securities and Exchange Commission acts like a cop; in Britain, the SIB acts like a coach). Seven thousand companies are listed on the London Stock Exchange, where millions of shares are traded daily, and the British are by far the largest share-owning and share-trading country in Europe. London's LIBOR (London Inter-Bank Overnight Rate) is a kind of Greenwich Mean Time of interest rates for borrowers and lenders, and LIFFE (London International Financial Futures Exchange) is a mêlée of daily trading in commodities, derivatives, options and other guesses about the future.

Lloyd's of London – the complex market of insurance syndicates

----

* When the City prospers, so does the nation. In fact, if you eliminated the profitability of the City from Britain's national accounts, the British economy would be parlous. Financial services in the United Kingdom make up about 14 per cent of Britain's exports, though they represent only 3 per cent of the domestic economy. Britain's surplus in financial trading came to £15.6 billion in 1995, and it is this positive flow of money in the balance of payments that keeps the British economic nose above the waterline.

and underwriters – buys and sells every kind of risk all over the globe. The Baltic Exchange trades in shipping capacity and freight futures. The Petroleum Exchange and the Metals Exchange set the international price for their goods. In the Square Mile, there are wholesalers and retailers for everything under the sun. And when night comes to the City, positions are taken, accounts are settled, computers are down-loaded, trading floors are swept and forklifts shift stacks of bullion around the vaults of the Bank of England. The City of London is a huge financial seascape of rip-tides and cross-currents, and in its depths swim the whales and the sharks of money and all the little fishes that feed on the bottom.

All of this must be serviced. And so British accounting firms are among the biggest and best in the world. London law firms write the international contracts for buy-ins and buy-outs (the legal apparatus which governs international transactions is almost always based on English or American law), and London's commercial courts are the accepted arbiters of international disputes. London printers and London publishers run off the reams of documentation that record international transactions, and firms of archivists store the material in huge warehouses for future reference.

The wired-up City of computers and telecommunications is one of the few examples in the British economy where advanced technology is commonplace. Reuters is one of the world's two premier financial information systems, and it produces a bubbling flow of details on which London traders make split-second judgments. There are actuaries and consultants and public-relations firms to embellish the margins of financial activity, and parties of headhunters roam the City jungles in search of talent to spirit away from one financial tribe to another. Security vans whisk sealed documents and floppy disks from institution to institution, and motorcycle couriers scoot along City streets to deliver urgent packages. And naturally everyone in the City carries a pink *Financial Times* tucked under his arm like a field marshal's baton. The City of London is a perpetual-motion machine at the centre of the world.

Big Bang intentionally opened up the City to foreign competition, and it was the Americans, naturally enough, who had the greatest impact. Like modern Vikings the American bankers in the mid-1980s stormed through the gates of the citadel. The muscular investment houses from New York – Goldman Sachs, Morgan Stanley, Merrill Lynch, Lehman Brothers, Salomon Brothers, J. P. Morgan – expanded their operations almost overnight, and they brought a sinewy, steel-rimmed look to the City and a heart-pounding, matrix-managing pace of money-making. The American interlopers were not universally acclaimed. One British banker sniffed to me that the Americans came to town acting as if they had invented investment banking whereas it was the British who were swapping currencies when the Americans were still dealing in beads and shells.

Nonetheless, the Yankees, especially the investment bankers, had ambitious global strategies and anywhere-anytime attitudes, and they sharpened their operations by putting their own capital at risk. Barely out of university, the legion of young Americans jogged before the sun was up, ate fruit for breakfast and were behind their desks or on a plane when most of London was still yawning. Installed in offices where the sheen was barely off the panelling, their no-nonsense intensity was almost military. They earned dazzling bonuses and intimidating reputations. And above all, they knew how to give service.

By the middle of the 1990s, the harshest observation about the City was the failure of British investment banking to take advantage of the opportunities which the reform of its own Square Mile had created. Big Bang opened up the City to the outside world only for the City to discover that the outside world was a rougher place than had been imagined. It was the foreigners – Americans, Japanese, Germans, Dutch, Swiss, all of whom regarded London as indispensable for their international operations – who made the running in London, while the British merchant banks fell further and further behind, and in some instances dropped by the wayside.

In 1995 Barings went down spectacularly, collapsing into receivership after more than two centuries of successful financial enterprise (in the old-boy days, Barings could have expected a safety net from the Bank of England, but this time there was only hard ground). Its wreckage was bought up by the Dutch bank ING for one pound. Kleinwort Benson, too, surrendered its 200 years of financial independence to Germany's second largest bank, the Dresdner. Morgan Grenfell had already passed into Germany's biggest banking hands. Merrill Lynch took over Smith New Court like a tycoon scooping up loose change from the top of a bureau.

Most distressing for the City, however, was the sale of S. G. Warburg to the Swiss Bank Corporation. Warburg's had been a relative newcomer to British merchant banking and had always prided itself on stealing the march on its more nonchalant City rivals. Of all the British banks in the City, this was the one that seemed to have the skills and ambition to sit down at the high table of global finance. But Warburg's ended up over-extended. Its pockets were too shallow and it folded its hand.

It is fair enough, I suppose, to say that British banks should not be expected to compete with the resources of the Americans or the Germans. But it is equally fair to say that banks from smaller economies, such as Holland and Switzerland, seem able to make the grade. In the explanations of failure, many of the familiar British bugaboos re-emerge: the British banks were self-satisfied and poorly managed; they had never really surrendered their snug corporate relationships in London; they did not invest in themselves and were too under-capitalized to compete; and they were by habit averse to risk. Whatever the explanation, the banks just couldn't come up with the first-class service which competitive international finance requires.

The City of London has such a vibrant history that this roll-call of failure may not matter very much. After all, foreign ownership is part of being international anyway. Smaller British merchant banks – Cazenove, Rothschild, Lazard, Fleming, Schroeder – retain the unruffled, unflappable character of solid British houses as they go about their business without fuss or bother. But these are bespoke banks, as if Savile Row had moved into finance where clients are for ever. Big British commercial banks, such as Barclays (with BZW) or National Westminster (with NatWest Markets), have spread their international wings only to have them severely clipped. The end result for the venerable City of London is that there is now not a single British bank which is counted in the top ranks of international investment banking. The British enjoy irony, and there is plenty of it here.

Britain is a services economy with a services deficit. Still, I have no question in my mind that the United Kingdom is singularly suited for the new economic age and should prosper in a fashion which has eluded it throughout this difficult century. There is an economic verve in Britain today that I have never seen before. And I think there is an accelerating convergence between national potential and national achievement. The principal political parties finally seem to share a lot of economic ground, and there is a much better match-up between British talent and British opportunity. None of this should be confused with an imminent *belle époque*, and it's still hard to get a ham-and-cheese sandwich around here. But I believe Britain now has as much future as past.

Advice and Consent

From time to time in the course of a year, the Diplomatic Corps in London is assembled as a single body. At the end of the nineteenth century, when there was only a handful of full-fledged ambassadors, this wasn't much of a logistical challenge. But these days, with 170 ambassadors and high commissioners roaming the capital, herding all of them into one place at one time is an organizational nightmare. On such occasions, the Marshal of the Diplomatic Corps becomes a cross between a prison warden and an air-traffic controller.

Most of the events to which the Diplomatic Corps is summoned are state occasions. Twice a year, for example, the Queen receives another head of state in London. These are grand affairs, so solemn and formal they seem almost funereal, and they are arranged so far in advance that they always seem to come at the wrong time.

Usually there isn't much for the British to say to whomever the state visitor happens to be, so the schedule is padded. And no one is better suited for filling up disposable time than a diplomat. So on the morning after the visitor's official arrival – the Sultan of Brunei, for instance, or the President of Bolivia – the guest is escorted to St James's Palace and stationed in a small ruby-red room where he is expected to shake hands with every member of the Diplomatic Corps as the troop of envoys files past. This kills a lot of time.

When I was minister at the embassy, I once substituted for the ambassador, Charlie Price, at one of these state functions. As a mere chargé d'affaires, I was placed at the far end of the diplomatic queue along with a few other stand-ins. On one side of me stood the chargé from North Vietnam, and on the other, the chargé from Cuba. As the United States enjoyed diplomatic relations with neither country, and as neither diplomat enjoyed relations with the English language, my morning at St James's Palace was less lively than I had expected.

As ambassador, however, I attended these events faithfully whenever they appeared on the calendar (I had purchased an overpriced morning coat from Moss Bros. and was determined to amortize the investment). I also had a much better draw in the lottery of diplomatic precedence, and when I went to St James's Palace I could at least look forward to some time with Kent Durr, the ambassador from South Africa, who was just ahead of me in order, and Ma Yuzhen from China, who was just after me. Great things were going on in both countries, so these little encounters were always worth while. Diplomats often feed on coincidence.

Once gathered inside a cavernous vermilion chamber, where monarchs of the past stare down from enormous gilt frames, the ambassadors are arranged along the walls according to the date on which they presented their credentials to the Queen. The Marshal and his assistants patrol the ranks on the lookout for unruly or straggling emissaries and politely whip them back into chronological shape. At this stage, the Diplomatic Corps looks like a long stag line shuffling around the outer edges of a big dance hall.

At the threshold of a far door leading into the room where the State Visitor stands, the envoys, like clay pigeons, are then fired off one by one for the stately handshake. When the name of the ambassador's country is announced, the envoy strides across the thick carpet, exchanges a brief word of greeting with the visitor over a fumbled grip of hands and departs by another door. I never knew what to say during this fleeting exchange. 'Welcome to the United Kingdom' didn't sound right because I was a foreigner too. 'The President conveys his greetings' would sound a little pompous, and untrue. Maybe 'Sorry for the inconvenience' would have been better. I don't recall what I said.

By the time the presentations are concluded, all the diplomats have again fallen into disarray in another room where champagne is passed around on trays and there is more chatter. The most experienced ambassadors drift to the outer margins of the crowd, towards the far end of the room, because once the State Visitor leaves the premises all the diplomats are free to go as well. The ambassadorial cars, however, are parked helter-skelter up and down the Mall and have to be summoned by loudspeaker. This takes a long time, so there is a premium placed on arriving among the first at the outside exit. At the appropriate signal in the grand reception room, all the morning-coated ambassadors break for the stairway, tumbling down the steps and into the long corridor in a controlled panic. In fairness to the diplomatic profession, I never witnessed a fist-fight.

The members of the Diplomatic Corps coagulate on other occasions as well. There is a glistening Diplomatic Reception at Buckingham Palace in November, where the Queen nods her way through the entire ambassadorial assemblage, and in June the Foreign Secretary always hosts a dinner for the corps. Douglas Hurd made a point of selecting imaginative venues for his dinners, and on one occasion we dined in the Dinosaur Room at the Natural History Museum surrounded by eerie creatures, and in some instances seated next to them as well.

Without doubt, however, the grandest event to which the Diplomatic Corps is invited is the annual State Opening of Parliament. I attended four of these occasions, advancing with time and seniority from a perch in the gallery overlooking the House of Lords to a diplomatic stall on the floor of the chamber at the right of the throne. Court dress is required, which for diplomats means donning white tie. For the British participants, the occasion is designated in the Palace calendar as a 'Collar Day', which means that all the chains, ribbons, medals, medallions, braids, aiguillettes and assorted decorations can be hauled out of the wardrobe and hung from whichever part of the anatomy can take the weight.

The State Opening of Parliament is like a *tableau vivant* of Britain's constitution. On this occasion only, all the instruments of governance are gathered together under one roof. In the centre of the House of Lords, ranged along the cross-benches and decked out in their red, ermine-edged robes, sit the various lords and ladies of the realm, both hereditary peers and life peers. In front of this noble sea of scarlet is the woolsack, where the Law Lords, in their black robes and tightly woven wigs, are arranged awkwardly like children on a large hassock.

On the benches which run the length of the chamber sit the bishops of the Church of England as well as more peers and peeresses and distinguished guests (women who are invited to the State Opening wear long evening gowns and sparkling tiaras, and when it comes to jewellery, the event is at the high end of the Richter Scale). The Chief of the Defence Staff, dripping with gold braid, is seated in the gallery, and there are other military officers dotted around the chamber. At the back of the hall, on the gallery level, are a few scruffy journalists crammed so close to the roof that they look like chickens in a roost. So before the Queen arrives the room has already assembled the lords and ladies of the realm, the senior representatives of the judiciary, the ecclesiastics of the church and the officers of the military as well as the professional voyeurs of diplomacy and journalism.

Punctuality is a modern trait of royalty, and at the precise stroke of 11.30, the royal procession begins. Through the doors on either side of the room, the panoply of state starts to seep into the great chamber. All rise. First come various officials of the household with puzzling titles such as Howard Pursuivant Extraordinary and Portcullis Pursuivant. Somerset Herald, Rouge Dragon Pursuivant, Maltravers Herald Extraordinary and the Gentleman Usher to Her Majesty file solemnly into the hall. No diplomat knows who these people are or what they do or why they are called as they are. But they are so resplendent it doesn't matter, and they take their places standing near the throne. The Equerry in Waiting enters and the Keeper of Her Majesty's Privy Purse along with Norroy and Ulster King of Arms. They are followed by the Yeoman Usher of the Black Rod and the Garter King of Arms, the Lord Great Chamberlain and the Earl Marshal. Who are all these people, you wonder. Do they govern Britain? Did they all come in the same bus?

A ribboned and starred field marshal brings in the Great Sword of State, so unwieldy that its hilt rests in an elaborate girdle strapped around the waist of this ageing warrior of the Queen. From the other side of the throne emerges the Leader of the House of Lords. He carries the Cap of Maintenance at the tip of a long upright stick and looks like a circus performer about to spin a plate. Only a handful of royal connoisseurs are quite sure why the Cap of Maintenance is carried in this ceremony, or even what it is.

After these dazzling preliminaries, the small area around the raised throne is almost filled up. Her Majesty then enters, or rather appears. She wears a billowing white gown and elbow-length gloves. She is crowned and bejewelled in regalia of exceptionally high wattage. She is accompanied by her consort, the Duke of Edinburgh, dressed as an admiral of the fleet, and carrying his own sword. Slowly the Queen climbs the stairs to the throne. Four jaboted young pages of honour arrange her train down the steps like a foamy white cascade.

In the Queen's slipstream come more denizens of the Household. The Woman of the Bedchamber, the Mistress of the Robes and the Lady of the Bedchamber float into the hall, followed by Gold Stick in Waiting and the Lord Steward and the Master of the Horse. Assorted equerries and aides-de-camp come in. Standing room starts to get scarce and there is some subtle jostling of epauletted shoulders. The Gentleman Usher to the Sword of State enters, and Silver Stick in Waiting. Now crowded around the throne like a crush bar at intermission, and bristling with batons, maces, sticks, rods, wands, poles and other pointy things, Her Majesty's attendants attend. For a republican outsider such as myself, it all seems a little comical. Only the British could carry off such sumptuous pomp with a straight face.

In the most famous part of the ceremony, the Lord Great Chamberlain despatches Black Rod to summon the Members of the House of Commons to the Queen's presence. Black Rod strides down the length of the House of Lords and disappears through the far doors on his parliamentary mission. This takes several minutes during which the Queen in magnificent silence surveys the assemblage. Everyone else fidgets, stirs, rustles, coughs and murmurs.

Black Rod, having executed the ritual pounding on the closed door of the House of Commons, bids the Speaker and the members present to follow him back to the House of Lords where waits the

Sovereign with surprising patience. A few moments later, the low buzz of the Lords is suddenly overtaken by the approaching din of the commoners. Led by the Speaker, the Prime Minister and the Leader of the Opposition, they spill through the entry of the House of Lords and push their way to a wooden barrier at the back of the hall, as if they were so much football rabble falling on a neighbourhood pub. Standing in their everyday suits and dresses, and crammed into their pen, the esteemed Members of Parliament are an unsightly intrusion upon the poised elegance of the House of Lords. Who invited them?

When order is restored, the Lord Chancellor climbs the steps to the throne. Bent over in deference, he reaches into a pouch hanging from his neck and presents the Queen with her speech. At every State Opening, the crowd watches as the Lord Chancellor, draped in his heavy robes, descends the stairs backwards, a treacherous journey of potential calamity, and every year the Lord Chancellor makes it.

The Queen reads the speech which the government, corralled at the other end of the great room, has written for her. The address from the throne is political ventriloquy. The words are as dry as attic dust. Customarily the Queen begins with a few nice things to say about foreigners and goes on to recite the list of legislation which the government intends to introduce in the forthcoming session of Parliament. There is no room for joke writers. There are no interruptions for applause. The speech lasts twenty minutes or so, and at its conclusion the ceremonial ebb tide quickly empties the chamber. The Queen returns to Buckingham Palace, where the Lord Chamberlain by tradition has stayed behind to guard one of the government whips taken as hostage against the Queen's safe completion of her rendezvous with Parliament. And Parliament settles down to start the business of the parliamentary year.

Like so much in British life, there is a fictional quality to the State Opening of Parliament. Elegant and colourful though it is, the occasion doesn't seem to represent what it is supposed to. But, given the choice between constitutional accuracy and constitutional pantomime, the British opt for the latter.

If the purpose were to display the components of the British constitution according to their powers and responsibilities, the ceremony, for starters, would take place in the House of Commons, not the House of Lords, and the Queen would be an observer, not the centre of attention. After all, in the array of power on view at the State Opening, it is only the MPs at the back of the room who have been democratically elected to office or subjected in any way to public scrutiny. Everyone else has either inherited his or her position or been appointed to it. But a constitutionally fastidious State Opening would be a pretty drab affair compared to the real thing, as unreal as the real thing is. And after all, the importance of the occasion lies not so much in the substance of the event as in its symbolism. The point of the elaborate exercise today is more to express British sovereignty than British authority. The Queen is simply blessing the Parliament.

When I attended this grand event, I inevitably thought about the American equivalent, which is the President's annual State of the Union message. The word 'State' is used differently here. It means 'condition', and the State of the Union is the President's yearly report to Congress on the general condition of the republic, like an annual check-up.

The President drives up Pennsylvania Avenue to Capitol Hill every year towards the end of January, just after the Congress has reassembled from the winter holidays, and there he addresses a joint session of the Congress, meaning that Senators and Congressmen are seated together in the bowed chamber of the House of Representatives.* The President, however, is a guest. He has no authority on the Hill, and there are no presidential props to reinforce his presence. The nine Justices of the Supreme Court attend, and so do the members of the Cabinet, and the chiefs of staff of the military services. They are unelected officials, and while they sit in the front rows, to the left, they too are treated as guests of the Congress. As in the State Opening of Parliament, all the important instruments of American government are brought together briefly under one roof. But the atmosphere is more like Wembley Stadium than the House of Lords.

Above the well of the chamber are two high-back chairs. In one

---

* In America, Senators are called 'Senators', and members of the House of Representatives are called 'Congressmen' or 'Representatives'; but because they are all Members of Congress, they are collectively called 'Congressmen'.

sits the Speaker of the House, the senior legislator in the land and third in line of succession to the presidency. Next to him is the Vice President. The American constitution does not assign many duties to the Vice President, but he happens to be President Pro Tempore of the Senate, and in a government where powers are strictly separated between the legislature and the executive, the Vice President is thus the only institutional link between the two branches. Even in this capacity, the Vice President does not have much on his plate, but if there is a tie vote in the Senate he has the casting ballot. He also is assured a good seat at the State of the Union speech.

Hanging behind the Speaker and the Vice President is an enormous American flag, the reredos of the American constitutional altar. Thanks to prime-time television (the American government would never consider scheduling the equivalent of the State Opening of Parliament in the morning), the State of the Union also starts punctually these days. 'Mr Speaker!' comes the announcement from the Sergeant at Arms at the central door. 'The President of the United States.' The President steps from the marble anteroom into the chamber. He is alone. In a rolling knot of waving, smiling, cheering, clapping, glad-handing and back-slapping, he works his way down the corridor of jolly Congressmen, as if he had just scored a touchdown in a crucial game. Bonhomie, not solemnity, is the watchword.

The President mounts the podium beneath the Speaker, the Vice President and the flag. The applause fades. The President begins with a few light words as everyone settles in. When he makes a joke, his party laughs harder than the other party. In a speech that is part inspirational and part propositional, the President then describes his priorities. He rarely takes more than forty-five minutes, though President Clinton in 1995 entered the Guinness Book of Records with an oration of eighty-two minutes. The press keeps score of the number of times the President is interrupted by applause. Once the speech is over, the President departs as he entered, jostling his way up the gangway with more handshakes and greetings.

When the Queen reads her government's speech at the State Opening of Parliament, she is politely informing the nation, on behalf of the government, what the government intends to introduce to that parliamentary session and what is almost certain to come out the other end, more or less intact. The Queen is announcing a parliamentary timetable and specifying which legislative trains are departing from which legislative platforms.

The American President, by contrast, is describing in his message to the Congress what he and his administration think about things, and the kind of legislation he expects is desirable. His political party may or may not enjoy a majority in the Senate or in the House, but favourable arithmetic is only part of the equation. In the end, the President must persuade the Congress to go along with his proposals. The Congress makes up its own mind. So the State of the Union message is more an appeal than an announcement. The President is describing the legislative balls he plans to put into the congressional scrum.

Customarily, the first observation about democratic government in the United Kingdom and the United States is that the former operates under an unwritten constitution and the latter under a written one. This is true, although much of the British constitution is in fact written down, even if the paper is scattered over the centuries. The British version is a kind of loose folio of documents strung together by precedent and convention. While the form and content may change, they do so only gradually and organically. There are no sudden moves, and, in that curiously British way, when something does change, it's supposed to look the same. Like the British weather, the constitutional pattern is steady, the shifts are moderate, and there are occasional patches of fog.

The American constitution is not so very different. It is more formal because it attempts to spell out the structure of the federal system, with its three separate branches, and how each branch is meant to relate to the other. Though reduced to a single document of surprising brevity, and protected from specious amendment by assorted convolutions, it is not a stone tablet. In our pluralist society, many constitutional principles turn out to be elastic. So what the American constitution means, as interpreted by the Supreme Court, is also changeable. But, like American weather, the change is often stormy.

Most of the principles written down in the American constitution come from the European Enlightenment and English common law.

The revolutionary aspect of the constitution, however, was the declaration that these common protections – such as the freedom of speech or religion or assembly – were so common that they were natural rights. And because they are bestowed by nature, a government may not infringe them. And if it does, it may only do so with the consent of the governed and the approval of an independent judiciary. The American constitution describes the limits of government, and the Supreme Court is there to make sure the government sticks to its side of the bargain. Or put another way, the constitution is a big No-Tresspassing sign explicitly fencing off as best it can the natural ground on which the government may not tread.

Calibrating the balance between government authority and individual rights is the central theme of American history. And sorting out who has a right to what is the central theme of American politics. The issue of abortion is a good example. Politically, abortion excites little comment in Britain, where the government has simply taken the measure of the popular mood and laid out the rules. There is no question whether Her Majesty's Government has the authority to do so. In America, however, abortion is a titanic controversy. This is not just for its moral dimension – though the debate often reaches pitched levels of moral fervour – but also for the constitutional question of whether the government should have any legal say in the matter, one way or the other. It is perfectly logical for an American to oppose abortion on moral grounds but equally to oppose the government interfering with its practice. A similar logic applies to gun control, and this is more or less the same for many other major constitutional issues that consume America's political oxygen.

The British, who are as much subjects as citizens, don't make too much effort to clarify their relationship with their government. In fact, there are no obvious limits to what a government may do, and the nation seems comfortable with this. After all, the same rights which are explicit in America are implicit in Britain, and they are protected by the common law and always have been, more or less. Freedom of the press, freedom of religion, freedom of assembly all thrive in robust condition, but largely by tradition, not by right. This is one reason why tradition is so fundamental in the British character.

Consent is important too, but the British have always placed more emphasis on liberty than on democracy. British liberty means whatever is left over after the government has acted. You can do what you want until the government tells you not to. Such a relaxed approach wouldn't work very well in a diverse society like the United States, but in Britain there seems to be an abiding confidence that the government won't overstep its bounds, and, if it does, that it will somehow be shouted back into place.

Still, an American in Britain, accustomed to black-and-white constitutionalism, finds it peculiar to live in a free place where basic rights are not precisely defined and safely locked away. Without a written constitution or, more exactly, an explicit Bill of Rights, some of the constitutional protections which are regarded as inviolable in the United States seem more vulnerable in Britain. The right to silence, for example, is chiselled into the American constitution, and 'taking the fifth [amendment]' in an American court is a common practice derived from common law without prejudice to the defendant. In 1992, the Home Secretary, Michael Howard, in attempting to reform the criminal justice system for the umpteenth time, proposed that judges could now take into account a defendant's silence. In America, this change in the law would go straight to the Supreme Court, where the frowning Justices, with only the quickest glance at the constitution, would doubtless strike it down in a single, swift stroke. But in Britain there is no constitutional recourse because there is no entrenched right.

Despite the different emphasis, however, both societies are sensitive to rights, and therefore both societies are literal and argumentative. As the British like to point out, Americans are excessively litigious. Legions of lawyers patrol the lines of conflict between the government and the citizen, and between one citizen and another, always on the lookout for whose rights are getting trampled and who can take whom to court.*

But, if Americans are exuberantly litigious, the British are inordinately legalistic. Inside every Englishman, I think, there is a

---

* There are almost a million lawyers in America, and there seems to be one lawyer joke per lawyerly head. Each year there are one million civil cases filed in America's courts, and on any given day there are ten million suits in the justice system. Half our Senators are lawyers and 40 per cent of our Congressmen, and the President is called the 'Chief Magistrate'.

solicitor struggling to get out. For example, English property law, with its multiple 'easements' and 'ancient lights', seems to have been handed down by Druids, and Stonehenge was probably the subject of a party-wall survey. The British know their rulebook, and a wagging finger and cold reproach await the innocent who commits the smallest infraction. To be British you are expected to understand the regulations, and obey them, which is how rights are best enforced.

So when it comes to rights, the Americans are absolutists and the British are relativists. For Americans rights are a national ideology, but for the British rights are sensible practicalities. Americans look for what is certain and the British look for what is reasonable.

As dissimilar as these constitutional attitudes may be, the end result is that we are both societies preoccupied by law, and over the years we have each rummaged around in the other's legal rucksacks. In the meadow at Runnymede, near a lazy bend of the Thames, there is a small tempietto built by the American Bar Association in 1936, on the ground where the Magna Carta was signed by an unwilling king. I once helped plant a tree near by. The open temple is not grandiose – just a dome set on a circle of columns – but it is a simple recognition of the connections between American and British law. Both countries believe the rule of law is about as good as any civilization is likely to get, and if there is anything of lasting importance in the relationship between the United States and the United Kingdom, it is this.

A more intriguing constitutional contrast between the two countries is the nature of sovereignty. Sovereignty is what makes things legal. It is a liquid substance and, like beauty, resides in the eye of the beholder.

Sovereignty is national psychology, and both the United Kingdom and the United States can be very prickly on the subject. British attitudes towards the European Union, or the earlier Common Market, and American attitudes towards the United Nations, or the earlier League of Nations, show just how touchy we can each be when it comes to sovereignty. In both countries, sovereignty has a mystical purity, like national virginity. Maybe this isn't so surprising in two nations whose frontiers have long been secure and whose territories haven't seen a foreign army in many years.

But the similarities stop there. For the British, sovereignty has always been a centralized commodity. Early British monarchs considered sovereignty a divine bequest which reposed exclusively in their regal person, and though there eventually came a time in British politics when the king had to be cut down to size – in one case, literally – the monarch today is still called 'the Sovereign'. Much of British history, from the Magna Carta to the Glorious Revolution and the Act of Settlement, has turned on events in which portions of this sovereignty have been extracted from the Crown and placed instead in Parliament. The fixing of sovereignty in Britain has therefore ended up a kind of compromise between monarch and Parliament, which the British awkwardly describe as 'the Queen in Parliament'.

Few people are quite certain what this formula means. It seems incomplete. The arrangement relies on practice and precedent, and some important constitutional questions are left dangling. This is a very British state of affairs, and to an American, sovereignty in Britain seems rather cryptic. By now, of course, the exercise of sovereignty has passed almost entirely to Parliament, in fact to only one House of Parliament, where real power lies. But British sovereignty itself remains a spongy thing.

The American Revolution turned the concept of sovereignty upside down. In the United States the idea is almost exactly the opposite of the British. Rather than sovereignty residing in a single, central authority at the top, which is devolved downwards, sovereignty in America rests at the bottom and is handed upwards. It is loaned to the government by the people, parcelled out carefully, and whatever is not specifically, in writing, doled out to the government is retained by the people. At least that's the theory. The preamble of the American constitution begins with the words, 'We, the people ...', which in eighteenth-century England must have invited peals of laughter.

On one occasion American sovereignty did break down disastrously. The states of the American South, in the middle of the last century, believed that the constitution of the United States was a compact entered into freely and individually by the separate states of the Union, and because the states had only granted limited and specific authorities to the federal government, they were legally free to withdraw that loan and secede from the compact. Abraham Lincoln insisted that a compact of consent could be broken only by consent, and that the Union in the meantime enjoyed a larger sovereign authority of its own which made its constitutional word the supreme law of the land. More Americans died in the ensuing Civil War than in all other American wars combined.

The concentration of sovereignty in the United Kingdom and the dilution of sovereignty in the United States explains a great deal about why the two political systems puzzle each other. One reason the British do not have a written constitution is because, to do so, they would have to tidy up a lot of loose ends. It is better simply to say that sovereignty is lodged with the Queen in Parliament, and if that leaves a bit of constitutional ambiguity, you can always clear it up as you go along. For Americans, it is preferable to write down exactly how much sovereignty the government is allowed to exercise on their behalf. So, when it comes to the organization of sovereignty, the Americans find the British imprecision a little complacent and the British find the American precision a little fussy.

But the distinction runs deeper than this. One of Britain's enduring legacies in the United States is the visceral American distrust of government. Thomas Jefferson said, 'The best government is the least government,' and most Americans would agree. In fact, most Americans would rewrite Lord Acton's famous aphorism about absolute power corrupting absolutely by saying that any power corrupts anyhow.

The constitution of the United States was composed with the purpose of insuring against the concentration of power in any single set of hands. 'In God We Trust' proclaims the cautionary motto on the dollar bill, a pointed notice to all elected politicians. The federal government is therefore broken into pieces which are designed to prevent each other from doing anything unilaterally. The presidency, the Senate, the House of Representatives, the Supreme Court and the individual states are more or less set off against each other. In America, power is shared, and everybody gets a piece of the action. That is seen as the best guarantee against abuse. Minimalist government is the American prejudice, in theory if not always in practice, and government remains one of the few things in American life where there is general agreement that the smaller the dimensions the more beautiful the product.

The brilliant group of Founding Fathers who designed the American constitution probably had in mind a delicate, clockwork mechanism which would operate in enlightened harmony. Instead, Americans ended up with a more cumbersome creation. But the point which seems hard for British observers to grasp is that there is a kind of perverse catch-22 in the American system which says that if the federal government isn't working very well, then the constitution is.

Given the complex way in which America has fragmented, layered and compartmentalized its sovereign government, you might think there would be a strong instinct to come up with something a little less dysfunctional. But on the whole Americans are satisfied with their constitution, even proud of it. Though we argue about what it means, and often trivialize its principles, amendments are few and far between. It remains the oldest written constitution in the world. There is room for improvement, without doubt, but, for all the dissonance, it seems to work well in a rumbling, pluralistic society.

Until recently, you could probably say the British were satisfied with their constitution too. After all, it has evolved pragmatically over centuries, and even if it seems a little vague at times, it has preserved the unbroken spine of British history. But, when I returned to London in 1991, one of the new features in British life I discovered was a broad-based discontent with established British institutions. This inevitably infected the constitution, or at least the constitution which is displayed with such flair at the State Opening of Parliament.

Part of this, I suspect, comes from the rapid growth of central government since the war, and the daily intrusion that naturally accompanies it. And part no doubt comes from the recognition that there are today few ways to brake the remarkable concentration of central government power. Whatever the cause, it seems that for the British nowadays almost everything about their constitution is in play.

Checks and
Balances

Towards the end of the last century, William Gladstone wrote, 'The American Constitution is, so far as I can see, the most wonderful work ever struck off at a given time by the brain and purpose of man.' This, I think, is true. On the other hand, Gladstone never tried to get a bill through the US Congress.

Watching the federal government at work is a little like watching sumo wrestling. Because of the push-me pull-you between the White House and the Congress, it sometimes seems that nothing in Washington is ever decided without the most colossal heave. It doesn't appear to matter much which political party is in control of which institution. A piece of legislation is built block by painstaking block. Everyone gets into the act.

Coming from this kind of fractured, fractious federal background, an American arrives on British shores astonished to discover how unfettered a modern British government is. When I first lived here, in the mid-1970s, it took me a long time to understand that a British government, with a simple majority in the House of Commons, can do pretty much what it wants to. If the party in power can count on having one more warm body in its lobby than all the bodies combined in the other lobby, there is nothing to prevent the government having its way. I kept looking for constitutional checks and institutional balances that could stay the will of a British government. But I could find none. In face of such arbitrary omnipotence, I could suddenly imagine myself as an American revolutionary, grabbing my flintlock from the wall above the fireplace and rushing into the forest to take a few potshots at the Redcoats.

Our respective national budgets are a good example of how government power is wielded differently in each country. In Britain, the budget is put together by the Treasury, behind closed doors. It is a strenuous exercise but an obscure one. When the Chancellor of the Exchequer emerges into the light of day, he poses for a few photographs and then heads over to the House of Commons to announce how much the government is going to spend and how much the government is going to tax. No ifs, ands or buts. If the Chancellor wants to put another penny on a pint of lager, that's what it will cost when the pubs open in the evening. The Chancellor's party will approve the budget (even if it disapproves) and that's it. In Britain, the legislative system seems about as sleek and streamlined as a Rolls-Royce purring along the motorway.

In Washington, on the other hand, the budget process reminds you of a clanking old Chevrolet jalopy you can barely coax out of the driveway without a fender falling off. The White House, the Senate and the House of Representatives always come up with different federal budgets followed by months of public bargaining, badgering, bickering and bluffing. Things are slipped into the budget and things are yanked out. And after all the trade-offs and log-rolling (and the agitation from most of the 80,000 lobbyists registered in Washington), the White House and Congress may agree. Or maybe not. In November 1995, while the Chancellor was breezing his way through the House of Commons, the Washington budget process broke down so badly that the entire federal government was shut down. The old jalopy just ran out of gas.

The principal reason the House of Commons seems so efficient is because the majority rules, literally. Party unity is the highest value in British politics, and if the majority party can keep its partisan loyalty intact, the government works. If not, you change governments. It all depends on keeping the party together.

I have lost track of the number of annual party conferences I have attended. I always felt awkward going to them, as if I had inadvertently stepped into someone's dressing room at a particularly embarrassing moment. But in Britain the party conference is an essential rite of unity, like a tribal ritual where the political slogans are chanted, symbols are paraded, chieftains are celebrated, loins are girded, gourds are emptied and war drums are beaten through the night.

For the two big parties, the conferences take place in seaside cities beginning with the letter 'B'. Bournemouth is the most salubrious location. Only recently has the town developed enough capacity to act as party host, and with a palm tree or two Bournemouth has the welcoming look of the *faux* tropics.

Brighton is sprightly, and George IV's Pavilion folly lends a suitable air of fantasy to a party conference. The Brighton beaches are hard and pebbly and almost always deserted, though I have seen a few hearty souls reclining in deckchairs, their faces turned to a fifty-degree sun and a forty-knot wind, and looking for all the world as if they were warming themselves on the Côte d'Azur. Blackpool, where the seafront looks like a large mudflat, is a forlorn bed-and-breakfast place, and the famous 'illuminations' I always found melancholy, like an old lady with too much rouge.

The Conservative and Labour parties rotate through these towns on a regular schedule, partly to show that the national party is aware there are other cities in Britain besides London, and partly to trap MPs in a location from which it is difficult to escape. Because these week-long extravaganzas are internal affairs, dissent is permitted at fringe meetings, where political poison is meant to work itself out of the system. But in the big conference hall, where each Cabinet member or shadow Cabinet member displays his skills, and where ordinary members can have a moment in the limelight, the emphasis is on tuning up the party engine and revving up the political motor. Sometime before a general election each party puts together its manifesto, and it is to this document that fealty is sworn by MPs and on which the British public is supposed to make its choice at the next election.

In America, party unity is an oxymoron. Political parties are organized state by state, as befits a federation, so national parties are simply loose amalgamations of state parties, which, like leap year, only come together once every four years in a star-spangled jamboree where the party nominates someone to run in the presidential election. Otherwise, state parties tend to their own affairs, which is perfectly understandable because it is in the states where most of the important elective offices are located. Neither the Republicans nor Democrats have a powerful, controlling central office, as the Conservatives do in Smith Square or Labour in Walworth Road.

When the former American Speaker Tip O'Neill said, 'All politics is local,' he meant not just the issues on which elections are decided but also the mechanisms which control the American political game. Most states today, for example, conduct primary elections in which the members of a party choose the candidates for whatever offices are up for election. In fact, primaries were designed to break up the dominance of wheeling-dealing party bosses who used to disappear into dimly lit, smoke-filled rooms and broker who the candidates would be.* But today candidates for almost any office have to submit themselves to party primaries. The fact that you may already hold that office is no guarantee the party membership will pick you again for the next election. It is as likely as not that someone from your own party will think he or she can do a better job, and throw down the gauntlet. Primaries are free-wheeling, wide open and local, just like the country, and the last thing in mind is party unity.

Primaries don't happen in Britain. It would be a remarkable sight to watch two Tory candidates in a Hampshire constituency, for example, fighting it out over European policy, or two prospective Labour candidates in Yorkshire publicly mauling each other over privatization. Instead, party candidates in Britain are vetted by party headquarters and have to be blessed before they can be selected by a constituency committee. American candidates are also expected to have lived in the constituency for a long time, the better to identify with local interests, but this sort of grass-roots identity is a recent development in Britain, and usually comes into play only after a candidate has won a seat. To an American eye, a new parliamentary candidate is almost always a carpetbagger.

---

* In a presidential election, it is the primary season which makes the contest seem so interminable. The election campaign itself only lasts about ten weeks, which, given the size of the country, is not so much. But the state primaries go on for ever.

Once an MP is elected to Parliament, he can expect to go unchallenged from within his own party for as long as he can hold on to his seat. To be an MP is not exactly a sinecure, but it's not a very vulnerable position either, at least not from inside. A sitting MP is hardly ever 'deselected' by his constituency. The British parliamentary system depends on exquisite party discipline (which is not easy in a society which prizes contrariness), but one reason the discipline holds is because an MP is almost never challenged in his or her constituency by another candidate from the same party. Security is exchanged for obedience. It sounds a little feudal.

In Britain, even selecting the party leader is an insider deal. In the Conservative Party, the leader can be challenged once a year, but this is a little like mounting a palace coup. If the leadership is contested, only sitting MPs can vote, and, if the party also happens to run the government, it is possible to end up with a new prime minister without any reference to the party membership as a whole, let alone the British electorate. The Labour Party is a little more experimental and participatory when it comes to selecting a leader, but in neither party can you be leader or prime minister unless you are already a Member of Parliament, and in a country of sixty million people this is a pretty narrow field.

So when it comes to elections in the two countries, the devil is in the verbs. In America, you run for office; in Britain, you stand for office. This is not simply different usage. It is different politics. And the result is that when an American congressman has to choose between voting the interests of his constituency or voting the interests of his party, he will almost always opt for the former. He knows where his bread is buttered, and in this sense all votes are free votes. In the House of Commons, on the other hand, to vote against the party is considered political treason and treated as such. For an MP the party is the butter and the jam. And that's what makes the British government work.

The only thing that is crisper in American government than in British government, or at least more predictable, is that Americans know exactly when their next general election will be – every four years, rain or shine. British elections always have an element of surprise about them.

In Britain an election is usually a straight fight with a clear-cut result. To an American, there is a razor-sharp finality about a British election: this party wins or that party. As much as pundits speculate about a hung parliament, it hardly ever seems to happen. The theory is that you support the party, not the individual, and a voter in a constituency decides which party he or she thinks should run the country and then ticks the box next to the party's candidate. Except for occasional by-elections and inconsequential local elections, there's never another chance to register a point of view until the next general election, which could be five years away. The British take their democracy neat.

In America the quadrennial elections are a democratic paroxysm. The place seems to go vote-happy right down to its boots. Americans vote for President and Vice President; for all the members of the House of Representatives and a third of the Senate; for state governors and state legislators; for judges, mayors, sheriffs, councillors, school boards and dogcatchers. At election time in America, anything that moves is liable to get elected to something. We vote on bond issues, referenda and propositions. And in between general election, there always seems to be a vote going on somewhere. Hapless members of the House of Representatives have to submit to the polls every two years. American democracy is constantly churning over in a huge, bubbling vat.

At the end of a general election, Americans know who won what office, but they don't really know how the country will be governed. One party may control the White House and the other party the Congress. The Congress itself might be split. In fact, since the war, this has been the pattern, and both branches have had to co-operate with each other in order to accomplish anything. The majority may rule in Britain, but in America it can only negotiate. Without some measure of bipartisanship, the President might veto what the Congress passes, and by the same token the Congress might override the President's veto if two-thirds of the members agree. But partisan warfare normally produces legislative gridlock, with both sides stymied. So, in America, all governments are coalition governments.

The British electoral system is designed to prevent coalitions. It is not too difficult for a single party to secure a commanding majority in Parliament. If there are more than two parties in a contest, which is usually the case, the first-past-the-post rule means that the divided popular vote can result in a huge majority of seats in the House of Commons. In Margaret Thatcher's three election victories, she never won more than 43 per cent of the vote, but each time this produced an unassailable majority. John Major also won 43 per cent in 1992 but only a slender majority. And Tony Blair in 1997 won 43 per cent as well and enjoys an overwhelming majority. In fact, you have to go back to 1935 before discovering a British government which took office with more than half the popular vote.* In British politics, there is little room for bipartisanship, and not much necessity.

Because these elections are uncluttered events, the British get right on with things. The change of government takes place lickity-spit. If the sitting government loses, the removal vans wheel into Downing Street the morning afterwards. (I've never figured out how the British do this. Does the Prime Minister pack before the election?) To an outsider, it all seems a little hasty and unseemly, and, you might think, better suited to America. In Washington, the change of government is more deliberate – or lumbering. Two and a half months elapse between the election and the inauguration, and in the meantime the outgoing administration and the incoming administration mill around the city like lost souls in a political limbo. In Britain, when an election campaign is finished, the bodies are buried warm. In America, they are stone cold.

Once in power, the Prime Minister chooses a handful of fellow MPs to form the Cabinet, and, along with three score or so other MPs, they comprise a ministerial roof atop the civil service structure in Whitehall. The civil service, which is justifiably one of the great prides of British governance, provides continuity and recall. But it is in the Cabinet, where the leadership of the party and the leadership of the government exactly coincide, that pure, unadulterated power in Britain truly resides.

When this small group of politicians gathers collegially around a long table in Number Ten and collectively decides on a course of action, the broad boulevard of national acquiescence opens up before them. They may be able politicians, or maybe not. They may

---

* The democratic exercise is a little harder to evaluate in the United States. Even in a general election, not much more than half the eligible voters go to the polls. So a president with 50 per cent of the vote represents only 25 per cent of the electorate. This is not the most laudable feature of American democracy.

be wise leaders, or maybe not. But if the Cabinet decides to press a piece of legislation or a policy position, there is no obstacle to its passage, provided the discipline of the parliamentary party holds.*

Discipline is the job of the party whips. Like a political mafia, they count noses, trade secrets, send signals, dispense favours, collect debts and occasionally kneecap the errant or stroppy backbencher. In keeping with the honoured traditions of the nation's navy, a British political party in power is designed as a tight ship on the open seas, with the captain and his officers commanding firmly from the bridge and a taut crew in the rigging.

When the British say 'winner take all', they really mean it, at least in politics. One party has all the power and all the others have none. So when one party says white, all the others say black. But like a criminal trial, with prosecution and defence, the system ensures that no point of view automatically prevails in the public mind and every proposal is challenged with knee-jerk predictability. What Parliament as a whole lacks in authority, it tries to make up for in accountability, and the democratic integrity of the system is fashioned by pitting one party against the others on virtually every issue.

As ambassador I often went to the House of Commons. Sometimes I would go there to hear a debate on a specific issue – the interminable exchanges on the Maastricht Treaty, for example – or sometimes I would drop by just to take a whiff of the political wind. The first row in the gallery, above the Commons entryway, is reserved for ambassadors. It was usually empty, and I could slide along the smooth leather bench to the middle, above the clock and opposite the mace and the Speaker's raised chair. From here I would look down on the government benches to the left and the opposition benches to the right.

On a good day the chamber was full, the MPs jammed together on the benches like starlings crowded on a fence, and when the Prime Minister walked in, or the Leader of the Opposition, there

* The only similarity with an American Cabinet is the name. American Cabinet members are appointed by the President. They hardly ever meet together, and it is the President alone, as the only elected member of an administration (along with the Vice President), who makes decisions and who is constitutionally responsible for the actions of the executive branch.

was always cheering and jeering and the rustling flutter of order papers, like wings flapping. From the gallery vantage, there were other fixed points as well. Below the gangway, for example, on the government side of the House, always sat Ted Heath looking like a white-topped newel post, usually inscrutable but sometimes scowling. And opposite him sat Dennis Skinner, in red tie and tweed jacket, ever ready to shout a taunt or leap to his feet on a point of order.

When Americans think of the British Parliament, they imagine the cut-and-thrust amphitheatre of Prime Minister's Questions. The event is popular enough in the United States that C-Span carries it on cable television. Jack Weatherill, when he was Speaker, was amused to discover he had become a media star in America, and Betty Boothroyd told me she was startled one day in Florida when a group of Americans recognized her in mufti. In 1993 a handful of envious Congressmen experimented with a Question Time in a hopeless effort to introduce a similar kind of debate to the floor of the House of Representatives (but, with the separation of powers, there is no one to question). Though the American President at least faces the press from time to time, the American Congress offers no real equivalent to the intense political confrontation you find in Westminster. Floor debates in the Senate or House of Representatives are more a series of speeches from a central podium, often for the record, and there is little room for political repartee. On any given day, you can stand in the well of the House and play frisbee without any danger of hitting a congressman.*

At Prime Minister's Questions, Her Majesty's Government is answerable to the elected representatives of the people. The Prime Minister must explain himself and his government. With one exception, no party leader, Tory or Labour, with whom I have spoken has ever had a good thing to say about this exercise, and all decry its vacuity. One of Tony Blair's first decisions as prime minister was to reduce the number of bouts from twice a week to once.

The single exception, naturally, was Margaret Thatcher. She

---

* The real work of the Congress, and the customary setting for American political drama when it occurs, goes on in the committee rooms of the Capitol or the buildings nearby. Congressional committees are the engines of the American legislature.

relished picking up the short sword and net and stepping into the sandy ring of the parliamentary colosseum. Rehearsed, fluent and histrionic, Thatcher's instinctive timing was masterful. Her phraseology was rarely memorable, and wit had no place in her armoury, but she had a way of patronizing the opposition and slapping back at just the right moment. For most of her tenure, she faced Neil Kinnock across the despatch box, but, for all his oratorical skills, Kinnock seemed to shrivel in the heat of parliamentary debate. Lacking a jugular instinct, he would usually arrive on the field just after the enemy had struck camp.

For the Prime Minister and the Opposition Leader, the episodic clashes on the floor of the House are less about legislation or policies and much more about their political authority within their respective parties. When the Prime Minister scores a bull's-eye in debate, his party on the backbenches erupts in hysterical approbation, with cheers and hoots, and the stamping of feet and kicking of benches. And when the Leader of the Opposition plants one square on the Prime Minister's jaw, orgasmic waves of pleasure cascade noisily down the rows behind him.

Because the essential ingredient in the British parliamentary system is the party, the leader's ability to command is the crucial element. The modern version of the House of Commons does not work very well unless, at the end of the game, the parties do what their respective leaders tell them to do. Floor debates are therefore like pep rallies. And if the Prime Minister, along with his Cabinet colleagues, can keep the respect of his party MPs, or at least their grudging subordination, there is nothing else to stand in the way of his government beyond procedural convention, political judgment and the sober reality that sooner or later he has to try to get his government re-elected.

So a British government, to an American eye, is a formidable invention. This concentration of power used not to be the case. Not so long ago, political parties in the House of Commons were looser organizations, and backbenchers more independently minded. And both the monarch, as the Sovereign, and the House of Lords, as the upper chamber, shared in the distribution of power and were much more than colourful props in national decision-making. But the constitutional checks and balances which once existed have been eroded over the years, and governance in Britain today is probably more unconstrained than it has been in the last couple of centuries.

In the House of Commons, the opposition parties are powerless to obstruct legislation. A government bill comes down the parliamentary highway like a juggernaut, and the opposition shouts and gesticulates as it whooshes past. And many backbenchers in the government's parliamentary party see themselves as not much more than window dressing for decisions made by the omnipotent Cabinet.

The Commons has tried to beef up the supervisory authority of its standing committees, but the British Cabinet is formed from the majority party in the House, and it is unlikely that a committee, whose membership is usually dominated by that same party, will subject its own government to harsh and independent scrutiny. It would be a little like a used-car salesman assembling a panel of independent mechanics to inspect his automobiles. Committees can arrange informative hearings and issue interesting reports, but they cannot originate legislation nor do they hold the strings of the public purse. Most backbenchers of all parties look longingly across the Atlantic at the independence, power and financing of their legislative brethren.

The House of Lords, as an unelected, semi-aristocratic chamber, is largely seen by the public as a geriatric mass which turns out in force only when the issue under debate is poaching. Still, the House of Lords can delay legislation and embarrass the government, and in British politics embarrassment is a powerful weapon (American politicians seem beyond embarrassment). The Lords combined can say whether they think a proposal is a good idea or a bad idea, and they can even vote against a government bill and so expose the shortcomings of legislation in a way which the regimentation of Commons politics does not allow. A peer can speak his mind without party constraint.

But the upper house is merely expressing an opinion which the government is free to accept or dismiss. It cannot prevent the government's will. The Labour government says it will reform the House of Lords by disenfranchising hereditary peers. But this still begs the question of the real power of the Lords, so the reform sounds more like redecoration than reconstruction. Alternatively, the Lords could be abolished altogether, though this would merely throw into gross relief the monopoly of power in the rival chamber. British politics is not radical politics, however, and any change is likely to be gradual. In the meantime, the second house doesn't do much to restrain or balance the first.

When legislation reaches Buckingham Palace, the Royal Assent is automatic. A veto is unimaginable in a parliamentary system, and a constitutional crisis would descend on the country if the Sovereign even hesitated to approve a bill which had passed through parliament. In matters of government, the Crown is a rubber stamp.

And once a law is in force, there is no set of objective constitutional standards, written or otherwise, against which the law can be measured in the courts. Judicial review applies only to the implementation of the law, not the law itself, and a court may not conclude that the government has constitutionally overstepped itself or that an inviolable right of an individual has been offended. As learned as the British courts may be, they cannot invalidate an act of the British Parliament.

Today, there are a few quasi-constitutional changes on the British agenda. The scornful Liberal Democrats, for example, have been banging the drum of European-style proportional representation ever since I first came to Britain. For an American, proportional representation isn't such a drastic idea. The Senate, which represents states as opposed to populations, is a form of proportional representation, and the two Senators from Kentucky, for example, have equal legislative clout with the two Senators from California. Proportional representation in Britain would surely produce a practical if not a constitutional restraint in Parliament. But the problem with proportional representation is that it would probably achieve electoral fairness at the cost of government efficiency. Most Britons don't seem to admire the way proportional representation works in continental governments and seem to prefer the clarity of a single party in charge, even if the single party makes a mess of things.

In a subtler example of constitutional change, decisions by the European Court have exerted an indirect pressure on the British judiciary to be more assertive. The United Kingdom is also a signatory to the European Convention on Human Rights (and the country most frequently found in breach of it). For the British judiciary, the authority of Parliament has always been a constitutional no-go zone, but these European bodies are a little like a Supreme Court, and they can overrule the British Parliament on certain points of law. So the British judiciary is gradually realigning its relationship to Parliament too. This is probably the most interesting and least clamorous constitutional story in Britain today.

Of all the reform proposals on the table, a genuine British Bill of Rights, interpreted by the Law Lords, is the one that makes most sense to me. And it is the most likely to be implemented responsibly. But this would be tantamount to a constitutional revolution, immediately undermining the Queen-in-Parliament definition of British sovereignty, and it would be an unusual House of Commons that allowed appointed judges to oversee its work.

If constitutional reform makes progress in Britain, it will surely come dripping slow. Reformers face a couple of particularly knotty problems. First, rearranging constitutional relationships might be desirable, but institutional changes are meaningless unless real power is transferred as well. An increase in the power of any institution, however, means a diminution of power in the House of Commons. It's not in the nature of political parties to give away power.

The second problem is even more of a dilemma. When a party is in opposition, the constitutional system looks dreadfully lopsided; but once a party is in power, the system looks about right. And only a party in power can initiate change.

In the meantime, the Prime Minister runs the Cabinet, the Cabinet runs the party, the party runs the Parliament and the Parliament runs the country. Parliament is supreme, and therefore so is the political party in charge of it. British government takes an American's breath away.

Root and Branch

When I was a boy, my parents took our family from New York to California by car on three successive summers. Each time we followed a different route, and each trip was an exploration.

We drove in a big, black Buick in the days before superhighways, and, like most Americans, we were fascinated by the road and where it led. Every night we checked into a motel in an era when a telephone in a room was a luxury item, and we ate in diners or stopped at roadside fruit stands or we made up picnics. Crossing the Mississippi was always an occasion for celebration, and so was the first sighting of snow in the Rockies. In the Western deserts, we hung canvas bags of water from the hood of the car against the chance of misadventure. And when, after thousands of miles, we finally reached the far coast, where the Pacific Ocean stretched out to an unbroken horizon, we knew we had been somewhere.

I wonder now at the fortitude of my parents in making those long journeys with three squabbling children in the back seat. But one way they kept us occupied was a series of I-spy games. See how many different brands of gas station you can identify. Count the number of bridges we cross. The toughest game was trying to spot an automobile licence plate from each state in the Union. For hours my brother, sister and I would stare at passing vehicles, hoping to discover a plate from North Dakota or Alabama. A licence plate from Hawaii was the Holy Grail.

Some state nicknames or slogans appeared on the licence plates: 'New York: The Empire State', for example, or 'Tennessee: The Volunteer State'. New Hampshire was a little unsettling for a young boy: 'New Hampshire: Live Free or Die'. We were also expected to memorize each state capital, each state flower, each state bird, each state motto, and so forth, and we were quizzed at the end of the day. As a result, we learned that every state had its special character and that the phrase 'United States' was not an idle choice of words.

So America is a pluralist state. The United Kingdom, on the other hand, is a unitary state. And it shows. Its licence plates are unimaginative and uninformative. There is no 'Kent: The Garden County' or 'Cumbria: Land o' Lakes'. I wonder what games British children play on long trips.

In matters of government, Britain is uniform. Services, benefits, taxes and licence plates are meant to be more or less the same everywhere. Central government divvies up the public purse and distributes the funds evenly across a homogeneous society. Who gets what is a national responsibility and a national preoccupation. Fair is fair. This egalitarianism is admirable, but it seems to encourage a disposition to look to London whenever anything goes wrong.

This difference between a unitary government and a pluralist one tells a lot about the difference between the two countries. In 1974, for example, New York City teetered on the edge of bankruptcy. The mayor at the time, Abraham Beam, claimed the city had run out of money because of its swollen welfare rolls. New York was the principal gateway for immigration, Hizzoner insisted, and the city was therefore carrying a disproportionate amount of the national burden. This was unfair. Having exhausted his credit in the state capital at Albany, the mayor turned to the federal government for a $4 billion bail-out. It didn't take President Ford too long to make up his mind. The *New York Daily News* carried a memorable headline: 'Ford to City: Drop Dead!'

I thought of Mayor Beam's troubles during the Liverpool

imbroglio ten years later. I was the minister at the embassy then, and it occurred to me that Beam should have been mayor of Liverpool. Under the profligate leadership of Derek Hatton, the Liverpool Council had embarked on a nose-thumbing, budget-breaking binge meant to defy and provoke the Tory government in London, and twist it into knots. And Liverpool got away with it because the city's finances were the ultimate responsibility of Her Majesty's Government, not of the council. In the mish-mash of British local government, all roads lead to London. Telling Liverpool to drop dead was not an option.

New York's financial doldrums were extreme but they were not exceptional. In 1994, Orange County, California defaulted after a run of calamities in the financial markets and the county is still sorting out its accounts with the banks. Miami is in trouble today. Most stories about American local government, however, are not disasters. In fact, sub-federal government in America – at the state, municipal or county level – is probably the most dynamic and creative feature of American democracy. State and local governments have real authority, and, if the authority is mismanaged, responsibility lies with whoever did the mismanaging. There is a close-in, street-level vitality about local government in the United States and this acts as a kind of safety valve for American diversity. The same thing is hard to find in Britain. For an outsider, this is a curious observation about a nation so proud of its ancient democracy.

In fact, the British don't seem to know what to do with their local government. Or even whether they should have much of it. The old counties of England have misplaced their identities, and this, I think, is a pity. It's difficult to put your finger on anything that expresses county identification these days except cricket teams. Otherwise, they seem to be a collection of administrative units, and even the boundaries of some parliamentary constituencies spill over from one county to another.

Since I first came to Britain, someone somewhere has always been trying to reorganize local government. There have been almost fifty bills in the last twenty years, so it's hard to keep the local structure straight in your mind. Districts and councils come and go. Two tiers of government dissolve into one, and maybe it's the other way around. It doesn't seem to matter much.

For all the rearranging of the local furniture, however, rarely does anyone propose that councils have more power, and rarely do you sense that councils are straining hard against the tight London leash. In fact, the phrase 'local authority' has become another political oxymoron. City councils, which are overseen by unelected, buggins'-turn mayors with big gold chains, possess no independent fund-raising capacity nor can they make laws. Nor can they speak with a distinctive political voice.

American states, in contrast, have their own constitutions and their own legislatures,* and they regulate most daily activity. They raise capital and they tax their citizens, both individual and corporate. The source of revenue varies state by state (property, income or sales tax, or a combination), but no state levies too much more than another lest the citizens vote out the state government or simply pick up and move to another state. Cities and counties can borrow money as well, so, unlike in Britain, if a locality wants to build a new school or repair a bridge or add a wing to the hospital, it can issue the necessary bond to secure the funds. The municipal bond market in the United States is worth more than a trillion dollars, and state and local governments have demonstrated more budgetary prudence over the years than the federal government.

States and municipalities are also the vehicles for alternative politics in America. Governorships are the customary incubators for future presidents, and elected mayoralties have become the platforms of black and Hispanic political leadership. Many state and local leaders enjoy national recognition. I can't name a single British mayor or local government figure, and I don't think many of the British can either.

With this kind of autonomy, American states also generate reform and experimental solutions to national problems. If you're hunting for creative ideas in American government these days, you should look at Wisconsin for welfare or Arizona for health care or Michigan for education. Even controversial social issues such as euthanasia (Oregon) or affirmative action (California) or prostitution (Nevada) fall within the purview of the individual states. There is no parallel in Britain.

It is safe to say, I think, that in the last ten years power has been flowing away from Washington and back into the local governments.

---

* There are about 17,000 elected state legislators in the United States.

And in Britain it is equally safe to say that power has been flowing away from the local authorities and back into London.

An American in Britain notices the absence of local political energy, even though the basic services are good in most places, and often better than what you find in America. I suppose the British have been suspicious of local government ever since the Magna Carta, and power has never been passed very far down the line. But the etiolation of local authority has accelerated over the last decade.

Prime Minister Thatcher regarded local government, especially in the cities, as the last redoubt of British socialism, where the loony left of British politics was holed up like a gang of desperadoes. She abolished the Greater London Council altogether, and London must be the only major capital in the world without a coherent governing authority (Washington might come a close second).* The ill-starred poll tax was meant to be a battering ram against feckless councils, though it ended up as one of the all-time shambles of post-war British politics. Mrs Thatcher, however, had a point: you are more likely to find responsible, efficient and accountable local government if a universal base of beneficiaries has to pay for it.

But the decline of local government was going on willy-nilly anyway. Big blocks of local council responsibility, such as education and housing, have been largely removed from council control. The taxes and budgets for what remains are capped by London. Today, local government raises only about 15 per cent of what is spent on local governance while Whitehall mandarins, who control the rest, cast a stern if benign eye over their satrapies in the outback.

Her Majesty's departments in London are assisted by hundreds of quangos† – boards, trusts, committees, commissions and regulatory agencies – which together form a kind of stealth government to supervise much of the country's public spending and regulate much of the country's public activity. There are some 40,000 appointments to these panels, but quango accountability is ambiguous. The appointments are not scrutinized by any public body. Their potential

---

* Prime Minister Blair intends to fill this vacuum with a popularly elected mayor whose putative powers are so far unclear but unlikely to be extensive.

† 'Quango' is an American invention meaning 'Quasi-autonomous non-governmental organization'. But the term never caught on in the United States, perhaps because it sounds too much like a marsupial.

for political patronage would make Tammany Hall drool, and it's a testimony to the public-spiritedness of the British that there has been so little abuse. But the end result is that practically every British social programme is run from London. The paternalism of British local governance is Britain at its most headmasterly.

An American instinctively wonders at the political wisdom of this super-centralism. Among other things, it means little political talent is attracted into local government. John Major must be one of the few national politicians who has ever sat on a local council. And because the public is largely indifferent to local politics, party cabals become more entrenched, not less so.* The feebleness of local government also means that any local incident can immediately escalate into a national issue. A controversy about a prison breakout, for example, or a bypass road instantly lands on the middle of a Cabinet minister's desk. And it means there are few local forums for real alternative politics in Britain. In a society which is more and more heterogeneous, the opportunities for real political expression at the local level are practically zero. If local government is directed from London in a semi-colonial fashion, local discontent has a way of building up without any natural form of ventilation.

This condition may be satisfactory for the English, but it seems to be decidedly unsatisfactory for the Scots.

There have been many proposals for redefining the relationship between Scotland and the rest of the Kingdom, and the agitation for devolution has been going on over all my years in Britain (I lived here during the stacked-deck referendum in 1979 when no one seemed to have much heart for it). The question should have gone away by now. After all, the English have been thrashing the Scots since time began, and you would think the Scots would have come around. But they haven't.

Because the Scots already administer their own legal and educational systems, they have always been unique within the Kingdom. Scotland has nonetheless agitated for greater autonomy, a prospect assisted by its oil wealth, financial prowess and general bloody-mindedness. And the land of Walter Scott, Robbie Burns, skirling pipes and wee drams doesn't lack for identity. After seven centuries,

* The turnout at recent British local elections isn't much better than America's.

the Stone of Scone finally returned north of the Tweed in 1997, and an empty assembly hall has been waiting in Edinburgh for the last two decades.

London has been understandably nervous about this. From Whitehall's point of view, devolution in Scotland might be only the first step down a slippery slope to full independence or, alternatively, to demands from other regions in the Kingdom for more autonomy, perhaps even leading to the break-up of the Kingdom. So the London civil service naturally views the Caledonian aspiration with some alarm. My experience in Whitehall, however, taught me that all slopes are slippery.

The Conservative Party has opposed constitutional change outright, and in a unitary state this is at least intellectually consistent if politically insensitive. It may also explain why there are now no Conservative MPs in Scotland. But the Labour government elected in May 1997, with its strong Scottish accent, put forward a fresh set of proposals to create a Scottish parliament with carefully restricted powers. And these were thumpingly approved in a September referendum.

How this legislative assembly in Edinburgh will relate to the Westminster Parliament, where the Scots are already over-represented, isn't clear. And no one has come up with a satisfactory answer to the famous West Lothian Question of how to run a system in which Scottish MPs can vote in matters affecting England, Wales and Northern Ireland, but English, Welsh and Irish MPs have no vote in matters affecting Scotland. You could even end up with a devilish parliamentary conundrum in which a Westminster government could command a majority on matters affecting the Kingdom as a whole but could not command a majority on matters affecting England only. So the constitutional mandate for a Scottish legislature is still pretty ill defined.

Creating a federal freak in the north of the Kingdom might be disruptive, especially without a legal umpire. But the British are a pragmatic people and none of these problems is likely to prove insuperable in practice.

My own opinion is probably distorted by my pluralist prejudices. If the Scots want to tax themselves by another penny or two, big deal. In fact, I think the Scots ought to be able to pass any law they want, provided it doesn't conflict with national law. Theoretically, a constitutional court would have to adjudicate a conflict if one arose, and this would take the matter out of Parliament's hands. But as John Wayne would say, that'll be the day. Westminster is only devolving authority to Scotland, not sovereignty, and what Parliament giveth, Parliament can taketh away. For all the muddle, however, it is clear that this single devolutionary step could do more to change the British constitution than anything since the Glorious Revolution.

A unitary state finds it hard to make exceptions. Wales too has its aspirations – the speaking of Welsh is on the rise and the natives have narrowly approved an elementary assembly for themselves. Cornwall also has its own special history; and it's hard to find a place more prideful than Yorkshire. Pluralism, however, may not work very well in a society which is so alert to who gets what.

Still, I think the United Kingdom would be more united if it were less uniform, and if local governments took more accountable responsibility for their own affairs. After all, democracy begins at home. And who knows? Maybe one day I'll come across a licence plate which says, 'Scotland: Kilt Kountry'.

Kith and Kin

D uring almost three decades in the lumpy fields of American
diplomacy, I had never been formally dressed down until
1 February 1994 when I was summoned to the Prime
Minister's office in Downing Street.

I had come to know the rabbit warren at Number 10 pretty well,
and I liked its squeezed-in, hunkered-down atmosphere. Number
10, after all, is a town house in a city street. The White House, on
the other hand, is a spacious country manor, built when Washington
was mainly dirt roads and swamps. Because the President is head
of state, the ground-floor rooms of the White House are grand and
airy; but the British Prime Minister is only head of government and
he can hardly turn around in the formal rooms at Downing Street
without knocking over a lamp. In both places, however, the leader
lives above the shop, and always at Number 10, and usually at the
White House, there is a muffled silence as you approach the seat
of power. Inside these two houses big decisions are made, and it is
here where the buck or the quid stops.

When I was minister at the embassy, it was frequently my duty
to escort one dignitary or another to call on Mrs Thatcher. The
Prime Minister was so popular in the United States that every
American politician who came to London wanted to see her. And

Mrs Thatcher always tried to oblige. Few congressional delegations were turned away, and a US senator could most always win an audience.

These meetings customarily followed the same pattern. The visitor would be taken upstairs, past the picture gallery of former Prime Ministers going back to Walpole. In one of the small sitting rooms on the first floor, Mrs Thatcher, prim and intent, perched herself at the edge of a sofa near a fireplace that was never lit. She rarely carried a piece of paper because she knew her message by heart, whatever it happened to be, and her mission was usually to stiffen the spine of whoever sat across from her.

The visitor would start the conversation with something such as, 'Thank you for seeing me, Madam Prime Minister' (Americans can never get the hang of saying just 'Prime Minister'), to which Mrs Thatcher would respond for about thirty minutes without drawing breath. The visitor nodded his head at suitable moments and would occasionally interject something like 'I see' or 'Yes.' When the meeting was over, the Prime Minister accompanied the guest to the door, usually adding one or two courtesy points about 'Ronnie', and say goodbye. Emerging into Downing Street, the visitor looked dazed, as if he had just gotten off the space shuttle. He would laugh to himself and scratch his head or pull his ear. 'What a woman!' he would say. 'What a woman!'

When I returned to London as ambassador, Mrs Thatcher had left office. But John Major was a friend from earlier days and I made a point of calling at Number 10 frequently, just to take the temperature of the place in London most likely to be feverish. I always tried to see him before one of my trips to Washington. Prior to a meeting, I would prepare myself carefully by first calling on other members of the Cabinet or senior officials. Douglas Hurd at the Foreign Office was usually the penultimate stop on my circumnavigation of Her Majesty's Government.

I normally found John Major relaxed, almost serene, and quite ready to chat on one subject or another as if he had all the time in the world. He was invariably thoughtful and considerate. Occasionally our discussions took place upstairs in his small study, but Major usually preferred to meet in the Cabinet room on the ground floor. He sat at his customary place, often in his shirt sleeves, halfway down the long table, and he would invite me to sit next to him.

On his left, the private secretary pulled up a chair and a clutch of sharpened pencils. Tea or coffee would appear.

John Major had none of the Thatcher flourish, but his command of detail was tenacious and his judgment of people shrewd. He was determined to the point of stubbornness. We usually ran through the business quickly, and then he would talk about whatever was on his mind, which more often than not was how to keep the Conservative Party from falling apart. The state of the Tories was never far from Major's calculations, and he sometimes spoke as if it were someone else's party.

On the February evening of my summons to Number 10, I was not looking forward to the occasion. I knew why I had been called to see the Prime Minister and I knew I was in for a drubbing. Over the weekend President Clinton had approved a visa for Gerry Adams to visit the United States. Until the President's decision, the Sinn Fein leader had appeared on anyone's standard list of terrorists. But Clinton had overruled his Cabinet advisers and dismissed the protests of the British government. He had certainly ignored what I had to say on the subject. Adams was already in New York, hopping from one television studio to another, promoting his brand of Northern Irish politics.

When I arrived in Downing Street that night, the porter opened the shiny black door. I walked down the long corridor that leads to the Cabinet room and turned into a little library off the coral-striped ante-chamber. After a few moments, Rod Lyne, the Prime Minister's private secretary, stepped through the door and sat down across from me. He looked as if he were about to perform an autopsy.

Lyne said the Prime Minister had wanted to talk to me personally but had just been called away to the House of Commons. Not wanting to delay the message, Major had asked Lyne to speak for him. I said that would be fine. I could guess the contents of the message anyway. Lyne pulled a stiff piece of paper from a folder and began to read to me. He paused after each point, punctuating his words with silence, and I nodded my head to fill the void. I did not recollect ever having been spoken to by a British colleague in such a prepared and formal manner. I don't think Rod Lyne liked the chore either.

Lyne left no doubt about the anger President Clinton's decision had caused from one end of Whitehall to the other. Working his way through the Prime Minister's notes, he pointed out that Gerry Adams had failed to meet the two conditions which the United States had itself laid down in considering whether to grant the visa. Adams had not renounced violence. Nor had he offered any commitment to peace on the basis of the Joint Declaration which the British Prime Minister and the Irish Taoiseach had agreed just a few weeks earlier. The purpose of the Declaration had been to isolate Sinn Fein and pressure the party to join democratic talks, Lyne went on, but this objective had been undermined by the American decision. The explanations offered in Washington had done nothing to set the Prime Minister's mind at ease. The British government hoped the Clinton administration would immediately reiterate its strong stance against terrorism, call on Sinn Fein to renounce violence and enter the democratic talks, and make clear that Adams' visit to the United States was an exceptional event that would not be repeated until terrorism had been irrefutably abandoned.

I had little in the way of response to Lyne's protest. I privately agreed with everything he had to say. The President's decision, it seemed to me, was either naive or opportunistic, or both, and it had debased America's long-established policy on terrorism as well as the value of relations with the United Kingdom. Nor did I think the gesture had much chance of converting Adams into a co-operative partner in constitutional talks about the province. When I stepped into Downing Street, I felt as gloomy as the chill February night around me.

With President Clinton's decision to issue a visa to Gerry Adams, the Irish Question returned full blown to the Anglo-American relationship, and so did a lot of Anglo-American history. Ireland has dogged relations between London and Washington almost from the beginning.

At the time of American Independence, there were a half-million Irish in the thirteen colonies, though the majority of these were Protestant Scots-Irish. You can't go to Northern Ireland today without being reminded by postcards, potholders and tea towels that a dozen American presidents descended from Ulster roots.

The independence of America also coincided with the first stirrings of modern Irish nationalism, and the United States soon became a refuge for thousands upon thousands of Catholics fleeing the repression and deprivation of their homeland.* The successive famines in Eire in the middle of the last century swelled the number of immigrants. Many Irish Catholics today believe that British policy in Ireland then was tantamount to genocide and that the famines were deliberately designed to drive them off their land or kill them on it. Deliberate or not, the famines were a shameful episode in Britain's past, though the story is mainly locked away in a dark cupboard of British history. For Irish Catholic immigrants in America, there was unfinished business left behind.

Irish secret societies proliferated in the United States, starting in the early 1800s. The Molly Maguires and the Irish Revolutionary Committee both advocated the overthrow of British rule in Ireland and sent arms and money to their brethren at home. The Fenian Brotherhood was founded in New York, and in 1866 Colonel John O'Neill, calling his band of 800 Civil War veterans the Irish Republican Army, crossed the Canadian border and momentarily occupied the British post at Fort Erie. Clan na Gael, a splinter of the Fenian Brotherhood, was established in New York in 1867, and in 1876 the Fenians inaugurated the Skirmishing Fund to support insurrection against the British in Ireland. Charles Stuart Parnell, on a fund-raising tour of the United States, addressed the US Congress in 1880 and met with President Hayes; and New York-born Eamon de Valera was the first leader of the Irish provisional government. The transatlantic network of political sympathy and material support goes back a long way. Noraid, which today sends a trickle of money to Northern Ireland, is a direct descendant from these earlier times. It has always been easy to make the case that Ireland, in seeking to rid itself of an English monarch and establish an independent republic, wasn't trying to achieve anything so very different from what Americans had themselves pulled off at the end of the eighteenth century.

The hardcore Irish in America never weighed very heavily in the

* There are today about forty-four million Americans of Irish descent, roughly divided between Catholics and Protestants. Most have become part of the everyday fabric of American life. But, for example, the Ancient Order of Hibernians, founded in 1836, still has 100,000 members.

balance of the nationalist struggle in Ireland, but they operated from America with relative impunity and kept alive the hope that one day things would change. In America, Irish Catholics nursed their wounds and nurtured their grievances. They recounted Irish legends and exorcized British demons. They neither forgot nor forgave. In the long Irish tragedy, Irish-Americans have played the Greek chorus, and it is this remembrance of bitter things past which the British today find so hard to comprehend.

The First World War delivered exhaustion to the British, influence to the Americans and opportunity to the Irish. London's suppression of the Easter Uprising in 1916 transformed a handful of nationalists in Dublin into international martyrs. When the war was over, the US Congress endorsed Irish self-determination. It seemed contradictory to most Americans that self-determination should be promoted for much of post-war Europe but denied in the backyard of America's wartime ally. Ireland was partitioned in 1922 and afterwards, for most Americans, became a poor, troubled European backwater of no great moment.

Only with the beginning of the Troubles in 1969 did Ireland re-emerge in the Anglo-American relationship in any tangible way, but by then there were bigger fish to fry. Irish neutrality in the Second World War, and in the Cold War that followed, had made Ireland irrelevant to the earth-shaking issues that preoccupied the United States and the United Kingdom. And for the broad American public, Ireland remained an incomprehensible, anachronistic and parochial affair.

For the British public today there is a curious remoteness about this rump province, as if it lay somewhere west of Greenland. Over my years in Britain, Northern Ireland has been a British responsibility but not a British concern. To an outsider, the impassivity of public opinion — except for the occasional atrocity on the mainland — seems odd. This is not, after all, some faraway colonial relic but a constituent part of the United Kingdom, whose representatives sit in the House of Commons, whose travails take a big slice from the national budget, and whose violence has so far cost more than 3,000 lives. Perhaps the public, inured by years of car-bombs and murders, has simply come to accept the low-grade turbulence of Northern Ireland as a natural feature of the political weather.

Northern Ireland always seemed to me to be an issue without a resolution, a vicious debate that had fallen into a revolving pattern, a circle that could not be squared. The province had been under direct rule from London ever since my first assignment to Britain, and there never seemed to be any prospect of a return to democratic government of any kind. The rest of the Kingdom might debate all manner of constitutional reform, but Northern Ireland was always beyond the constitutional pale. Like the British public, I watched the province from the corner of my eye.

When I returned as ambassador the political parties in London still looked at Northern Ireland as a millstone around any government's neck, frustrating in its intractability and costly in its administration. To be named Secretary of State for Northern Ireland was generally regarded as a one-way ticket to political exile.* The fervour of Unionism had largely disappeared with the last generation of Conservative Party leadership, though there remained a handful of old-guard Tory backbenchers who would spiritedly remind you that the official name of the party was 'Conservative and Unionist'. The Labour Party, having earlier bent its own political sword in Northern Ireland, rarely gave the government a hard time. Neither party was active in the province, and Irish affairs offered a rare example of bipartisanship in domestic British politics.

Whenever I visited Belfast I found a one-subject town where the horizons were claustrophobic. The Third World War could be raging across the face of Europe, but talk in Belfast would still be about the future of the province. Nothing else seemed to matter. Every day both Catholics and Protestants gathered around the bonfires of their communal memories where they summoned the ghosts of ancient heroes and listened to the echoes of ancient events. Every serious conversation struck small sparks of political dispute. Every political word concealed a barb and every symbol held a history. The Falls Road and the Shankill Road cut through the centre of the city like jagged gashes. Makeshift walls of brick and corrugated steel, streaked with graffiti and draped with coils of razor-wire, divided the town into sullen enclaves. There was an inescapable edginess about the place, and during the Orange and

---

* Patrick Mayhew was an exception. At considerable danger to himself, he plunged into the fray for five strenuous years.

Green 'marching season', the triumphs and treacheries of the past were kept as warm and close as yesterday.

The Protestants of Northern Ireland felt their majority eroding. Besieged and friendless, Protestant leaders were suspicious of betrayal by London and paranoiac about intentions in Washington, and they clung to British sovereignty like a drowning sailor to a piece of wreckage. Until the Troubles, Catholics had been second-class citizens. Kept in place by discrimination and intimidation, they too felt betrayed, sold out by the Catholic south and condemned to everlasting inferiority in the Protestant north. Though life had improved over the years, progress seemed slow and painstaking. Extreme Catholics hung on to the revolutionary vision of the IRA and believed that Catholics would never be free and safe until the British oppressors were finally driven off the island.

So the paramilitaries from both communities, in their balaclavas and black berets, had for a generation carried on an aimless, nasty para-war against each other. Both sides used the trappings of guerrillas and the techniques of gangsters. The British army and the Ulster constabulary tried to police a conflict that seemed to have little point and no end. Armoured cars crept along city streets past bunkered posts, and meandering rural lanes threw up checkpoints where jumpy soldiers hassled touchy civilians. Along the provincial border – in Armagh and Newry and Tyrone – lookout points dotted the hilltops. By the early 1980s, Northern Ireland had become a military stalemate.

Most people in Northern Ireland, I saw, carried on their daily affairs with a quiet, law-abiding normalcy. The men went to pubs, the women went to shops, the children went to school and everyone went to church. Of course the pubs, the shops, the schools and the churches were all sectarian. Centuries of hostility lay behind the tranquillity, and the two communities steered clear of each other.* But this was not especially noticeable to an outsider. You couldn't tell one denomination from another without a hint. Most places in the province looked peaceful, even dreamy, and most places were.

---

* I have a Protestant friend who was brought up in Northern Ireland, attended Queens University and moved to London for a job with an international company. In London, he married a Dutch woman who happened to be Catholic. His parents refused to come to the wedding, and so did his best friend.

When something violent happened, it was like a stone tossed into a still pool.

Periodically, Irish-American activists in the United States pressed for a more vigorous American involvement in the problems of Northern Ireland, and occasionally visited the province to stir the pot. The British tolerated the interference because they had to. But the responsible Irish-American leadership was as repelled by the thuggery and violence of the IRA as anyone else. And so long as relations between Dublin and London remained civil, and so long as the British government continued to put forward negotiable options for the constitutional leaders of the North to discuss, genuine American interests were not affected. Most Catholics were committed to peaceful negotiations and so were most Protestants, and the British government had the constitutional responsibility for bridging the historic mistrust between majority and minority. In 1994, the Clinton White House took little account of these simple constitutional and democratic facts.

The stasis of Northern Ireland started to change form in the spring of 1992, not in a fundamental sense but in the way that new cards are dealt around the table in an all-night casino. John Major won re-election and remained prime minister in charge of a party so weary and restless that his majority on any given issue in Parliament was problematical.* The handful of Ulster Unionists, who for more than a decade had sat in the Siberian reaches of the Tory-dominated House of Commons, suddenly acquired a new prominence in the calculations of Conservative nose-counters.

Meanwhile, Governor Bill Clinton was working his way through a series of wing-and-prayer campaigns in the springtime Democratic primaries in the United States, seeking his party's nomination to run against a president who at the time appeared unassailable. Irish-Americans in New York, whose Democratic Party has always been a jumble of ethnic interests, welcomed the Arkansas Governor's generous distribution of political promises. President Clinton later admitted to John Major that his campaign pledges seemed a good

* On the weekend following the election, the IRA detonated a bomb in the City of London which shattered the Baltic Exchange. I remember the rattling of the windows in Winfield House a couple of miles away. Three people were killed.

idea at the time, and, for a relatively unknown Southern politician in a North-eastern state, they probably were.

Once in the Oval Office, President Clinton nominated Jean Kennedy Smith to be ambassador to Ireland. She was not an individual noted for her grasp of foreign policy, but Dublin had always been a plaything for American presidents who wanted to score a point or two with the Irish-American electorate. Still, it was a curious selection,* not because of Mrs Smith's inexperience but because she was both wilful and skittish, a dangerous mix. From Clinton's point of view, however, a Kennedy was a Kennedy. The new President, whose election victory seemed almost accidental, needed all the help he could get. If giving Mrs Smith the Dublin post made Senator Ted happy, it was cheap at the price.

I did not know Mrs Smith. But shortly after her arrival in Dublin it became obvious she wanted to promote the reunification of both parts of Ireland, even if one of the parts happened to lie in the United Kingdom. We collided almost from the beginning, and when I refused permission for her to make political contacts in Belfast, Ambassador Smith was upset. Kennedys have a hard time absorbing refusal.

When Mrs Smith came to London, we met alone at Winfield House. It was a tense encounter. As hard as I tried, she seemed unable to comprehend that her responsibilities as ambassador to Ireland did not extend north of the border and that she was meant to represent administration policy as opposed to her own. I told Mrs Smith that I recognized my political weight in Washington was feather-like compared to hers. Nevertheless, I was paid to give my judgment about American interests in the United Kingdom, of which Northern Ireland was still a part, and her political involvement in the province was inappropriate at the time. Ambassador Smith claimed a personal mandate from the President to oversee Irish affairs in their widest range. I replied she should then have little difficulty persuading the President to overrule me. But, until that happened, she was to stick to the arrangements I had approved. We went back and forth in this fashion for two stiff hours. I have

---

* Her niece was married to an IRA activist named Paul Hill, whose convictions in two cases of murder had been overturned on appeal because of police mishandling.

never had a more unpleasant encounter with an American diplomatic colleague.

I had made an enemy. And a serious one at that. But she stayed away from the north. Later I learned that Ambassador Smith told anyone who would listen that I was a Republican 'hold-over' with Republican sympathies from a Republican administration; that I was intentionally subverting President Clinton's policy in Ireland; that I was in the pocket of the British government; and that I was anti-Irish. Even from London I could smell my goose cooking.

Diplomatic squabbles aside, the critical figure in the events that followed was John Hume, the leader of the SDLP in Northern Ireland, and a man of considerable courage and faith who was ready to put hope ahead of experience. His private discussions with Gerry Adams had achieved a major if ambiguous breakthrough, and on numerous trips to the United States he set about spreading the word of the IRA epiphany. In America, John Hume legitimized Gerry Adams. He insisted Adams was finally on the hook, and a little boldness in Dublin, London and Washington could reel in the peace.

London and Dublin did in fact seize the opportunity. The Downing Street Declaration stated that Britain had no ulterior strategic or economic motive in maintaining its authority in Northern Ireland. After centuries of anxiety, Britain was no longer worried about Spanish galleons, French legions and Russian submarines at its back door. Dublin, for its part, disclaimed any unlawful ambitions north of the border and agreed that the future of the province should be decided only with the consent of the majority who lived there.

In effect, the Downing Street Declaration said the British wanted out, and only the manner of their leaving remained to be resolved (it did seem odd to an American that the Declaration implied London's principal interest in a part of its own Kingdom was a matter of arithmetic). Of more immediate interest, the Declaration was designed to test the intentions of Sinn Fein/IRA and to corner Gerry Adams. At least that was the idea.

Gerry Adams had a long way to go before establishing his democratic credentials. Adams may not now meet all the technical requirements to qualify as a genuine terrorist, but in a democratic society he approves of violence as a legitimate instrument of political expression. I don't know whether Adams ever pulled a trigger or set a timer, but a mountain of intelligence information puts him in the front rank of the plotters and planners of political violence. He sees himself as a revolutionary in the radical, messianic tradition, and the chosen messenger of Irish liberation. When he became leader of Sinn Fein, he gave the IRA an intense and intelligent voice, though the party never commanded more than 10 per cent support in the island as a whole. Adams was a known quantity to any American who cared to pause a moment over the information available. On eight previous occasions, he had been refused a visa to enter the United States. America, which had suffered so often at the hands of terrorists around the world, should have been the last place to offer a platform to Gerry Adams, but in the end this is what the President did.

It was not too hard to appreciate the depth of British hostility to Adams and what he represented. The IRA had killed British subjects and British soldiers in the province and on the mainland for many years. There were thousands of victims dead or injured. The IRA had attempted to assassinate Margaret Thatcher in a horrific explosion at the Grand Hotel in Brighton in 1984. The Queen's cousin had been murdered. Three MPs had been killed by the IRA. The wife of the Leader of the House of Lords had died in the Brighton attack and the wife of Lord Tebbit was confined to a wheelchair as a result of the same atrocity. Shortly before my arrival in London, the IRA lobbed two mortar shells into the garden at Number 10 while the Cabinet was in session, and when I went to see Richard Ryder (the Chief Whip and an old friend), he showed me the pock-marks in the walls. Unless one believed Gerry Adams had no association with these and other exploits of the IRA, a relaxation of the American restrictions against him would be seen as a flagrant disregard for British life as well as British sensibilities.

Many Irish-Americans saw the Downing Street Declaration as a vindication for Sinn Fein's years in the cold. The British appeared to acknowledge that the cherished goal of a united Ireland was only a matter of time. The Taoiseach in Dublin declared that peace was just around the corner.

Two prominent Irish-Americans, Bruce Morrison and Niall

O'Dowd, who were the most serious and persuasive advocates of the Irish cause, took up the campaign for a visa. They believed a visit to the United States by Gerry Adams might bolster his position in IRA councils and be just the gesture to tip the balance for peace. There were other arguments in his favour as well. The British government itself had been in secret contact with the IRA. The overturned cases against the Birmingham Six and the Guildford Four proved that British justice was a malleable thing when it came to Ireland. And, anyway, peace and reconciliation were breaking out all over the world – in the Middle East and in South Africa.* Even the film *In the Name of the Father*, which had just been released in America, affected the atmosphere, and St Patrick's Day was just a few weeks away.

Within the Clinton administration, the State Department, the Justice Department, the FBI and the CIA were all ranged against the admission of Adams. Tom Foley, the Speaker of the House and the most sophisticated gauge of Irish affairs in the Congress, had assured me he was also dead set against a visa. Adams had done nothing and said nothing to change his record, and the United States had a well-rehearsed position on dealing with anyone who sanctioned terrorism. But, unlike previous occasions when Adams had applied for a visa, there were now sympathetic ears inside the administration to listen to the arguments of Irish-Americans on the outside.

Jean Kennedy Smith, who distrusted her own staff and penalized them for their dissent, became a promotion agent for Adams. Too shallow to understand the past and too naive to anticipate the future, she was an ardent IRA apologist. But her influence by itself would not have made much difference. Her brother was another matter. For Clinton's political staff, a visa for Adams seemed a relatively trivial give-away for the powerful Senator's support. Moreover, Senator Kennedy faced a serious re-election challenge in Massachusetts, and he was an anxious man in the market for favours.

And Nancy Soderberg, who had been appointed to a staff position

* Unlike the Palestinians on the West Bank or the Africans in South Africa, however, the Catholic community in Northern Ireland lived in a democratic society which offered democratic alternatives to violence.

at the National Security Council, was a dedicated Adams advocate long submerged in the Irish cause. Soderberg's influence flowed from her previous ten years on Senator Kennedy's staff, and she became the in-house coach for the Irish lobby. Her new boss was the National Security Adviser, Tony Lake, a quiet, scholarly man with Harvard and Cambridge degrees and an ego more disciplined and subdued than Washington is accustomed to. Lake came from the Wilson–Roosevelt wing of the Democratic Party that has historically opposed colonialism, and, for him, no country was more imperial than Britain and no place more colonized than Ireland.

From London I tracked the Adams case with a concern that eventually graduated to alarm. At first I did not believe any American administration could be so nonchalant about a matter involving terrorism. In the 1980s the United States had insisted that Yassir Arafat renounce violence before coming to talks, and to condemn terrorism whenever it occurred. It was a hard bargain but an effective one. Surely no visa would be granted to Adams without extracting something in return. But just before the crucial meeting in Washington to decide the visa, I despatched a final cable starkly stating the case against and warning of the consequences.

Unless we ignored all the evidence, I said, Adams was involved with the IRA right up to his elbows. To suggest that a visa would make him more amenable to democratic dialogue was dead wrong. It would give him a way to avoid it. A visa would confer respectability on him and condone the violence he advocated. Adams should be told plain and simple: renounce the violence first and then get the visa. To do otherwise would subvert America's established policy on terrorism and damage the Joint Declaration. And Washington should make no mistake about the severity of the British reaction in the Parliament, the press and the public.

I could not have been blunter. I suppose I belong to the old school of diplomacy whose cardinal rule says you don't give unless you get. And in the Adams case there was still a lot of getting to be gotten.

In reply the embassy was instructed to invite Adams to the consulate general in Belfast. There he should be asked whether he was prepared to state publicly that 'you personally renounce violence and will work to that end, and that Sinn Fein and the IRA are committed to the end of the conflict on the basis of the Joint

Declaration'. To me, the conditions for the visa were exactly right.

Adams failed on both counts. But, at a hasty White House meeting the next day, Clinton succumbed to Irish-American blandishments and ordered the visa. Having established two strict conditions for Adams' admission to the United States, he promptly abandoned them.

Adams received his visa at the embassy in Dublin and departed for New York on the next flight. In the days that followed, he said nothing which could justify the President's exceptional decision. In Britain, an avalanche of protest poured down the hillside. The President started to scurry backwards, but it was too late. Clinton's aides retreated into a prickly defensive posture of adolescent name-calling, claiming the only drawback to the decision was that it would annoy the British, which was perfectly acceptable so far as the White House was concerned. The Adams affair disintegrated into a fiasco of political amateurism.

And so it was that I found myself talking to the Prime Minister's private secretary that gloomy evening in Downing Street at the beginning of February 1994. In the weeks ahead, I had to reach deep into my professional reservoir to explain the Clinton decision. I did not like the role. Two days after my meeting at Number 10, I attended a long-scheduled, on-the-record luncheon with the parliamentary lobby correspondents in the House of Commons. Lunch was indigestible.

The *quid* for the Adams visa never produced its *quo*. Instead, Adams and his American supporters, like Oliver, asked for more. And they got it. Through the following months, the Clinton White House made one concession after another (fund-raising, official recognition, high-level meetings, presidential photos and so forth), and again and again it backed away from its own conditions, usually over the furious objections of the British. In this fractious atmosphere, London even stopped passing sensitive intelligence to the White House because it often seemed to find its way back to the IRA. In Washington, Gerry Adams reached a state of political beatification. His stature immeasurably enhanced, he had managed to place himself on a par with the British government.

The IRA announced a cease-fire in August 1994, and, though a cease-fire had always been on the cards, an imitation of peace descended on the province for a while. In the autumn of the next year, President Clinton conducted an impressive, triumphal tour of the province and the Republic. To the men of violence, he declared their 'day was over'. Ten weeks later, in February 1996, the IRA detonated a bomb in Canary Wharf, on the banks of the Thames, ending the cease-fire. In the spring, a bomb devastated the centre of Manchester, and by the summer Catholics and Protestants were again taunting each other across police barricades. In the summer of 1997, another cease-fire was declared, and Sinn Fein came to the negotiating table. The tactical manoeuvring of who is wrong-footing whom continues. But Gerry Adams has never renounced violence and he has never condemned it. And so it goes.

At the time I realized the matter of a visit for Gerry Adams was hardly the centrepiece of the Anglo-American relationship. This was no Suez. Its effect on grand global strategy, insofar as there was any at the moment, was negligible. Nonetheless, the British were disheartened by the immaturity of decision-making in Washington and discouraged that the substance, let alone the nuance, of their intentions in Northern Ireland seemed to have escaped the senior reaches of the administration. This little débâcle also demonstrated that British interests – on a matter of deep importance to Her Majesty's Government and minor importance to the United States – did not weigh heavily in the political scales of the Clinton White House. Whether this was an aberration in the post-war pattern of close co-operation or a signal that the nature of the relationship itself had shifted fundamentally with the end of the Cold War was a question left hanging in the air.

Ireland has bled at the British side for centuries. Today the separation of two Christian communities along denominational lines seems hopelessly palaeolithic in modern Western Europe, but it is an unhappy fact of political life. The Protestants in Northern Ireland are a majority because they are concentrated in the vestigial counties of an artificially partitioned island. The Catholics are a minority because they are unnaturally severed from their homeland. Demographics are gradually changing the provincial balance and economic development in some areas has softened the edges. The people want peace. But fundamental change is a long way off.

To an outside observer, the only durable solution to the division of Ireland is to unite the island. It seems as plain as the map. How to do this peaceably, however, is a constitutional riddle. It will surely require multiple compromises, joint supervision, awkward structures of power-sharing and a remarkable evolution of communal trust. In the meantime, Northern Ireland will remain the turbulent priest of British politics.

PART FIVE

Love and Anglo-American Relations

Betwixt and Between

Not long after leaving office as American secretary of state, Dean Acheson observed, 'Britain has lost an empire but not yet found a role.' This is the most widely quoted remark about Britain by an American in this century.

Acheson's comment in 1962 was not well received in London. The suggestion of British befuddlement came across as patronizing, hardly the appropriate tone for the American upstart to use about the British scion. Nor was Britain accustomed to Yankees making haughty declarations about Britain's destiny. It was usually the other way around.

The source of the comment was equally unsettling. For an American, Dean Acheson was about as English as you could get. Tall and angular with a trimmed moustache on his stiff upper lip. Acheson was Ivy League and East Coast Establishment to his core. His closet was full of double-breasted suits and old-school ties. He drifted in and out of government, between New York and Washington, with the natural insouciance of a nineteenth-century grandee, and he was as comfortable in a Mayfair salon as he was in a Georgetown dining room. If an Englishman looked in an American mirror, he would see Dean Acheson. So when this particular American statesman seemed to talk down to America's closest ally, it stung.

Even more unforgivable, Acheson's comment sounded uncomfortably close to the mark. His words captured the gigantism of British events in the years after the Second World War, a period when the world seemed to turn upside down. Europe was no longer the epicentre of the globe, and Britain had undertaken the painful process of dissolving its Empire and dismantling large parts of its history. Though a victor in the war, Britain also seemed somehow diminished by it. Economic decline accompanied imperial decline, and for a country which had always been preoccupied by status, the reduced circumstances were hard to reconcile with the memories. There was an embarrassing disconnection between the loftiness of Britain's behaviour and the reality of Britain's power.

Acheson's diagnosis, as it turned out, was wrong. Or at least premature. The sun may indeed have been setting on the British Empire, but in many ways it was a false twilight. Britain was thrown back on its own devices, and discovered its own devices were still considerable.

In the generation after the war, and especially in the period following the shock of Suez, Britain managed to adjust its role in the world with a deftness that has usually characterized its worldly ways. Because the Cold War was principally a question of security, it enabled Britain to transfer its wartime alliance with the United States into a peacetime collaboration of unique intimacy. Great power rivalry was a game the British knew well and had practised for centuries. For America, Britain was the ultimate been-there, done-that ally. And because Britain was so accomplished on the global stage, London's relationship with Washington meant it could enjoy the vicarious benefits of power without the crushing costs.

America's pre-eminence might have been a little hard to swallow, particularly when it seemed clear to British eyes that the United States still had a lot to learn about the tricks of the trade. But if the ungainly new superpower needed a little friendly coaching along the way, so much the better. In a statement equal in renown to Acheson's, Harold Macmillan observed that Britain would hence-forth play Athens to America's Rome. Macmillan outdid Acheson in both condescension and insight.

Britain's Cold War influence in Washington was much more than whispering in the ear of the king. Britain was a nuclear power in its own right. Though the military doctrine for an 'independent nuclear deterrent' was never very convincing, Britain's nuclear weapons ensured that London's interests had to be accounted for in the great superpower balance. The British Army of the Rhine was stationed along the confrontation line that cut through the middle of Europe, and the Royal Navy patrolled the strategic sea lanes of the North Sea and the North Atlantic.

Britain's sophisticated intelligence network remained intact and so did Britain's cool-hand diplomacy. British garrisons in Belize, Oman, Cyprus, Diego Garcia, Ascension Island, Hong Kong and so forth might have been scattered remnants from the imperial robe, but they were enough to make Britain an important player in the global competition. The United Kingdom was a permanent member of the Security Council and most other world clubs, and the British knew how to keep a secret. From an American point of view, Britain remained in a different category from most other nations. Britain was almost always able to find a seat at the global table, and in crisis after crisis the British always had something to ante up for the game, and willingly did so.

Working out a post-imperial relationship with the European continent, however, did not flow so smoothly. Following the war, Britain preferred to regard itself as extra-continental, like the Americans or the Russians. Britain might participate in some of the designs for Europe – the Marshall Plan or NATO, for example – but not if they were exclusively European. After all, the British enjoyed a range of relationships around the world, and thinking of itself as primarily European rubbed against the historic grain. Britain was not just another European nation.

When the other European governments gathered in Messina in 1955 to negotiate a common market, Britain attended as a remote if interested observer, while the thought of actually signing the Treaty of Rome seemed downright demeaning. London might encourage continental integration, but there was no obvious reason why Britain should be part of it. European aspirations seemed a little woolly, after all, and typically European. In retrospect, it's easy to say now that Britain's strategic pretensions on the global level caused it to make a strategic blunder in its own backyard.

The great Cold War issues of defence and deterrence, however, could not disguise Britain's frailty. Its performance on the world stage was marred by its threadbare costume. As one disappointment followed another, the harsh realities of the economy forced it to narrow its horizons. The withdrawal from East of Suez was the best demonstration of this inadequacy, but retrenchment had been driving the British budget for years. Events at home made it painfully apparent that Britain could not discharge its international political ambitions unless it better secured its regional economic base. This meant reconsidering its relationship with Europe.

For some, it seemed perfectly plausible that Britain on its own could develop economically into a kind of independent Hong Kong, beavering away just off the coast of the European landmass; but for others it seemed equally obvious that Britain, detached from Europe, would more likely become a kind of Sicily drifting on the deprived margins of European economic development. By the 1960s, Britain concluded that Albion bound was better than Albion unbound.

Having made the decision to go into the Common Market, Britain was at first refused admission at the door. Charles de Gaulle, who had an irritating habit of being right, charged that Britain was as much American as European. Joining the European enterprise was a psychological commitment as well as an economic one, he insisted, and Britain failed to meet the standard. It took the British another decade to polish their European credentials, and, even after signing up, Britain never really resolved the in-or-out dilemma. Britain wanted to be in Europe but not of Europe. And because it wanted half a loaf, its commitment was half-baked.

In the mid-1970s, when I first lived in the United Kingdom, the British seemed unsure what they really were. But they were pretty sure what they were not. They were not a superpower. Nor were they just a regional power. They were not wholly American in orientation but neither were they entirely European. They were not what they used to be but they weren't what they would yet become. They were, as the French say about the shadowy twilight, *entre chien et loup*. Britain was something in between. But this in-betweenness had also become Britain's principal source of post-war, post-imperial influence. The position was perhaps not as tidy or glamorous as the good old days, but it nonetheless gave the British ample room for manoeuvre, and manoeuvring is what the British do better than anyone else.

Britain has always enjoyed a talent for keeping its options open, picking its way through the rough terrain of international affairs one step at a time with the sure-footed dexterity of a mountain goat. Throughout most of the Cold War, the British exploited their midway position between Europe and America with consummate finesse. The security relationship with the United States meant Britain could speak with greater authority in Europe, and Britain's membership in European councils meant its voice was stronger when consorting with Americans. The British acted as a kind of intermediary between two continents, and if they jiggered the message a little bit along the way, it was usually for the better.

Transatlantic and trans-channel, the British found that each position amplified the other, and they seemed content with the unusual equipoise they had managed to achieve. If this apparent ambivalence postponed fundamental decisions about the long-term future, that too suited the British character. For the time being, it was the best of both worlds. Britain could firmly plant a foot on each stool, and so long as the two stools didn't start to slide apart, it could cock a snook at Achesonian analysis.

When I returned to Britain in the spring of 1991, the Cold War had largely ended, and so too, it seemed, had the period when Britain was able to work both sides of the street. The finale of the Cold War came so silently that most nations found it hard to assess the consequences. When the Berlin Wall came down, the political map of Europe changed almost overnight. Germany was unified, enlarging itself by a third; the Soviet empire quavered on the brink of collapse and Russian forces were streaming back to their Eurasian hinterland; Yugoslavia fragmented and then resurrected the nightmares of the continent; and the nations of the East were suddenly free and on their own. In fact, it was hard to think of another time in modern European history when such sweeping change had been let loose across the continent without a precipitating war. For all nations, including Britain, the givens of two generations were suddenly in doubt, and Europe set about looking for a new kind of order to replace the old one.

The principal problem for Europe, including Britain, was the standard one: Germany. For a century and a half, Europe has grappled with the German Question, and none too successfully.

One of the great miracles of post-war European politics, however, has been the Franco-German rapprochement, an achievement so monumental that another war between these two countries is all but unthinkable. The progression from the Coal and Steel Community to the Common Market to the European Community to the European Union was primarily a Franco-German endeavour, and in this institutional ground they buried their ancient hatchet. This was good for Europe and good for Britain.

In 1990, however, the unification of Germany upset the sensitive balance between the two continental partners, causing alarm in both capitals and in most of the rest of Europe as well. Set smack in the middle of the continent, the new Germany overnight became disproportionate in size and power compared to other European states. Moreover, its frontiers were more notional than natural, its history was as much a source of shame as of pride, and its modern nationality seemed defined more by its currency than by any other feature. Within living memory, Germany had invaded each of its neighbours, and Germany's impeccable democratic record since the war had not completely steadied European nerves. So Paris and Bonn were determined to accelerate the pace of European integration and to make permanent the denationalization of European politics. Even the Germans agreed that Germany was a national Gulliver that needed to be tied down in a tangle of unbreakable European bonds.

The British have never shared this vision of European unity as an antidote to European nationalism. The unification of Germany set off amber lights in Whitehall as well, but Britain is not by nature a fretful country. Moreover, for the British, Europe is a place, not an idea. It is a necessity, not a mission. Europeans may see their Union as a natural descendant from Rome, Christendom, Charlemagne, the Holy Roman Empire and Napoleon, but Britain always found the concept of a Concert of Europe, however expressed, disharmonious, and had little tolerance for it. Britain usually had other options.

The experience of two calamitous wars in the first half of the twentieth century was also different for the British. After all, Britain was victorious in both. No continental power was really victorious in either. European countries saw their frontiers violated and redrawn; their territories invaded by foreign armies and their own armies disgraced and defeated; their roads clogged with refugees and their cities piled in rubble; their minorities victimized, their institutions destroyed, their governments overthrown and their peoples betrayed by their own leaders.

Europe in this century has been a nasty business, and this makes it much more understandable why the continental nations have been willing to deposit their troublesome sovereignties in a common European pool. For Europeans, it is important to hold up a vision of unity, no matter how romantic or fuzzy, that promises a better, safer future. For the British, it is impossible to recreate this emotional continental history because Britain does not fear its past.

It doesn't take long for an American to realize that being in Britain is not the same thing as being in Europe. Sometimes there seems to be a greater distance between Dover and Calais than there is between London and New York. The British still refer to 'Europe' as if it were a place apart, which it is, and the fog has never lifted entirely from the English Channel.

To an outsider, Britain often seems pulled in opposite directions – towards Europe and towards America – as if it were developing a hybrid system lying somewhere midway between the two. The similarities with the United States, as opposed to Europe, are recognizable to an American in such trivial matters as the sound of a telephone ringing or the taste of a cup of coffee. On the other hand, an American also notices that electrical voltage in Britain is lethally European and that the regulation of the simple things in British life, such as weights and measures, is increasingly European.

Britain today trades primarily with Europe but invests primarily in America, and, if you look at social benefit spending or total taxes, Britain comes out somewhere between the two poles. The British pound and the British Stock Exchange seem to trail their American counterparts, but the national budget looks more European in its priorities. Historically, Britain has admired the compassion of Europe's welfare system and the dynamism of America's market system, but European welfare is too pampering for the British to accept economically and the American market is too crude for the British to accept socially.

The British government is parliamentary, like most continental states, but European governance seems too corporatist and intrusive to fit the British spirit of liberty; the American model of government, on the other hand, is too decentralized and chaotic to satisfy the British sense of order. At heart, Britain doesn't want to buy either version completely but instead take what it likes and leave what it doesn't. In national disposition, Britain is the Middle Kingdom.

All of that said, however, one of the principal contrasts between my first assignment in Britain and my last one is the degree to which Britain has been absorbed by the business of trying to be European. I recall, at the beginning of 1993, asking a senior Foreign Office official what the FCO's priorities would be for the new year. He listed three issues, each having to do with the structure of the European Union. Given the great events going on in Russia, China, Yugoslavia, South Africa and the Middle East, this surprised me, but it was an accurate reflection of what preoccupied British diplomats.

Moreover, the line between foreign affairs and domestic affairs, at least so far as Europe is concerned, has blurred. Britain's position on innumerable issues is shaped in a European mould. Cabinet members nowadays are constantly flying back and forth to Brussels, and a minister's calendar is littered with European meetings. A quarter of the British budget flows through the Union, and almost everything affecting trade or agriculture or industrial standards has a European dimension decided in Brussels. European directives make their way through Westminster faster than in most other European legislatures, and Britain pays its considerable European bills on time.

On the whole, Britain has done pretty well in Europe, especially for a latecomer. A lot of the economic benefit of EU membership might have happened anyway, but Britain has helped clear out the clutter of internal barriers to trade in Europe and remove the external ones. British reforms at home, such as privatization and deregulation, are imitated by other European governments, and Britain has influenced the political agenda of Europe on such important issues as separate defence and enlargement eastwards. The British are so sensible and practical that their advice usually leavens European decision-making, and the smaller European states, leery of Franco-German dominance, like to have the British around.

When the Channel Tunnel opened, it was more than just a hole in the ground.

Sometimes it seems that managing relations with the continent has become an exercise in self-definition. Europe today cuts across most of the major issues which the British debate among themselves. The monarchy, Scottish devolution, Westminster, the judiciary and so forth all look different in a European context. If Europe is headed for a quasi-federal system, how much authority would remain for the British to decide their own affairs? Can they really go along with all this, or will the European reach exceed the British grasp? These questions have given the British the sense of Europe closing in and options closing down.

British political parties can barely stand the strain. Ever since I can remember, Europe has lurched around British politics like a drunk at a tea party. The 1975 referendum on British membership divided Labour and Tories alike. In the beginning of the 1980s, four MPs – all former Cabinet members – bolted the Labour party as much over relations with Europe as any other point of difference. The only apparent advantage to Labour's long season in opposition was that it could paper over its internal divisions, and from my talks with Tony Blair I concluded he was instinctively sympathetic to the European cause but dubious about its course.

Conservative governments, which have taken the real battering over Europe, signed the Single European Act and joined the Exchange Rate Mechanism (late, as usual), but when Geoffrey Howe challenged Margaret Thatcher's chronic Europhobia, her government came apart. I don't think the Tories ever really recovered from their own act of matricide, and Europe – troublesome enough on its own – became the instrument for settling other scores too. The truth is that continental-style Europhiles in either party are still as scarce as hen's teeth.

When I was ambassador, European issues tied the Tory government in knots, with no Houdini in sight. John Major started his tenure declaring he wanted to be 'at the heart of Europe', but other parts of the anatomy were more in evidence. With a restless, suspicious party at his back, he negotiated the Maastricht Treaty, preserving rearguard British options as best he could. The ratification was an interminable parliamentary agony. After the 1992 election the Prime Minister lashed his economic policy to the ERM and suffered the humiliation of deserting it.*

More than anything, this failure of sterling legitimized deep-seated Tory antagonism to things European. Afterwards, every European issue that came along – fishery policy, the encroachment of the European Court, the quality of British beef – made Europe seem predatory and drove the wedge deeper and deeper into the Tory establishment. By the middle of the decade, it seemed to me that no Conservative leader could take the party where the rest of Europe wanted to go, and for some Conservatives it was better to lose power than to proceed any further down the European path.

The Prime Minister believed the issue of Britain-in-Europe divided the party so profoundly that it was the modern equivalent of the Corn Laws. His own historic legacy, he thought, would be the simple feat of preventing the party from splitting in two. But the harder he tried to keep the party together, the more the party divided. Europe made the Conservative Party virtually ungovernable and lit the fuse for Tory implosion.

For much of British opinion the bridge too far in Europe is the creation of a single currency. For Europeans the monetary union is designed to make integration irreversible, and in the process to make Germany more continental than national. To achieve this goal, European countries have to surrender their individual control of monetary policy, which in one step is about as close to sacrificing sovereign decision-making as you can get. Binding currencies together in a monetary union has never happened before, and this is a brave and hazardous undertaking. It is also an undertaking of political elites, and there is little evidence in France or Germany, for example, that a single currency has the enthusiastic support of their populations. But for most European governments the political goal is worth the economic risk.

Not for Britain. The British, even pro-Europeans, have deep

---

* A couple of days after the pound fell out of the ERM, I accompanied the American Secretary of Defense, Dick Cheney, to see John Major in his temporary office in the Admiralty (Downing Street was under renovation). As we sat down there was a large crash of something in the hallway on the other side of the door. 'What was that?' said the Prime Minister, looking startled. 'The pound?' I suggested. Major turned to Cheney: 'Tell the President I want another ambassador.'

misgivings about whether this project is well conceived, and whether Europe can cope with the political strains that will inevitably follow. Monetary union will lock in inequalities among the European states just at a time when Britain itself seems to have recovered its economic bearings. Moreover, in order to work, monetary union will require more political union, which is exactly what European governments say they want and exactly what the British say they don't.

But British apprehension runs much deeper than judgments about a single currency. Monetary union brings Britain face to face with the same dilemma left unresolved by its midway position through all the years of the Cold War. The British never took the goal of European unity seriously, and for a long time didn't have to. But now the Union is telling all its members to put your money where your mouth is. So Britain has to ask whether it is part of this European experiment or not. Is Britain better off joining the enterprise, no matter how troubling the risks, or is it best to leave the Europeans to get on with it?

I don't think Britain can bring itself to decide this, at least not for now, even though it is one of the most important strategic issues Britain has confronted since the end of the war. Both major parties think the political union of Europe has gone about as far as it should and that an *à la carte* 'Europe of nations' is about the right level of institutional maturity. Only the Liberal Democrats are consistent Europhiles, but their influence is still too wispy to count much.

On the one hand, the success of European integration is wholly in the British interest. If monetary union produces one of the world's major trading currencies, it is logical that Britain should enjoy the benefits too. And because integration is the best guarantee of Europe's safety, it is also Britain's best guarantee. If European success is in the British interest, the success is much more likely if Britain is in instead of out. Nothing could be worse for European stability than a Union which overreaches itself and brings down the whole structure. This is less likely to happen if the wily, rational, straight-thinking British are part of the exercise.

On the other hand, there is no compelling reason why Britain should want its comfortable nationality siphoned off into a muddy

European pond. The British will never be part of the Franco-German core of continental management because Britain has neither the geography nor the psychology. And there is no convincing analysis which says that the British will suffer measurable economic damage if they are outside a monetary union rather than inside. Britain has plenty of problems, and, without the Cold War, self-confidence is probably one of them. But there is no certainty the British can resolve this by pretending to be something they obviously are not.

Hobson had better choices. John Major's government ended up with a position on monetary union which was almost a parody of classical British diplomacy: wait and see. The serious thinking in Tony Blair's government isn't much different. But this position is probably about right, touching as it does the outer boundary of British boldness. The British are a cautious race and the least likely nation to rush into a proposition which may be misbegotten. If monetary union goes ahead, and if it can withstand the political weight, and if the British business and financial communities begin to see a costly disadvantage in being left out, then Britain will try to catch up and, like the dog's tail, be the last one over the fence. But this will be on European terms, not British ones, and Britain's late arrival will further diminish Britain's position within the Union.

I used to think that joining the monetary union was so obviously in the British interest that there could be little question. After three years at the embassy, I'm less sure. Many EU decisions don't make it very easy for the British, but the real problem remains that the British are not, at heart, European. I'm told the younger generation feels differently. Maybe. But the drawback to the younger generation is that it gets older.

Recently the option of leaving the Union altogether – unthinkable at the beginning of the decade – has struggled into the debate. Such a course would be a pity, for Britain and for Europe. Some hold up the American connection – a revivified 'special relationship' – as a viable alternative to full-blooded Europeanness. But this is a flimsy proposition, unlikely to gain much traction except with the graspers of straws. When push comes to shove, America has a greater interest in European unity than in British sovereignty.

Standing between America and Europe used to be a British

advantage. Now it's a British dilemma. But it was never either or. It always had to be both. The same formula holds true. If Britain is not part of important European decision-making, it is less likely to be important in American decision-making, and vice versa. If Britain is aloof from developments on the continent, it is bound to be more marginal in America.

This isn't to say that Britain cannot make its way as a European maverick. There may even be some advantages to standing clear. And there's always the chance that, as Mr Micawber would say, something might turn up. Perhaps. But, if anyone is shaking his head, it's Mr Acheson.

Movers and Shakers

I once asked Ted Heath a question which showed I still had a lot to learn about the subtleties of diplomacy. We were lunching at his weekend home in Salisbury, just across the flat green lawn from the great cathedral. The former Prime Minister was giving me a hard time about American policy in the Middle East, where he thought – as he always thought – the United States was making a hash of things. I was ready to change the subject.

So I asked my question: 'Of all the relationships between a British prime minister and an American president since the war, which one do you think was the best?' Heath didn't hesitate more than a nanosecond. 'Heath and Nixon,' he replied. I almost choked on my asparagus.

The next time I asked this question I was a little smarter. Margaret Thatcher had also left office, and we were sitting in her comfortable office in Chesham Street. I said, 'Of all the relationships between a British prime minister and an American president since the war, which one do you think was the *second* best?' I was pleased with my reformulation. But this too was a mistake. Lady Thatcher wasn't sure there had been a second best.

I went back to the first formula when I saw Jim Callaghan, this time over a luncheon table in the House of Lords. Callaghan pondered the different combinations out loud. He didn't want to select from the obvious choices nor did he want to toot his own horn. And even as an elder statesman he didn't want to concede anything to the Tories. This didn't leave a very long menu. In the end, he said, 'Attlee–Truman.'

I doubt any relationship between two countries has invested so heavily in the personal compatibility of its respective leaders. Before the Second World War, personal relations across the ocean mattered hardly at all. With the exception of Teddy Roosevelt, almost every previous President mistrusted what the British were up to, usually with some justification, and for the most part Downing Street paid scant attention to Pennsylvania Avenue. For some unaccountable reason, Andrew Jackson and Queen Victoria took a shine to each other, and they exchanged portraits. But at the political level personal contact of any kind was limited.

The modern paradigm of Anglo-American partnership comes down from Winston Churchill and Franklin Roosevelt. In many ways, they were a match for each other. Both were patrician, with long family histories, and Churchill's mother was born in Brooklyn.* Both were eloquent and witty in a time before God invented speech-writers. In their political intrigues and public relations, each was as manipulative as the other. And both were warriors.

They did not always agree. After all, one was a dyed-in-the-wool Tory and the other a visionary Democrat. Their worldviews were distinctly different. Churchill worshipped the British Empire and understood European history better than any American was likely to do. Roosevelt, for his part, had no intention of fighting a war to preserve British colonialism and thought European history offered more problems than solutions. Military strategy was a contentious bone between them and they often exasperated each other. But these two leaders – wrapped in lap rugs on the deck of a battleship in the North Atlantic or watching a desert sunset from a Moroccan tower – cast a spell over Anglo-American relations through all the years that followed.

Most presidents and prime ministers since then have tried to

* FDR's lineage went back to Dutch settlers in the Hudson River valley; in American politics, you can be well-to-do and pedigreed so long as you're a Democrat.

preserve this aura and to disguise disharmony when it occurred. This was not always easy to do, nor was it always successful. And as the balance in the relationship became more lopsided, British prime ministers had to try harder. The Churchillian term 'special relationship' was never an important part of an American president's vocabulary, but in Britain it became a kind of political mantra, as if its repetition would somehow make it truer. Prime ministers were therefore more vulnerable to its ups and downs. While London made it axiomatic to consult in Washington before making any significant move, Washington was more erratic in reciprocating.

As Lord Callaghan said, Clement Attlee and Harry Truman were a successful pair, though their personal relations were nothing more than proper. Politically, they were a little like John Major and George Bush a generation later. From parallel parties, Truman and Attlee had each succeeded towering figures when dramatic changes were under way in Europe, and they together fought a limited war in a remote part of the globe. But neither felt a particular need for gesture diplomacy. In fact, a week after the Japanese surrender in 1945, Truman abruptly cancelled Lend–Lease, and he later signed the McMahon Act, which suspended nuclear co-operation between the two countries.

The onset of the Cold War, however, pushed them together.* Truman was the first president to see that, if you wanted to sell something foreign at home, you had to have allies abroad. And because of the war, Britain was by then the most likely candidate and politically the most acceptable one. That was a big change.

Attlee, on his side, was the first to see that, if you wanted to play with the Americans, you had to bring something to the game. So, even while Britain was abandoning its positions nearer to home (in the eastern Mediterranean, for example), British troops showed up for the fight in faraway Korea. Attlee also learned to exploit Britain's special access to Washington's councils. He rushed there when he thought Truman might drop an atomic bomb in Asia, just as Margaret Thatcher hurried to Washington thirty-five years later

* This was due more to the activism and grasp of Attlee's Foreign Secretary, Ernest Bevin, than to the Prime Minister, whose preoccupations were almost entirely domestic. On the American side, George Marshall and Dean Acheson were the primary movers of post-war policy.

when Ronald Reagan seemed ready to bargain away the nuclear arsenal.

When Dwight Eisenhower became president in 1953, he knew the British well enough. He had spent two years in London directing the Allied campaign on the continent and sorting out the endless wrangles between British and American generals. And Anthony Eden, when he finally succeeded from foreign secretary to prime minister, thought he knew the Americans well enough too.

To have been foreign secretary, or even a senior member of the Cabinet, is always a distinct advantage for a British prime minister. You already know your way around.* By contrast, no American president in this century has earlier served as secretary of state. In fact, the route to Downing Street always runs through the Cabinet, but the route to Pennsylvania Avenue never does. The parliamentary system also offers a measure of predictability about who will wind up in Number 10 – it's always one of a handful. The federal system, on the other hand, is full of surprises, and the White House can end up with a peanut farmer from Georgia or a former actor from California.

Theoretically, things should have run smoothly between Eden and Eisenhower. But all of Eden's experience didn't help the relationship much. He was arrogant and vain, with an abysmal sense of timing, and he was confident he could handle ex-colonials, either in Egypt or in America. Eden was intent on asserting the independence of British action, even when it seemed obvious to everyone else that independent action was the last thing Britain could afford. No event in post-war Anglo-American relations has ever surpassed the misjudgment, deceit and calamity of Eden's Suez fiasco.

Eisenhower and Harold Macmillan got on much better. They were friends from wartime days, when Macmillan had initially been assigned to Eisenhower's staff, and their regard was mutual. Though Macmillan had been deeply involved in the Suez shenanigans, he afterwards retreated so rapidly it seemed he had spent the whole time in a monastery. Macmillan entertained few illusions about British power, and he was the first prime minister to appreciate fully

* Since the war, five prime ministers have first been foreign secretary: Eden, Macmillan, Douglas-Home, Callaghan and Major.

the change in Britain's international fortunes. He also recognized that good relations with Washington could be helpful electorally, and with the arrival of the media age he exploited his friendship with Eisenhower shamelessly.*

Very British because he was very theatrical, Macmillan was ready to act any role. From Eisenhower's point of view, this adaptability made Macmillan a little slippery. The Prime Minister's willingness to compromise with the Soviets on virtually any issue, especially Berlin, made Eisenhower wary of Macmillan's interventions.

Harold Macmillan was the first British prime minister I met. When I was minister at the embassy, he had long since left office. But after I asked to call on him, he invited me to come to lunch at his home in Birch Grove, and I drove down there one fine October morning. I recall pulling into the driveway and seeing Macmillan framed in the doorway. I don't know how long he had been waiting there or how he knew I had arrived. Perhaps the crunching gravel was his cue, and Harold Macmillan never missed a cue. He was an old man by then. His dark suit was voluminous and hung from his bent shoulders in folds. With drooping face and weary expression, he leaned forward on two walking sticks. The light of the morning in front of him and the shadows of the corridor behind him created a chiaroscuro effect.

We talked for a long time, though this was mainly Macmillan telling stories. His conversation often went back to the First World War (the British, he said, were not always very good at peace but they were splendid at war), and he spared nothing in disparaging both political parties (the Conservative Party was full of accountants and solicitors and the Labour Party full of union stewards and school teachers). Of all the subjects covered, however, it was his relationship with John Kennedy to which he returned most frequently.

Like Churchill, Macmillan had an American mother, and through the Hartington family he was indirectly related to the young President. Kennedy, for his part, was the son of a former ambassador to the Court of St James's, and as a charming, witty sophisticate he

---

* Just before the 1959 election, Macmillan inveigled the President into a joint love-in on British television.

had once happily roamed London society. Kennedy's elder brother had died in the European war, and his sister was buried under the shade of a yew tree in the small churchyard on the Chatsworth estate. The President admired the English graces, and his Anglicized White House mixed Avalon with Broadway and came up with an American Camelot. When Kennedy became president in 1961, everything transatlantic seemed to fall into place.

Macmillan and Kennedy overlapped for only two and a half years, but, as the old Prime Minister recounted that day, they together seemed to have found the perfect hand-in-glove relationship. Macmillan consoled Kennedy at Chequers after the President's first brutal encounter with Khrushchev in Vienna. Kennedy saved the Prime Minister's bacon by finding a new formula for nuclear partnership after the awkward Skybolt affair. Macmillan was faithful to Kennedy during the Cuba missile crisis, and together they achieved the Nuclear Test Ban Treaty. Macmillan also flooded the White House with personal messages designed in part to simulate the Churchill–Roosevelt ambience.

Occasionally, Kennedy found Macmillan a little dippy, and Macmillan's influence was more shallow than the Prime Minister supposed. But they were genuinely fond of each other. Both had a sense of history and a sense of humour. In fact, the casting was almost too good: the youthful, eager President embodied the robustness of America, and the avuncular, patient Prime Minister reflected the wisdom of Great Britain.

It all went sour soon enough. Kennedy was killed in Dallas in November 1963, just as American troops were arriving in Vietnam, and Macmillan, dispirited and ill, resigned six weeks later, leaving behind a party sapped of vigour and wracked by scandal.

Personal relations afterwards were a muddle, at least for a while. These were tough years for presidents and prime ministers alike. The Oval Office was an unstable place to be (after Kennedy was assassinated, Lyndon Johnson was driven from office, Richard Nixon resigned, Gerald Ford hadn't been elected by anybody, and Jimmy Carter was defeated after one term). Number 10 wasn't much better, with Heath and Wilson teetering along on friable majorities, and Jim Callaghan stepping in when Wilson suddenly resigned. Domestic strife overwhelmed incumbents on both sides of the ocean.

Lyndon Johnson could barely conceal his disdain for Harold Wilson. He once referred to him as 'a little creep'. A Texas Democrat, the President was suspicious of anyone who called himself a socialist, especially a pipe-smoking foreigner who wouldn't recognize a spittoon if he tripped over one. He regarded Wilson's mollifying trips to Moscow not as mediating but as meddling, and as Johnson was sucked more and more into the quagmire of Vietnam, Wilson's refusal to send so much as a 'platoon of bagpipers' made the Prime Minister seem little better than useless.

Strangely, Wilson thought his friendship with Johnson was harmony itself. In fact, he believed he was so close to Johnson that it was a political problem for him at home, which it was. Wilson was the first prime minister for whom a good relationship with an American president was a domestic liability, and his tip-toe manoeuvring on Vietnam, as deft as it was, still made him seem a White House toady to his critics (a progenitor of the Thatcher poodle). But Wilson liked American stroking. When I went to see him one day, his memory was failing badly, but he waxed rhapsodic about his visits to the White House and the LBJ ranch. Looking at the record, it's hard to see how Wilson thought he had achieved any rapport with the overbearing Texan. Except perhaps for Eden, no other prime minister so misread the runes.

Richard Nixon, on the other hand, liked Wilson. This pair made strange bedfellows, but Nixon admired the Prime Minister's donnish intellect and political cunning (Nixon knew a thing or two about cunning). The fact that one was Republican and the other Labour didn't seem to make much difference. Perhaps they got on because they had fewer expectations of each other. In any event, as Henry Kissinger once observed, America was not so replete with friends in those days that it could afford to ignore the few who came calling.

Ted Heath had no wish to come calling. To prove he was a good European, Heath conspicuously distanced himself from the Nixon administration, rejecting any hint of bilateral collaboration and declaring that Britain would henceforth consult with its European partners before voicing any opinion directly to the Americans.

During the Yom Kippur War in 1973, he obstructed American efforts to supply Israel. From Heath's point of view, a deliberately stiff relationship with Washington was good policy. The White House, on the other hand, found his logic perverse and his behaviour bizarre.

As I discovered at lunch in Salisbury, however, Heath believed his relationship with Nixon was the best on record because he was the only prime minister in the post-war relationship who gave the Americans as good as he got. Unlike Macmillan before him or Thatcher after him, he would not do the American bidding. As prime minister, he said, he didn't confuse respect with chumminess (hardly a notable trait in Heath's case anyway). Heath recalled a meeting with Nixon and Kissinger in Bermuda when the two governments were bickering over the Indo-Pakistan war in 1971. For strategic reasons, the Americans wanted Heath to support Pakistan, but Heath said he set both of them straight, and he wouldn't budge. The Americans were impressed. Britain, Heath thought, wasn't an American satrapy unless it behaved like one.

Whatever the political chemistry of the Heath–Nixon tandem, the personal relationship ended in mutual contempt, and, once they left office, the old lions were barely civil to each other.

When Jim Callaghan thinks of transatlantic relations, he thinks of Gerry Ford. They overlapped for less than a year, but to this day they correspond frequently and see each other when they can. Their compatibility may have something to do with their keen appreciation of political fickleness. Both came to office in the wake of resignations and neither ever won a national election.

For most of Callaghan's time in Number 10, however, Jimmy Carter was in the White House. Their relationship was solid and workmanlike, Callaghan says, but on a personal basis he never penetrated much beyond the President's mirthless grin. Their shared naval backgrounds and parallel party affiliations made little difference.

Still, the President and Prime Minister co-ordinated on a host of issues, especially in the Middle East and southern Africa. Sometimes Carter seemed to treat Callaghan like a member of his own Cabinet, sending him little notes that were more like inter-office memos. At the Guadeloupe summit Callaghan dropped by Carter's bungalow just as the President was about to take a nap, and with Carter seated in his underwear, Callaghan extracted an American commitment to supply the new Trident submarine to the British. Carter and Callaghan were more than cordial but less than convivial.

During these awkward middle years of the late 1960s and 1970s, the Anglo-American dance card was not well arranged. Both countries were preoccupied and frustrated. Personal relations at the top were uncomfortable. But the framework of the Cold War was so well established by then that neither side was willing to upset it, at least not in Europe. In fact, transatlantic security was so solid that it didn't seem to matter much which party won office in either capital or what one leader really thought of the other. And anyway, the relationship between prime minister and president was about to enter a phase of almost delirious mutual admiration.

When Margaret Thatcher strode into Downing Street and Ronald Reagan rode into the White House, the compatibility rating soared off the scale. They held office simultaneously for most of the 1980s. No Anglo-American duo has come close to this record.

At first glance, Thatcher and Reagan were an odd pairing. The Prime Minister was an indefatigable worker, long on energy and short on humour. She was a formidable advocate of her political views and consumed reams of information. Reagan, on the other hand, was genial, distracted and an inexhaustible source of one-liners. His political beliefs were simply held and simply stated, and they could usually be squeezed on to an index card. In the political maelstrom, Thatcher was a bare-knuckle street fighter and Reagan was a folksy pussycat.

Still, one was a Conservative and the other a Republican. They had both emerged from wings of their respective parties which hadn't had a grip on national power for a long time. Thatcher was middle class and anti-Establishment, and, as a woman, she was by definition an outsider. Reagan was middle class and anti-Washington, and, as a grade-B actor, an aberration from the mainstream of American politics. They both hankered after Victorian virtues and each counted old-fashioned patriotism among the highest values of public life.

Thatcher admired America. Whenever she returned from a visit to the States, she was buzzing. This too was different from most of her predecessors. Old-line Tory thinking had customarily looked at America as a volatile, overgrown juvenile that would be much improved if it could just learn to be a little more British. Thatcher reversed this by saying that Britain was a fine old place but should learn to be a little more like America. Reagan, on his side, admired Thatcher for her conviction, forcefulness and flirtatious femininity, and through her he came to regard Britain sentimentally as a bastion of democratic straight thinking notably distinct from the fuzziness of the continentals.

Unusually for American and British politics, both were ideological leaders. They saw the world in stark terms of light and dark. Their conversation didn't distinguish much between foreign policy and domestic policy. In both arenas they were trying to achieve the same thing: throw back the state – vile communism abroad and suffocating bureaucracy at home. Reagan and Thatcher saw themselves as crusaders, riding out in suits of armour to challenge the enemy wherever it appeared. For them, the sword of the open market would slay the dragon of state control.

Nonetheless Margaret Thatcher was sometimes left in the cold. America's incursion in Grenada and Reagan's nuclear bargaining at Reykjavik seemed to overlook that the British had particular interests to protect. And the Prime Minister, at least at the beginning of the Falklands campaign, was disturbed to find that Reagan's apparent sympathy didn't translate immediately into American support, though things turned out all right in the end.

Still, there were few American politicians and no foreign leaders with whom Reagan conferred more closely. Single-handed Thatcher put Reagan's SDI on a more coherent basis, and once Gorbachev took power in Moscow she became a genuine intermediary between the superpowers. When Thatcher gave the green light for the American raid on Libya in 1986 – even knowing the reaction in Britain would be severe – she became a heroine in American public opinion. Thatcher was more of a domestic political asset for Reagan than the other way around. This was unprecedented.

These two leaders, so different in background and personality, so contrasting in political style and political appeal, were together righteous warriors, and they infinitely admired each other's efforts. And one reason they got on so well privately is that they almost always talked past each other. In Reagan and Thatcher, American Gothic met British Gothic.

*

As irony would have it, it was George Bush and John Major who actually fought a real war together. No two leaders in the relationship have ever been so suddenly thrown together in such dramatic circumstances. When Major arrived at Number 10, American and British forces were already deployed in the Gulf and the clock was ticking down to war.

On the surface Bush and Major were not an obvious mix either. The President came from a mainline New England family and had done all the right things to qualify as East Coast Establishment except he had moved to Texas. Stepping from one government job to another, Bush's political career was more British in its pattern, and, for once, America had produced a leader with more international experience than his British partner.

Major's career, by contrast, was more American in style. He came from modest origins and began his politics in local government. He possessed none of the usual credentials for Tory validation except a devotion to cricket. With no university education and an accent that one would never hear at White's, he was an up-by-the-bootstraps politician. 'Meteoric rise' is not a phrase often heard in British politics, but scarcely had Major entered the top ranks of the Cabinet than he became prime minister.

Underneath, however, the President and Prime Minister had a lot in common. Each had replaced formidable predecessors and had to suffer the comparisons. The foundation of their leadership in their respective parties was unsteady. Neither was ideological in outlook or fervent in manner, and neither had a gift for inspirational oratory. Instead, they were pragmatic and practical, and, in their easy-going, mild way, they were also good listeners (Bush had come to think of meetings with Mrs Thatcher the same way he thought of visits to the dentist).

The Gulf War was a stunning political success for Major and Bush and it sealed their friendship. Bush recalls his first private conversation with Major when they were driving in a car to Camp David in the Maryland mountains. Bush told the new Prime Minister everything that was on his worried mind and what he expected to happen in the weeks ahead. Major listened carefully and offered unreserved support. With his penchant for choosing not quite the right phrase, Bush told me a couple of years later, 'I love that guy.'

Bush and Major spoke frequently and frankly. They took an

active interest in each other's political fortunes, and I think it's probably true that Major felt more comfortable in Bush's company than he did in the company of most of his Cabinet colleagues.

If anything, the President and Prime Minister were too close. Bush assured Major in early 1992 that he would avoid anything that might complicate the Prime Minister's chances in the general election, and Major sent the same private message to Bush when the President was campaigning later in the year. This would have been fine if both had won. But only one did.

For twelve cosy years Republicans in Washington and Conservatives in London had grown accustomed to each other. In this era of good feeling and camaraderie, party officials naturally exchanged techniques and information, as if they were like-minded members of a transatlantic trade association. A few weeks before the American election in 1992, two functionaries from Conservative Central Office went to the United States to advise Bush's campaign managers on how to pull a rabbit from an electoral hat. They brought along charts and slogans and surveys, and they were too obvious and too smug in doing so.

At another point in the American campaign, it seemed the Home Office had riffled through its files with the thought of dishing the dirt on Candidate Clinton. On the eve of the American vote, Douglas Hurd momentarily set aside his diplomatic discretion and sent Jim Baker a good-hunting message. These clumsy little incidents planted the seed of transatlantic recrimination.

When he won office, President Clinton was an obscure politician from an obscure state. There was an audible sigh of relief in London that at least Clinton had spent time at Oxford as a Rhodes Scholar, and it even seemed for a moment that there would be more Oxford degrees in Clinton's Cabinet than in Major's. Surely this boded well for Anglo-American affairs.

But Clinton felt he owed little to the British and nothing to the Conservatives. Oxford had taught him mainly about British privilege and snootiness, and, as far as he was concerned, the Tory Party had done its best to prevent his election. His coterie of score-keeping advisers was even more embittered at Conservative interference. Equally important, the Cold War was over, and the transatlantic relationship had lost the sobering structure and rehearsed vocabulary which two generations of presidents had inherited with the job.

As was the custom, John Major went to Washington a few weeks after the President's inauguration. I preceded him by a couple of days in order to scout out the tricky political terrain. The visit itself was hard enough to fix in Clinton's schedule. The British press was almost ghoulish in its anticipation of rancour at high levels. Just before the Prime Minister arrived at the White House, Clinton was sitting with a few aides in the Oval Office. 'Don't forget to say "special relationship" when the press comes in,' one of them joked – a little like 'don't forget to put out the cat'. 'Oh, yes,' Clinton said. 'How could I forget? The "special relationship"!' And he threw his head back and laughed.

In the event, the encounter went well enough. The President recognized the University College tie which Major's Cabinet secretary, Robin Butler, was wearing, and when the press mob trundled in from the Rose Garden Clinton proclaimed his hallelujah faith in the 'special relationship'. The Prime Minister and President talked fluently about international economics, and on Bosnia and Northern Ireland each cut some slack for the other. But as the relationship ripened the strains became more obvious. Clinton was cavalier about British interests, especially in Northern Ireland, and at one point Major was ostentatiously unavailable to receive an emollient phone call from the Oval Office. Their personal relations stayed on a grin-and-bear-it basis. So, with Bush and then Clinton, John Major knew the best of times and the worst of times.

An aura of New Age camaraderie enveloped Bill Clinton and Tony Blair from the beginning – energy, eagerness, empathy, earnestness and a high-tide confidence in high-minded reform. In May 1997 the President made a detour from his European itinerary to come to London and welcome the new Prime Minister into the international fraternity of leadership. Outside Number 10, the pair could barely contain their mutual admiration. 'Clinton blazed the trail,' Blair enthused. 'We copy each other shamelessly,' gushed the President. The refraction of political light between New Democrat and New Labour was unmistakable, and was reminiscent of the Thatcher–Reagan fellowship. What goes around comes around.

The atmosphere at the top doesn't necessarily affect all the other working relationships in Anglo-American affairs. Eisenhower's Secretary of State, John Foster Dulles, with his Calvinist convictions, scared the wits out of most British he encountered in the new nuclear age. Henry Kissinger had a soft spot for the British, especially their appreciation of balance-of-power politics, but in office he never really developed a strong personal relationship with any of Her Majesty's foreign secretaries.

Alexander Haig called Peter Carrington a 'duplicitous bastard', which amused both of them. Cyrus Vance and David Owen happily tilted against innumerable windmills while in office, and continued to work closely together afterwards. George Shultz and Geoffrey Howe, both of whom were physically and intellectually bulky, seemed like two peas in a pod, and in Washington or London they always found time to talk about the metaphysics of monetarism. And Douglas Hurd and Jim Baker regarded each other as unsentimental equals, though their meetings often seemed like conversations between brain surgeons.

In the unglamorous trenches of the bureaucracy, personal relations are usually undisturbed as the politicians at the top come and go. One reason I liked my job so much was because of the many friends stationed at important junctions in the British civil service, some of whom I had known for years. I regularly stopped in at the Cabinet Office to see Robin Butler, and we almost always talked alone about problems between the two governments, signalling to each other the likely accident spots down the road. The succession of private secretaries at Number 10 – Charles Powell, Stephen Wall, Rod Lyne – were old friends, and so were the Prime Minister's foreign policy advisers, first Percy Cradock and then Rodric Braithwaite. Michael Quinlan's door at the Ministry of Defence was always open, and on military matters, Peter Inge, the chief of the defence staff, was always ready for a chinwag.

Perhaps most regularly I went to see David Gillmore, who was permanent under secretary at the Foreign Office. As often as not, he would pull a bottle of whisky from his desk drawer, and in the evening light of his gigantic office we would talk and sip and try to get to the bottom of things. And since 1974 I had worked closely with Robin Renwick, in one capital or another, and he went to Washington as British ambassador at almost the same time I came to London. As ambassadors to each other's governments, we plotted together to make things work, and sometimes to make them not work. I once proposed that Robin and I should switch jobs to see if anyone noticed.

Whether the personal relationship between a president and a prime minister matters much is anyone's guess. Looking at the record, it's hard to find too many examples of one leader, for the sake of personal rapport, deciding to do something which he or she might not otherwise have done. Nations rarely do each other favours, at least not favours that cost anything.

Nor does coming from different points on the political spectrum seem to make much difference to personal compatibility. On the other hand, the common domestic agenda which Thatcher and Reagan shared clearly reinforced their partnership, and the budding relationship between Blair and Clinton has obviously been enhanced by their new-generation look.

One wonders what things would have been like with Margaret Thatcher if Jimmy Carter had been re-elected. Or with Ronald Reagan if Michael Foot had won in 1983 or Neil Kinnock in 1987, though the likelihood of poor transatlantic relations is one of the reasons neither did.* And certainly things would have been smoother for John Major if George Bush had succeeded in 1992.

A good relationship at the top works at the margins of decision-making, not at the centre. For a president and prime minister, it means a willingness to talk to each other and to listen, an instinct to pick up the telephone for a quick word, a readiness to compare notes about one thing or another. It also means access at the critical moment. Often this has to do with timing – not whether to do something but when to do it. Good allies bend just that extra inch to take account of the other's interest. They are just that extra degree more aware of the consequences for the other, and this is more likely to happen when the relationship between the leaders is open and uncluttered. But good or bad chemistry between the respective leaders should never be confused with what the Anglo-American relationship is all about.

---

* When Kinnock and Denis Healey called on Reagan in 1986, the President was confused about which one was which. The meeting was a joke. A few years later Kinnock and Gerald Kaufman met with Bush's Vice President, Dan Quayle. 'What did you think?' Kinnock asked Kaufman after they had left the office. 'Well,' said Kaufman, 'I never really understood the meaning of the word "dickhead", but I think I do now.'

Rhythm and Blues

When I became ambassador I vowed I would never use the phrase 'special relationship'. In Anglo-American affairs this was close to diplomatic apostasy.

I didn't harbour any particular aversion to the term. But, like a brass plate on a church floor, the words seemed a little worn from years of hard rubbing. By the beginning of the 1990s, I also thought the formula was misleading, especially with the rapid unravelling of the Cold War. In Britain, however, 'special relationship' remained a kind of knee-jerk catch-phrase, almost like an advertising jingle, and it overlooked that the official partnership was a relatively recent state of affairs, and a pragmatic one.

Not everyone in Britain saluted the 'special relationship'. For some, it was only a subliminal alibi for avoiding all the nettlesome questions about Europe – a bromide should Europe ultimately prove indigestible. And the further right or left you moved on the political scale, the more certain people were that the 'special relationship' was merely a euphemism for roll-over British sub-servience. There was also a merry band of revisionists who said the 'special relationship' was a figment of the imagination and had never really been what it was cracked up to be. So devotion to the term was hardly universal.

For the broad middle of British opinion, however, the phrase still carried the reassuring resonance of wartime triumph and captured the spirit of an exceptional alliance between two countries which didn't take naturally to alliances. The 'special relationship' implied a steady rhythm of collaboration between the United States and the United Kingdom as well as a transatlantic code which promised that things would probably turn out all right on the night, and usually they did.

But the two countries had never been diplomatic doppelgangers, nor had the bilateral alliance acquired a life of its own apart from the specific conditions which had created it. And those circumstances were changing fast.

When I arrived in London, the partnership was already undergoing some stress. The success of the Gulf War disguised this, but the Gulf War was the last hurrah of the old regime. My first private meeting with John Major was to inform him that the United States had decided to cancel a missile programme to which the British military had already committed itself. This was a small harbinger which the Prime Minister didn't fail to appreciate.

The main reason for the gradual shift in relations was obvious. For fifty years or so, the Anglo-American relationship had taken its shape from a single, strategic fact. Concentrated in the centre of Europe stood a large military force controlled by a hostile, totalitarian regime – first Nazi and then Soviet – which wished neither of our countries much good. Confronting this threat was the political bedrock of the 'special relationship'. Cold War doctrine said that Chicago was on the front line just as much as Coventry, at least in theory, and that the security of Europe was indivisible from American security. As Roosevelt said to Churchill after Pearl Harbor, we were in the same boat. The 'special relationship' wasn't only about this but it was largely about this. And once the continental threat dissolved, things were bound to change.

The theme of 'common adversary' wasn't new to Anglo-American affairs, but until the Second World War it was unspoken. One reason the American colonies and the British metropole stayed together through the seventeenth century, and most of the eighteenth, was the shared perception of Catholic France as a threat – to England via Scotland and to America via Canada. Spanish domination in Latin America was viewed pretty much the same way, and Britain cheered the Yankees in the Spanish–American War. The military rise of Germany at the turn of the century produced the same effect, and America cheered the British in the Boer War and broke with its own past when it finally sent troops to Europe in the First World War. So there had always been a rough instinct of common cause or common interest, even when bilateral relations between Washington and London were not particularly affectionate. In fact from an American point of view, the principal foreign threat to the United States through most of its history was Britain.*

The celebrations at the end of the Cold War didn't last long. Yugoslavia suddenly appeared as the grisly ghost at the European banquet, and events in Bosnia made the new realities in transatlantic affairs more apparent. Americans at first thought the disintegration of Yugoslavia was a problem which the Europeans should handle themselves, and the Europeans, at the outset, also thought the Balkan haemorrhage was an opportunity to show they could now look after continental security on their own.†

In 1992 British and French army units (and others) started operating in Bosnia, trying against the odds to suppress the three-cornered killing in that atavistic land. The new Clinton administration floundered around the Bosnian blood-letting, on the one hand venting its outrage at the slaughter while on the other ducking any commitments that might help stop it. The Americans chastised the Europeans, including the British, for not doing more, and the Europeans criticized the Americans for not doing anything at all. Americans looked across the ocean and saw the shadows of appeasement, and Europeans looked across the ocean and saw the shades of isolationism. The policy gap was so deep you could sometimes smell a whiff of Suez.

In the spring of 1993, however, Warren Christopher, the Secretary of State, came to Europe to deliver a new American position on Bosnia. Christopher is an inscrutable, courteous man with all the

---

* In the 1920s the US Navy still kept up to date the 'Red Plan', which laid out how to sink the British fleet should events make that desirable and fortune make it possible.

† The British were much too sensible to believe this was so, but they nonetheless allowed the Germans to bamboozle them into recognizing Bosnia prematurely.

intelligent precision of a California lawyer but none of the flamboyance. His serious, careful, upright style stood out in the Clinton administration like an adult in a kindergarten, but Christopher always seemed smaller than the events around him.

The new plan in Christopher's briefcase was called 'lift and strike', meaning that we would lift the UN arms embargo against the Muslims so they could build up their forces on the ground and we would strike the Serbs from the air if they tried to do anything about it. But there would be no American troops. It was largely a plan designed to satisfy the cantankerous Congress, and it meant that America would step in to change the Bosnian situation without exposing itself directly to any of the consequences if things went wrong. It was a cockamamie idea.

The Secretary of State arrived in London on a weekend, and together we drove down to Douglas Hurd's official country residence in Chevening on a bright Sunday afternoon. In the car, Christopher showed me his talking points, which had been put together in final form just as his plane was landing at Heathrow. When I finished reading them, I said I thought the British reaction would probably range somewhere between shock and horror. There was no way Her Majesty's Government, with 2,000 troops strung out over Bosnia's muddy mountain passes, could possibly agree to a proposal whose only certain result was military chaos. Nor was it clear how this plan would contain the fighting instead of widening it. At a minimum, I said, we should be ready to explain what we would be prepared to do if the plan didn't work, which it wouldn't. Christopher looked out the window.

Chevening is a fine old Jacobean house with many brick chimney pots and brass rim locks. It sits at the end of a country lane, just past the parish church of the little village. The house once belonged to the Stanhope family (inevitably pronounced 'Stannup'), but was turned over to the Foreign Office as a retreat when the Stanhopes could no longer afford the upkeep. In the large entry hall, the walls are covered in forbidding armorial patterns of old shields and swords, but off to the side there is an airy, chintz-filled drawing room, and this is where Douglas Hurd steered us and Judy Hurd gave us drinks. The Defence Secretary, Malcolm Rifkind, arrived shortly afterwards, and the Prime Minister, fresh from a cricket match, came in a half hour later. For a weekend, this was a remarkable turn-out on the British side.

We all went upstairs to a panelled sitting room where we arranged ourselves on opposite sides of a table. The tabletop was covered with a green baize cloth, which the British like to do, and it felt as if we were sitting down in a casino, which I guess we were. There was a loud clattering of cups and saucers as tea was brought in. The British like to do this too, mainly to test your concentration.

Christopher pulled out his papers, tapped them carefully into order and started to lay out the American proposal. His words had all the verve of a solicitor going over a conveyance deed. I watched the faces of the three ministers opposite me, trying to catch the little flickers of disbelief as the plan unfolded. At one point Christopher said the Holocaust Museum had just been dedicated in Washington and this had naturally agitated congressional concern about genocide. The other side nodded sympathetically but seemed doubtful whether a museum opening was a sound basis for formulating foreign policy.

When the presentation was over, the British sat in silence. There was some clearing of throats and a few sideways glances. 'Well, ah, yes …' Major, Hurd and Rifkind each asked two or three what-if questions. There were long pauses. Christopher had no real answers.

After a couple of sterile hours, the meeting adjourned. We all went downstairs again, where we mingled in the drawing room before dinner. The atmosphere was downbeat and awkward. I suggested to the Prime Minister that he take Christopher aside and tell him straight that, leaving apart the wisdom of the American plan, he couldn't possibly deliver his sceptical Cabinet to such a risky proposal. It was, in the jargon, a non-starter. This the Prime Minister proceeded to do, guiding Christopher by the elbow to an alcove where they chatted privately for several minutes. We then ate a dinner of strained conviviality, following which the American delegation disappeared into the Sussex night.

For a while afterwards, I wondered whether Christopher had intentionally put up this plan as a kind of target for the British to shoot down and thus end an internecine debate at home. This was a time-honoured, bureaucratic gambit in Washington – bring the British into an internal squabble provided they tip the balance in your favour. It was one of the minor themes of the 'special relationship' which both sides played willingly. But I abandoned this line of speculation when I later received a middle-of-the-night call from the Secretary's aircraft asking whether I thought the British would veto a lift-and-strike resolution in the UN. The administration apparently intended to go ahead even without European support. My revised speculation was that there was a screw loose somewhere in downtown Washington.

I also wondered whether President Clinton was trying to work himself into a comfortable political position on a tricky policy issue. He could now tell the Congress that he had proposed a bold plan to salvage Bosnia but the Allies wouldn't let him do it. And this, in fact, is what the President subsequently did, at one point publicly divulging Major's private conversation with Christopher about the British Cabinet. This might have been good domestic politics but it was lousy foreign policy.

The Christopher visit in itself was not significant. Eventually, the administration managed to cajole the different Bosnian parties into a jerry-rigged peace, though this was due as much to changes in the military situation as to any diplomatic strong-arming, and Bosnia may yet prove a tar baby. But the visit did show one thing. At a time of almost manic killing on European territory, the British and Americans seemed unable to find common ground. During the Cold War, this might not have been unusual in other parts of the globe. But in Europe, with the British leaning forward and the Americans hanging back, it was a first. Whatever the relationship had been before, it wasn't going to be the same again.

Beneath the surface sore of Bosnia there were much deeper things at work which were also infecting the health of the post-Cold War 'special relationship'. Americans barely noticed these trends, but when I was at the embassy the British asked about them all the time. These apprehensions were often exaggerated, I thought, but they were real, and there was enough truth in each to give everyone something to worry about.

The first anxiety concerned the word that every British school child seems to learn about America: isolationism. After all, at the end of the First World War, American troops were out of their trenches and into their boats before the armistice ink was dry. The same thing happened at the end of the second war, and by 1947 an American army of millions in Europe had dwindled to a couple of divisions. When it became obvious that the Soviets didn't suffer from the same withdrawal symptoms, however, this was quickly reversed. The third war – the cold one – set in, and Americans came back for the third time.*

When you think about it, this is an extraordinary tale. There are about 6,000 miles from the middle of America to the middle of Europe, and for most of our history American presidents warned the nation against 'entangling alliances' with corrupting Europeans. European countries, particularly the British, were accustomed to sending expeditionary armies to faraway places – in fact they seemed to relish doing so – but this was usually to control an established colony or to tip a political balance. Unlike the British, however, Americans have always thought that military forces were for military purposes, not political ones, and this has caused myriad headaches in the past.

Moreover, the United States, as a nation of immigrants, mostly thought of Europe, with its pompous monarchies and petty wars, as a place to get away from. The further the better. This was not an unreasonable attitude, and America enjoyed the geography to make it possible. For the United States any overseas commitment was a radical departure from our national past and our natural disposition, and if no obvious reason exists for being over there, it's the last place we want to be. So the British wondered whether America at the end of the Cold War would once again revert to type, packing up its gear and heading home.

This is a trick question, and the answer is maybe, but not yet. Over the two generations of the Cold War, under Republican and Democratic administrations alike, there was a consensus in the United States that a substantial American presence in Europe anchored the transatlantic peace. There was also an appreciation that, without an American presence, there was no such thing as European security. Paradoxically, the same kind of consensus was harder to find in Europe. Even in Britain the Labour Party was hardly an ardent advocate of NATO doctrine. In fact, it was not

* From the end of the 1940s to the beginning of the 1990s, there were always at least a quarter-million American troops in Europe. I once calculated that, over the course of the East–West stand-off, more than twelve million Americans had rotated through Europe on military duty.

too difficult to argue that during the Cold War the isolationist shoe was on the other foot, with Europe retreating into a regional shell and seldom taking responsibility beyond its immediate horizons, and America up to its neck in global events where everything seemed connected to everything else.

Without a great moral struggle, however, America's course is now more difficult to chart. With each new election, the composition of the Congress churns over, and experienced senior legislators fall by the wayside. The meagre budget for foreign affairs is cut, and then cut again, and politicians on the left and right are always on the lookout for foreign scapegoats. The American media today seems involved in a conspiracy to keep the nation ignorant. It's not a picture to inspire long-term confidence.

On the other hand, America does remain engaged in Europe more than six years after the Cold War's end – a little half-heartedly, perhaps, but engaged nonetheless. By contrast, it is the Europeans who have become even more self-absorbed in their internal debates and who have rapidly reduced the size of their armed forces. In fact, if there is a measurable danger to the traditional content of the 'special relationship', it is the British miniaturization of its own military forces.* Britain could not do now what it did in the Gulf, let alone in the Falklands.

There are plenty of isolationist instincts in the backwoods of American politics. But there also remains, I think, a vague national judgment that the luxury of our distant geography will never again provide for our national safety. And it is equally obvious that America's economic prosperity depends on overseas markets in a way that has never been the case before. Pure isolationism is no longer a serious option. The real risk is that the United States, distracted or petulant, might simply stop paying attention to what happens abroad. This is different from isolationism, but the effect can be near the same. The first Clinton administration almost turned foreign policy into a vaudeville act, and, in the end, the answer to the isolationist question will depend on the quality of American political leadership.

*

* The American defence budget today is also running down, but it remains larger than the budgets of all the NATO Allies combined; and the number of American forces still overseas is larger than the entire British military.

The second British worry I regularly ran across was directly related to the first. This said that America would find it easier to go home if Europe were better organized to handle its own affairs. Many British thought the United States was such an enthusiastic supporter of European integration that it might be prepared to sacrifice the 'special relationship', if that was the price of a more cohesive Europe.

It is true that the United States has always encouraged greater European integration, especially when this seemed unlikely to happen. Washington never tried to prescribe any particular formula or schedule for European unity, but the general support has been more than lip-service. The Marshall Plan, for example, aimed to encourage greater integration in a reconstructed Europe, and NATO, though conceived as a bulwark against an external enemy, was equally intended to suffocate the old nationalist rivalries of Europe's past. Other American enthusiasms were less successful: the European Defence Community in the 1950s, which the French torpedoed; the Multi-Lateral Force in the 1960s, which was too ridiculous to work; and Henry Kissinger's Year of Europe in the 1970s, which established a new gravity record for lead balloons.

It is logical for Americans to think that the Continent would be better off together than divided. This is manifestly true on defence issues, and the NATO military command remains one of the best examples of tying together European sovereignties. A single European market is more attractive to American business than an economic patchwork, and one reason for the enormous American investment in Britain is access to the broader European marketplace. And to Americans, naturally, the F-word ('federal') is not offensive, even if its meaning in Europe is different and its prospects virtually nil.

Practical experience with the European Union, however, tends to temper American eagerness for more unity. Brussels is a cumbersome decision-maker, and when it finally arrives at a position, it is often determined by the lowest common denominator among its bickering members (in fairness, American decision-making is hardly a thing of beauty). The United States has always worried that a wholly European defence system, if it ever came to pass, would operate with all the streamline efficiency of the Common Agricultural Policy. And on trade issues, too, the image of Fortress Europe is never far from the American mind, even though America is usually the one accused of protectionism. On monetary union, the United States is largely agnostic, provided it works and provided other economies are not penalized. And America has always recognized that the more united Europe is the less influential Washington will be. As a practical matter, therefore, the United States doesn't always mean what it says.

But, as a matter of principle, we continue to support European integration, more as a process than a goal, and more as a desirable alternative to Europe's ruinous past. And we have equally encouraged the British to be a part of it, largely in the expectation that Europe would be less likely to do foolish things with Britain in than with Britain out.

The British often seemed to think that American support for the concept of European unity inevitably meant Germany would displace Britain as the object of Washington's affections. The fallacy in this thinking is the British tendency to view the 'special relationship' as functioning independently from the broader complex of issues in Europe as a whole. This is an illusion. The truth is that the United States has never looked at Britain as something separate from the continent. While Britain may have dealt with America as a more or less coherent whole, America has dealt with Britain as a piece of a larger European puzzle. For decades, America's transatlantic policy has been European in scope – one continent to another – not a series of compartmentalized, bilateral policies.

And so the substance of the 'special relationship' – in security or economics – has revolved around the role which Britain has played in Europe, not away from it, and while Britain's membership in the European Union has been indisputably complicating to the Anglo-American relationship, it has also been indispensable to it. I always had a hard time getting this across.

There were two other chestnuts I often heard about the future of transatlantic relations. First, the British seemed to worry a lot about America's demography. After all, the theory ran, by the middle of the next century barely half America's population would be non-Hispanic white. The Anglo-Saxon axis of the past was eroding, and a mongrelized America couldn't possibly keep up the same affinity for the old motherland.

This situation is hardly new. America's ethnic furniture is always in the midst of rearrangement. And in any democratic nation, foreign policy is naturally constrained by its domestic constituencies. In America's case, policy-making in Washington has habitually resembled a noisy bazaar of competing lobbies and interest groups, many of which are ethnic in character.

The Irish-American community is only one hyphenated example. Middle East policy is impossible without consulting the Jewish-American lobby. In my Washington years, I was regularly surprised to discover the political clout of Armenian-Americans when it came to relations with Turkey, or Greek-Americans when thrashing about for a policy on Cyprus or Macedonia. America's black population means that no American administration can be indifferent to events in Africa. The Cuban community tilts Cuba policy, and America's cautious reaction to the Falklands crisis was mindful of America's large Latin population.

But the logic of this concern should not be a simple numbers game. In the heyday of the 'special relationship', for example, only about one in eight Americans could trace their roots to British ancestry. This didn't seem to make much difference. And in the nineteenth century, when America's political establishment was almost wholly composed of British stock, the country enjoyed its longest period of alienation from Britain.

So strict demographic analysis doesn't really hold up. It too easily discounts the metamorphosis of Americanization. It also overlooks that a nation's foreign policy, in the first instance, is based more on its foreign interests than its genetics, however appealing the theory may be. Nonetheless, I would agree that the intensity of the Anglo-American relationship is bound to diminish as America's ethnic kaleidoscope continues to change. And I worry about America's social fragmentation. But the effect is likely to be less automatic than British arithmetic anticipates.

The other chestnut about the 'special relationship' postulated that America's interests in the Pacific were outstripping America's interests in the Atlantic, and this too would stifle the Anglo-American connection. Maybe. But I was always a little startled by what seemed to be the sudden British discovery of the Pacific Ocean when the Pacific Ocean has been there all along, and so has America's attraction to it.

From the beginning the American population has moved westwards, seeping over the eastern mountain chains into the endless land beyond. 'Westward Ho!' has long been an American rallying cry (and, inexplicably, a small town in England too), and Horace Greeley advised, 'Go west, young man.' In 1912, the business magnate Henry Huntington proclaimed the Atlantic the ocean of the past and the Pacific the ocean of the future. America's two most recent states, Hawaii and Alaska, are set deep in the Pacific, and, unlike most European countries, America borders Russia, but from the other side – a map always looks different depending on where you're standing when you look at it.

Even in the era of High Isolation, the United States was much absorbed by the Pacific – in China and Japan and the Philippines. America entered the Second World War through the Pacific door, not the Atlantic door, and both our major wars since then have been fought on the Asian mainland. So, for Americans, nothing about the Pacific is very new.

It may be true today that greater economic opportunity for the United States is shifting to the Pacific (it is for Britain too). Just as armies follow the sound of the guns, economies follow the sound of the cash register. It is probably also true that there is now a greater danger of strategic instability in Asia than in Europe, and this attracts American attention as well (which the British should applaud). That said, however, it doesn't necessarily follow that American foreign policy will be a simplistic zero-sum game, with commitments in the Atlantic declining in a predictable ratio as commitments in the Pacific increase. Just as Britain's interests in Europe and America are complementary, so are America's interests in the Pacific and Atlantic.

One evening during the Queen's visit to the United States in 1991, President Bush took her on to the second-floor balcony of the White House, from which you can look across the Mall to the Tidal Basin and the Jefferson Memorial. Painters were recoating the outside of the White House at the time, and layer upon layer of old paint had been peeled away. Leaning over the railing, the President pointed out a thick, bare pilaster where you could see the scorch marks from 1814 when British troops torched the place. The next day the Queen dined in the rotunda of the Capitol, where the same troops had piled all the congressional furniture in the middle and set it ablaze.* If you take a long view, the official relationship has made a lot of progress since then.

But, even in the Cold War, the Anglo-American relationship was never as seamless as both sides usually wished it to appear. On one issue or another, the Americans often suspected the British of trying to fix the game. The British, for their part, often thought Washington handled its power clumsily. The Americans sometimes believed it was more effective to deal directly with the Soviets, going over the heads of their British allies. The British sometimes feared the American cowboy instinct might one day drag them into an unnecessary confrontation with Moscow. The British often complained that the Americans did not consult but only informed, and the Americans complained that consultations only gave the British an opportunity to object. So it was never smooth sailing. But on the whole, when everything is added up, the Anglo-American contraption worked pretty well.

And in many ways it still does, even without the old, hard-edged strategic focus. At the embassy, I saw this almost daily. The collaboration between London and Washington does put the relationship in a league by itself. For almost any diplomatic initiative in Europe, London is customarily the first port of call, and it's a rare British initiative that isn't first aired in Washington. The integration of operations and personnel between the respective military services is legendary. We exchange sensitive intelligence with each other by the bucketful.†

American codebreakers serve at the British electronic head-quarters in Cheltenham and British eavesdroppers work at American headquarters in Maryland. The FBI, the Drug Enforcement Agency and US Customs – comparatively recent arrivals in Grosvenor Square – also trade secrets with their British counterparts and plan joint operations against assorted terrorists, smugglers, money launderers and international crooks. So there remains a lot about the day-to-day relationship which is unique. Even the alphabet helps: at international meetings the delegations from the United

---

* Thomas Jefferson briefly entertained a plot to burn down St James's Palace in retaliation.

† So far as I could tell, both sides stuck to the agreement never to spy on each other.

Kingdom and the United States are seated side by side, unless the French are writing the place cards.

To declare a relationship 'special', however, does not make it so. Nor are relations between states often advanced by sentimentality. Nations pursue their interests, and important interests tend to remain stable. This is how nations behave.

What is remarkable about Anglo-American affairs is the degree to which our respective national interests have historically coincided. And it is this phenomenon of natural history which is the fundamental ingredient in the relationship. One reason is the obvious impact of geography, and another is a common language which enables us to communicate with a facility not available in the relations of other major powers – we can talk to each other in nuance.

Perhaps most important, America and Britain share an accumulation of historical concepts given body over generations – human and civil rights, liberty, the common law and the rule of law, tolerance and equity, the manners of property, the basic freedoms. We may practise these imperfectly, but all of them mixed up together mean that we think about things in a similar fashion, and on one issue or another we are as likely as not to arrive at pretty much the same conclusion.

This is not always true but it is often true, and the relationship emerges from the repetition of this pattern. I suspect our international priorities won't match with quite the same frequency as they once did, and the overlap of our strategic interests may not be quite so extensive as before. But, anyway, the important, durable part of the relationship flourishes outside the official government-to-government framework, and it is here where it is most 'special', as it always has been.

One thing is sure: neither nation could possibly replicate this relationship with any other country.

Warts and All

You can't judge a book by its cover, my grandmother used to say. But P. D. James can. Or at least she says she can tell a British book from an American one. When her latest crime novel goes to print, there will be one dustjacket for the British edition and another for the American. The British, it seems, lean to softer pigments and more representational designs. Americans, on the other hand, respond to bolder colours and more abstract covers. America and Britain are different countries.

The military historian John Keegan recalls his first encounter with Americans. He was a boy in Dorset, and in 1943 the county was flooded with GIs. The soldiers were boisterous and cocky, and Keegan says that when he first saw their swaggering, confident ways, he thought Americans were exaggerated versions of the British, though he never again doubted who was going to win the war. It was not until he was older, and had begun his many visits to the hallowed battlefields and military institutions of the United States, that it dawned on him that America was not a derivative of Britain but another country altogether.

So the elemental lesson about the United Kingdom and the United States is that they are different places. This is not always easy to appreciate. The differences are more real than apparent. But we each walk in our own way, talk in our own way and even eat in our own way. Americans, for example, are corn-fed: corn bread, corn muffins, corn dogs, pop corn, corn grits, corn pone, corn oil, corn whiskey, cornflakes and corn-on-the-cob. The British, on the other hand, consume more sugar per capita than any nation on earth, and the country is a large trolley of cakes, jams, marmalades, tarts, biscuits, confections, sticky buns and all manner of sweet, treacly things. Americans grow their own corn whereas the British have to import their sugar, and therein lies much history.

But if America and Britain are different, they aren't quite foreign. George Bernard Shaw's well-worn epigram that 'England and America are two countries divided by a common language' misses the point. I wish I had a nickel for every time I've heard this quotation. One of the hardest parts of my job was looking dutifully delighted whenever someone served it up again (variously attributed to Oscar Wilde, Will Rogers, Mark Twain or Winston Churchill). Shaw was a clever writer but also wrong. We are least separated by a common language.

Usage, of course, is sometimes different. Many words in our common vocabulary mean the same thing but end up in different positions. In America, for example, you mail a letter through the post and in Britain you post a letter through the mail. But there's nothing puzzling about what is meant. There are also plenty of words whose shade of meaning varies by a degree or two. I have a British friend who once boarded a flight in Dallas and was momentarily alarmed when the pilot announced the plane would be taking off momentarily. And a Briton in America learns pretty quickly never to say how much he enjoys fags, while an American in Britain learns never to ask if anyone wants to shag.

Caroline and I have both assimilated into our vocabularies such useful Britishisms as 'chuffed', 'plonk', 'bumpf' and 'bonk', though we have to edit these when we're at home. And we're always juggling 'crisps' and 'chips' depending on where we eat them.

American slang and colloquialisms seem to penetrate British society with remarkable ease, and some modern American words are supplanting their British counterparts. The dominance of 'radio' over 'wireless' or 'ketchup' over 'tomato sauce' or 'dieting' over 'slimming' are examples. This horrifies many British, who see the defence of their own distinctive versions as the linguistic equivalent of Rorke's Drift. The British are equally alarmed by 'gotten' and any number of nouns which Americans convert to verbs, and they frequently take pot-shots at American expressions such as 'Have a nice day' or 'downsizing' before going on to adopt them.

Pronunciation and accent are more obvious differences, though there seems to be as much variation within each country as between them. I recall taking my first trip on British Rail and wondering what a 'buffy car' was. One of the sharpest instruments of social triage in Britain is the pronunciation of 'herb', but most mannerly Americans have been brought up on an unaspirated *h*. And to hear a cultivated Englishman say he 'et' his food startles an American who just ain't used to it.

Americans in Britain also notice an uncommon amount of subtle stammering and lisping ('The ... the ... the pwime minister wetunned fwom Bwussels'), which is usually explained as an affected upper-class imitation of a long-dead and linguistically challenged monarch. The English glottal stop is as hard for Americans to understand as American street-talk is for the British, and down-home vernacular is also difficult for an outsider to follow – a dialogue from *Huckleberry Finn*, for example, or a poem by Robbie Burns. And there have been occasions in Liverpool and Glasgow when I wished I had had an interpreter by my side, while British friends have found parts of the American South as linguistically impenetrable as Uzbekistan.

There is some truth, I think, in the broader observation that the British tend to understate things and the Americans to overstate them, and that Americans in speaking are usually more explicit than the British, though not always so in writing. I remember my first encounter with British understatement shortly after I came to live here in the 1970s. There was a rowdy demonstration at Stirling University when Prince Charles visited there one autumn day, and several people were hurt in the ruckus. On the television news that evening, the screen showed a picture of two plain-clothes cops kicking a long-haired student who had fallen to the ground. The news reader, using his most serious good-citizen voice, said, 'A man is helping police with their enquiries.'

America, on the other hand, is such a voluminous, boisterous country that you have to exaggerate things just to get your point across. Part of my job as ambassador was to make sure both sides understood that the British usually meant more than what they said and the Americans less. But the real point is that the English language, in all its rich variety, makes the two countries uncommonly accessible to each other.

I think George Bernard Shaw would have been more accurate and less amusing if he had said, 'England and America are two countries divided by a common idea.' This seems to be true in everything from government to sports. Sometimes the differences are imperceptible and sometimes they are substantial. We usually go about our common problems in our own distinctive ways, and both countries come up with different answers to similar questions.

History explains much of this, though even our appreciation of history is different. The British are much more aware of history and enthralled by it. Their history is Grade I listed and nothing is ever thrown away. America, by contrast, is the ultimate disposable society and often seems so unanchored by history that it is skittish and easily blown off course. American history promotes the idea of solving problems while British history suggests problems are to be managed. Americans are therefore given to reinventing the wheel whereas the British believe they invented the wheel in the first place.

Looking backwards, it's not easy to pinpoint when British colonists in America evolved into American colonials. It was a gradual metamorphosis and the political union of the United States only came at the end of a long Americanizing process. This broad, slow emergence of nationhood is different from the British experience, where Britishness was largely an imperial phenomenon and followed the political union of the United Kingdom rather than preceding it. Massive immigration to the United States has also made nationhood a continuing, unfinished process, like kneading yeast into dough, whereas the British have historically resisted immigration (but both countries are remarkably tolerant – America more by law and Britain more by disposition).

The modern histories of the two countries are hopelessly entwined with each other. The threads are separable but not quite separate, and this is why the relationship isn't ordinary. For example, you can look at the English Civil War in the seventeenth century, the War of Independence in the eighteenth century and the American

Civil War in the nineteenth century as an Anglo-Saxon continuum of domestic strife and constitutional development. On both sides of the Atlantic, there has been a steady progression of events which have defined rights, liberties, democracy and the rule of law. A sage friend of mine once commented that 1688 and 1776 were the only successful revolutions in history, and the American conflict between North and South might have been just the Roundheads and Cavaliers having another go at each other.

You can also argue that some of the old tensions in Britain's tightly structured society were played out in America's wide open spaces. What might have happened in Britain did happen in America. Puritanism, non-conformity and Cromwell's republican Commonwealth seem to have blossomed in America after they were smothered in their homeland. Or social divisions in Britain, once transferred to America, broke down and recomposed themselves in a different way.

The result of all this political chemistry is an amalgam of the familiar and the bewildering, depending on your point of view. In America there is much more emphasis on individual rights in a transparent, mobile, pluralist, anything-goes society. In Britain there is a deeper sense of communal rights and paternalist responsibilities in an opaque, subdued, unitary, not-so-fast society. The British, I think, are disturbed by the noisy, roiling, aggressive, contradictory polity of America, and Americans, for their part, find British politics too reliant on government, too arbitrary, too exclusionary, too status-conscious and too secretive.

For all the historic and temperamental contrasts, however, one characteristic of the relationship has remained steady over the years. This is our natural inclination to experiment and to explore. In fact, the calibre and variety of intellectual interplay between the two countries is probably the most important feature of Anglo-American affairs, and it has been going on since the beginning. Some of this exchange takes place in the corridors and conference rooms of government – economic analysis, for example, or geo-strategy – but most of the lively trading of ideas goes on outside the official framework and it is this which is genuinely special about the relationship.

The United States itself was an Anglo-American intellectual

creation, as much a product of Locke and Hobbes as it was of Jefferson and Monroe. As political philosophers, Burke and Madison were Tweedledee and Tweedledum. Tom Paine, though a little eccentric in that fidgeting British way, provided the manifesto for the American Revolution, despite arriving in Philadelphia only a year or so before the outbreak of fighting.

Through the nineteenth century, American experiments with democracy were so influential that it sometimes seemed the dis-enfranchised in Britain had adopted American political ideals as their own. I was surprised to discover that Ulysses S. Grant – hardly the most vividly liberal of American presidents – was given a liberator's welcome when he visited Newcastle in 1877 after his retirement. For Britain's traditional elite, there was always something vaguely seditious or reckless about the political goings-on in America. But, for most British, American democracy has been chaotically exciting.

For better or worse, the electric impulses back and forth across the ocean still stimulate our politics, though the traffic is more of a one-way flow from America than it used to be. The American civil rights movement in the 1960s inspired events in Northern Ireland, and I remember the same sort of liberationist atmosphere when, with jaw slightly dropped, I watched Neil Kinnock and the Labour Party leadership lock arms on a Brighton stage and sing 'We Shall Overcome'. On the other hand, the British thought of state pensions and social security long before the Americans, and John Maynard Keynes stood behind much of America's post-war boom. Monetarism is an example of joint intellectual development from the 1980s and 'reinventing government' is an example today. Political parties on both sides of the Atlantic regularly trade ideas and techniques with a candour you don't find in the partisan dialogue between other countries. Political themes are frequently the same in both nations and so are political moods, and these can be traced in election after election.

But the cross-fertilization is much more than political. Virtually every point on the cultural spectrum has been affected. Abolitionists in the first part of the nineteenth century and trade unionists in the latter part carried on a long transatlantic dialogue of mutual encouragement. So did suffragettes and evangelicals, each side working with the other. Muckraking was common to both sides of the Atlantic at the turn of the century, and so was the doctrine of Anglo-Saxon invincibility.

Feminism and environmentalism are contemporary examples of cross-fertilization. The respective movements are essentially seamless, though their expressions and successes vary in each country. Almost every reformist organization in Britain today has its counterpart in America, and vice versa. The argument about health care in the United States regularly draws lessons from the British system. Relatively trivial debates, such as the pros and cons of Sunday trading (for the British) or the pluses and minuses of school uniforms (for the Americans) have each been informed by the experience of the other, one side peering over the fence to see what the other was up to. Even the much maligned political correctness, whose most egregious manifestations deserve all the ridicule they get, nonetheless has a serious underlying purpose applicable in different ways in both countries.

Academic theories have always flown back and forth across the ocean, and so have the scholars who espouse them. The traffic covers everything from archaeology to zoology. Financial markets in both countries look to each other for ideas, and business alliances abound. Both countries learn from each other on penal reform, tax reform, welfare reform and innumerable experiments in education. There has been a bubbling transatlantic intercourse on all these subjects for decades. The press and the media feed off each other. Medicine, research and technology are unencumbered by nationality, and it's hard to think where the Nobel Prizes would be without the Anglo-American community of doctors and scientists. Someday someone will write the story of 'The English Look' as contrived by the American designers Nancy Lancaster and Sister Parish and then fed back to British and American consumers alike, and Ralph Lauren has proven how well ersatz Englishness still sells.

The story of the Anglo-American relationship is replete with anecdotes of collaboration. Most Americans wouldn't know that the Smithsonian Institution was a gift of one Englishman and the Boy Scouts the inspiration of another, or that Burger King is owned by a British company. One of today's foremost scholars on the American Civil War is a Brit. Most British wouldn't think that two Americans wrote 'The White Cliffs of Dover' or that Jaguar is owned by an American company. A mystery writer who entitles her books after British pubs is an American. Among our friends we count a British curator of an American museum and an American Vice Chancellor of a British university. And the double-helix puzzle of DNA would probably have remained unsolved were it not for the partnership of a British scientist and an American scientist.

Some of this enriching, non-stop interchange can be measured, and while the figures aren't too important, the dimensions are. Trade and investment are obvious examples, and these are interesting because they are together so much greater between America and Britain than they are between any other combination, even when other economic partners are nearer to hand. Capital is drawn in both directions because it is treated in much the same way in both places and because it is seen to be safer there than almost anywhere else.

On any given day, there are several thousand students studying in each other's institutions, and it is no more unusual to come across an American in a British newsroom than it is to discover a Brit behind an American editorial desk. In the course of a year, there are now between six and seven million visits to each other's shores, and the purposes are as varied as the destinations. Most of the travel is by air, and in 1996 there were about 41,000 flights between the two countries, and the number keeps rising. At one point in my time here, about a quarter of the plays on Broadway had first opened in the West End and a quarter in the West End had first opened on Broadway. Music and movies are exceptionally well-travelled two-way streets. Some of the best and wittiest shows on British television are American, and British productions have an avid middle-size audience in America.

My preferred measurement of Anglo-American relations is telecommunications. The first transatlantic cable was laid in 1858, a remarkable technological and maritime feat which occasioned exuberant celebrations in both countries. Queen Victoria sent an inaugural message to President Buchanan which consisted of ninety-nine words and took more than an hour to transmit. The Queen, with commendable royal restraint, declared she was certain the President would 'join her in fervently hoping that the electric cable ... will prove an additional link between the two nations, whose friendship is founded upon their common interest and reciprocal esteem'. The drafter of this prose, I believe, is still working at Buckingham Palace today.

The President responded with customary American fulsomeness. 'May the Atlantic Telegraph, under the blessing of Heaven, prove to be a bond of perpetual peace and friendship between the kindred nations, and an instrument destined by Divine Providence to diffuse religion, civilization, liberty and law throughout the world.' Buchanan's 143-word signal took two hours in transmission.

Things grew from there. In 1996 there were more than one-and-a-half billion minutes of telephone conversation between the United States and the United Kingdom, or, put another way, roughly three millennia of talk in one year.

In the end, both societies in their own way are liberal, progressive, inventive and reformist, bursting with creativity and always on the lookout for a better way of doing something. These things often explode in America because Americans are more impetuous and daring, while they emerge in Britain because the British are more cautious and exacting. The Americans lurch; the British sidle. But the United States and the United Kingdom influence each other's intellectual development like no other two countries.

One thing is certain about all this. Neither country has needed much convincing about its elevated exceptionalism, though in recent years each has stumbled over its own limits. But both remain pretty sure they enjoy a special benediction which others don't, and this is one reason why we are so self-flagellating about our own frequent failures. Insularity, the Protestant ethic, commercial success, military prowess have all contributed to this self-regard. The Americans proclaim, 'We're Number One.' The British just think it. But both enjoy an inner sensation of destiny and the expectation that, if anyone comes close to regaining paradise, it's likely to be a Brit or an American. Deep down, Britain remains a sceptred isle of sunlit uplands and America remains a city on a hill.

None of this is to say that things have ever been easy between the two countries. In fact, the similarities tend to exacerbate the differences. Certainly one American movement that failed in Britain was prohibition – unthinkable in this spirited country, though it didn't last long in America either. But Americans, for example, can't figure out why the British have so many cathedrals and churches and so few people in them, and the British can't quite understand why American devotion brings half the population to religious services every week in a country so notoriously violent. American moralizing, whether in a revivalist tent or a presidential proclamation, sounds sanctimonious to the British and makes them feel queasy, and the thought of perfidious Albion still finds a place in the musings of some Americans.

Even the humours sometimes don't seem to click. The British gift for parody and satire are hard to translate and so is the American proclivity for tall tales. Americans often find British humour strangely scatological, while the British find American humour juvenile on the subject of sex. Socio-psychologists explain all this with multiple theories about America as a matriarchal society and Britain as a patriarchal one, and there are plenty of Freudians around to talk about oedipal complexes and anatomical envy. There's no end to the analysis, which itself is worth a laugh.

Despite the reams of commentary on Anglo-American relations, ignorance still has a lot to answer for. Neither country knows as much about the other as it pretends to. American studies only started at British universities in the 1960s, and British studies in America these days no longer enjoy primacy. Both countries have always found it difficult to overcome the well-established stereotypes about each other, though whether this comes from too little knowledge or too much is debatable. In any case, our mutual stereotypes portray the British as jaded and the Americans as jejune. America is boastful and Britain is arrogant. Britain is untrustworthy and America unreliable. America is philistine and Britain phoney. The British are whingeing and the Americans mawkish.

Some British like to regard America as a vulgar upstart whose contributions to civilization are little more than technological, a gadgety nation of little distinctive cultural value. And some Americans like to portray Britain as priggish and effete, a tuckered-out nation with no moral centre. Pundits in both countries have always enjoyed standing in front of their glass houses and throwing stones at each other. Sidney Smith and H. L. Mencken were masters of transatlantic insult, and their kind of *bon mot* guerrilla warfare has been going on for as long as the two countries have been around.

Harold Nicolson said simply that an American is 'not the sort of person we like', a sentiment echoing Samuel Johnson's earlier observation that 'I am willing to love all mankind, except an American.' James Russell Lowell, for his part, commented that

England 'has a conviction that whatever good there is in us is wholly English, when the truth is that we are worth nothing except so far as we have disinfected ourselves of Anglicism'. G. K. Chesterton once wrote, 'There is nothing the matter with Americans except their ideals. The real American is all right; it is the ideal American who is all wrong.' And the American drama critic John Mason Brown, responding to a particularly tactless toast proposed by his English host, replied, 'Mr Chairman, you have observed that while you don't care for Americans in the mass, individual Americans are delightful people. With the British, I find the reverse is true.'* Even when the British have meant to be generous, they can have a hard time managing it. The Earl of Buchan, writing in 1788, said, 'The Americans may lose in the inland parts of the country the habits of Europe ... in which case, six or seven centuries would go far to making them an interesting people.'

And so it goes. Auberon Waugh's *faux* curmudgeonliness continues the tradition today, just as the American writer Ivan Fallon finds it hard to pass up a transatlantic dig whenever the opportunity presents itself. Both seem to do it more for sport than any other purpose.

For most British and most Americans, none of this matters very much, except it's funny. As ambassador I never encountered any real hostility to Americans, at least nothing serious. On one occasion a man came up to me in a crowd, grabbed my hand, smiled and said, 'I don't like Americans,' and disappeared again. I liked him instantly.

If there is a problem these days, it probably lies in the sheer overwhelmingness of America. Americans believe that anything worth doing is worth overdoing, and this willingness to exceed the boundaries is often disconcerting to the more staid and stable mentality of the British. In the United States you can find the extreme of anything, good or bad. In its kinetic, razzmatazz way, America seems always to be spinning off fashions, fads, fast-foods and new-fangled ideas which wash along the Gulf Stream and

---

* Tom Wolfe's essay on 'Mid-Atlantic Man' fired in both directions at once, striking out at Americans who emulate the louche, mannered ways of the English and at the English who feign the loose, snappy ways of the Americans.

pound against the foundations of Albion. The British feel a little helpless before the pandemonium of America's material and cultural barrage, and this is hard because it's only recently that the British have seen their own power to intimidate diminish.

The British seem to think that America is full of communicable social diseases – violence, divorce, crime, drugs, obesity, discourtesy, illiteracy and so forth, and they are very vigilant about these things. I remember when a British professor told me disapprovingly that the American grey squirrel had almost entirely displaced the native red squirrel, and he made me feel guilty. And when you hear the phrase 'American-style', you can be pretty sure that what follows is unlikely to be flattering, as in 'American-style politics' or 'American-style schools'. In 1993 the BBC issued a censorious 'stylebook' admonishing news readers, among other linguistic infractions, not to use Americanisms, or at least not without a condom. And I once heard a woman interviewed on radio, who, when asked for her opinion on the subject at hand, said perfectly straight that there were two ways to deal with the issue: the civilized way or the American way. I took a shine to her too.

America and Britain are different places. But on the whole we get along, despite whatever our governments happen to be up to at the time. While I may be careful about the term 'special relationship' when I think about official relations, I find the term doesn't begin to capture the breadth and depth of what otherwise goes on between us.

In the Foreign Office, there is an old story – apocryphal, no doubt – about a young man who was taking his examination to enter Her Majesty's foreign service. This happened before the Second World War. Sitting in front of his stern examiners, he was asked the following question: 'What do you think are the most important things in the world?' He thought for a moment. 'Love,' he answered, 'and Anglo-American relations.'

Hail and Farewell

During the three years Caroline and I spent at the London embassy, we sometimes felt we were shooting a set of whitewater rapids in a narrow stretch of the Anglo-American river. The ride was exhilarating, and it hardly seemed to have started before it was over. I never enjoyed a job so much. If I had had my druthers, I would have taken my little diplomatic canoe right back up to the headwaters and started paddling all over again.

Our diplomatic lives in London had almost come to a premature end in November 1992 when America decided to change presidents. On the night of the American elections about 130 guests came to Winfield House for dinner. These were mainly members of the Cabinet and shadow Cabinet along with a number of luminaries from the media. The house was swathed in red, white and blue, and each round dinner table was named after an important state. Life-size cut-outs of the candidates formed the receiving line, and I passed out mock ballots listing George Bush, Bill Clinton, Ross Perot and John Cleese. Cleese won in a landslide.

After dinner we all repaired to the embassy in Grosvenor Square where we joined another 1,500 people who were invited to watch the real returns come in from America. The ground floor and basement had been converted into a big election centre, with television monitors, bunting, posters and a huge scoreboard to list the results as they were announced by the various states. In the best British tradition, the evening was an immense, teeming bun-fight. But no one doubted the outcome. Clinton's lead in the polls was commanding, and Bush seemed to have lost heart. Perot cornered the plague-on-both-houses vote. So the electoral hand-writing was already on the embassy wall.

No previous ambassador in London had survived a change of party in the White House. All my predecessors had been political appointments, and because an ambassador serves 'at the pleasure of the President', a new president is unlikely to take much pleasure in being represented by a member of the opposing party. And when it comes to appointments, as everybody knows, the London embassy is one of the juiciest fruits in the presidential orchard.

By tradition all ambassadors offer their resignations after an election in order to give the President a free hand, and I sent in my letter a few days after the vote. But I was a career diplomat and, though I had been appointed by a Republican, it still remained to be seen how displeasing I would be to a Democrat or whether I would be caught up in the post-electoral purge.

Many British friends, so long accustomed to this American peculiarity, anticipated our immediate execution. We too half expected a tumbril to clatter through the gates of Winfield House and cart us away. Several people sent us condolence notes, and I recall one woman, a couple of days after the election, asking in a dolorous voice whether we had started packing. The press inevitably speculated about who our successors would be.

So the weeks following the election were unsettling for us. There was no word one way or the other from Washington. We were aware of a spontaneous lobbying effort on our behalf, and touched by what it meant, but we kept silent. It was awkward. Caroline and I decided simply to keep doing the job until someone told us to stop. As it turned out, the reports of our diplomatic demise were exaggerated, though it was not until March 1993 that I was told President Clinton wanted me to continue for another year. This was as much of a miracle as coming to London in the first place.

It was during that period of suspended animation, however, that I decided to end my diplomatic career. When my assignment at the embassy came to a close, I would also resign from the foreign service. I thought there was no better time to call an end to a career than when it was most gratifying. Though I would surely miss the stuff of foreign policy, the political tumble of Washington and my foreign service colleagues, I was still young enough to try my hand at something else. In the year that followed, the foreign policy record of the Clinton administration made my decision easier.

One springtime Sunday afternoon, as we were driving back to London from Peter Carrington's house in Buckinghamshire, Warren Christopher reached me on the car phone to propose another post in a distant clime. Caroline and I pondered this option for a day or so, but our minds were already set and I declined. We made our plans to leave in May 1994.

One reason I was disappointed to depart the embassy when I did was that I would miss the fiftieth-anniversary commemoration of the Allied landings in Normandy on D-Day, scheduled to take place just a few weeks after our departure. No single event in Anglo-American history better captures the depth and dedication of what has gone on between the two countries than that dangerous, daring endeavour.

The commemoration had a personal meaning for me because my father, at the age of thirty-six, had commanded an American regiment that went ashore on Omaha Beach that harrowing morning. In the way of old soldiers, he never talked about it much. But the immensity of the event was part of my youth, and to mark the half-century anniversary of this great Anglo-American enterprise would have been a kind of rounding-off for me.

I had been to the Normandy beaches several times before, the first occasion on a summer day in 1960, when my father, my stepmother and I drove over from Munich, where my father was stationed at the time. We stayed the first night at a small auberge in Bayeux, and we visited the museum in the centre of town where we saw the famous tapestry depicting another invasion in the opposite direction many centuries earlier.

The next morning we went out to Colleville-sur-mer, a little village at the top of a shallow valley that runs down to the sea. My stepmother and I, barely swallowing our emotions, stood to one side as my father walked the empty beaches. It was a blue, gentle day. The water was flat and grey, and in those days you could still see an occasional rusting tank trap poking through the surface. Otherwise, there was little evidence of the great events from sixteen years before. Cows grazed on the hillside. Gulls drifted overhead.

After a half-hour or so, my father rejoined us. Looking a little bewildered, he shook his head and said, 'I don't recognize a thing.' The peacefulness of that morning bore no resemblance to the horror he remembered. It was another time and another place.

We started back up the sandy pathway to the village. He paused once at a spot where he thought he recalled a friend of his, a young captain, had been killed. But he wasn't sure.

Afterwards we visited the American cemetery at St Laurent, where there are thousands of serried white crosses standing over neatly trimmed graves. There is a similar American cemetery in Madingley, just outside Cambridge, but the one at St Laurent is bigger. Behind the cemetery, on a small promontory overlooking Omaha Beach, there is an obelisk erected to the First Division – the Big Red One, as it is known. On three of the faces are the names of the many soldiers who had died in the D-Day operation. My parents and I stood there in timeless silence, looking down the long lists, just as Caroline and I in later years have read the melancholy rolls of honour in countless parish churches in Britain. And it was here, as he was reading the names of regimental comrades from long ago, that something gave way inside my father and he wept.

I never forgot that. And I think, at this simple moment, the memory of one generation was passed on to the next.

My mind went back to that picture in the autumn of my final year at the embassy. I was interviewed on the radio programme *Desert Island Discs*. This is another one of those sturdy British institutions that goes on year after year and hangs in the air like the smell of a Sunday joint roasting in the kitchen. To be interviewed on the programme is an honour so rare that it is akin to a Garter Knighthood. And during the exchange with Sue Lawley, I happened to mention that my father had fought on the beaches on D-Day.

Three days later I received a letter from a Mrs Betty Sewell, an English widow in Hertfordshire, who said her husband, Brigadier Sewell, and my father had been friends in those wartime days. In fact, shortly after the war, the Sewell family had briefly stayed with my family at First Army Headquarters in Governors Island, New York. Mrs Sewell recollected my mother recounting how she had sat in a darkened room, by the glow of a murmuring radio, listening to the early, tense reports of the D-Day landings, and she and my mother had told each other stories.

I immediately wrote back. I said that even though I was only seven or eight at the time, I did recall an English family that had stayed with us. I remembered how envious I was that they were about to board the *Queen Mary* and sail all the way back across the ocean. I also recalled that one of her children, in an abnormal act of adolescent generosity, had given me, just before they sailed, a silver dollar as a souvenir of friendship. And by some peculiar accident, I had managed to keep hold of that coin through all the intervening years when I had lost or misplaced virtually everything else I must have owned at that time of childhood. In fact, the silver dollar was sitting in a small leather box in my bedroom.

A couple of days later, as I was seated at my desk in Winfield House, I received another letter – this time from Major-General Toyne-Sewell, who was about to retire as Commandant of the Royal Military Academy at Sandhurst, and he informed me that he had been the English boy who had given me that silver coin all those years ago.

A month before I departed the embassy, I drove down to Sandhurst and, on the green field that lies before the grand academy, I stood with General Toyne-Sewell at his last Sovereign's Parade, the silver dollar safely in my pocket.

Caroline and I had decided to rent a small house in Trevor Square in Knightsbridge and spend a few months there while making up our minds what to do next and where to do it. So our departure from the embassy and from Britain was more psychological than physical.

The weeks before we left were a marathon of farewells. We dined with the Queen and Prince Philip in Windsor, and John and Norma Major hosted a jolly goodbye dinner in Downing Street. Two friends – one American and one British – put together a splendid bash at Spencer House in St James's, where Caroline and I felt we were attending our own memorial service. Just before packing up Winfield House, we hosted an open-house mêlée, and we stood in the same spot for more than four hours shaking hands and embracing many people whom we had known over many years. I paid my last respects to the Anglo-American community in a Pilgrims speech at Claridge's. On my last Friday in Grosvenor Square, the embassy staff assembled in the ground-floor atrium, where I thanked them as true friends and colleagues. Goodbyes are hard and long goodbyes are hardest.

We spent one last weekend in Regent's Park and took the dogs for one last stroll through the gardens. On the Sunday morning, we said our farewells to the household staff and then climbed into the armoured Cadillac for the last time. John Bryant, our driver who had manoeuvred us through the London maze for three years, sat behind the wheel, and Rick Persich, our principal Special Branch escort and certainly the funniest, sat next to him. We didn't have far to go. But we put the American flag on one wing of the car and the ambassadorial flag on the other, and we decided to take a farewell tour of London. Our years in Britain had taught us that a little ceremony is good for the soul.

We glided up the Strand and Fleet Street to St Paul's Cathedral and then along the Embankment where the Thames was in full flow. Caroline and I sat in the back seat, staring out the window, still noticing little things that had escaped us on all our previous prowls around the city. London is that way. There's always something you've missed.

Flags snapping, we went twice around Westminster Abbey and St Margaret's Church, past the Houses of Parliament, and then turned down the government valley of Whitehall and into the open plain of Trafalgar Square. I thought about all our years here – altogether more time in London than in Washington. Of course I still didn't understand Britain, though living here helped me understand my own country better. A foreigner can only understand bits of Britain, never the whole.

Coming in and out of Britain over a quarter-century or so, I had noticed many changes. And a lot of things that hadn't changed too. The country seems so full of peculiar contradictions and funny flukes. But, despite all the divisions and misgivings and occasional bouts of gloom, Britain still seems somehow able to come together at intimate moments of national sorrow or joy. And anyway, the British have never counted consistency among their prime virtues.

Our car drove through Admiralty Arch and down the grand Mall to Buckingham Palace, and then back up past St James's Palace. There was hardly a building we saw that didn't bring back memories. What to make of all this? I suppose after my time here I had concluded that Britain is caught in a vice between its past and its future. Who isn't? I had no idea how the British would resolve their problems, but I knew the British, for all their caution, are chance-takers, and having made the calculations about their chances will usually act on them. And I had also long ago concluded that, pound for pound, Britain contained more intelligent, witty, interesting, creative people than any country in the world. This may be just another one of those illusions at which the British are so masterful. But I don't think so. I think it's more like some sort of genetic mutation. Whatever the explanation, no place on earth compares. And so, for all the troubles, I was confident the British would sort things out in their own good way and in their own good time.

We drove the length of Piccadilly and around Constitution Hill, and then at Hyde Park Corner turned into Knightsbridge. I looked at the little flags fluttering on the front of the car, and I smiled. There is much about Britain which Caroline and I admire and which makes us happy. My pulse still jumps when I see the spire of an old country church beyond a hedgerow lane, and I float away when I hear an English choir. I tingle at the crinkly sound of a footfall on frosty Scottish grass. I know nothing kinder than a British nurse nor braver than a British soldier. Surely nowhere is more peaceful than an English churchyard nor is anything more beautiful than the palette of an English spring. We like the coal fires of a British winter, the long, lingering light of a summer night and the dream of an English swan drifting on an English pond.

Our little house in Trevor Square was stacked with packing boxes, and it was too much of a task to start to sort things out that day. We were too limp. In the late afternoon the doorbell rang. Standing on the stoop was Nico Henderson, the former British ambassador in Washington and Paris, and a man who knew a thing or two about saying goodbye to a post. He was holding a great green hatbox from Harrods with a big red bow tied around it. Mary

Henderson had filled the box with succulent Harrods bones for our dogs.

As night came Caroline cooked spaghetti in a battered pan and heated up some pesto sauce. We found a lamp and stood it on top of a crate in the small dining room. The bare bulb threw blotchy shadows against the walls. The Girls settled at our feet, gnawing at their house presents. We were too tired to try to find proper utensils and plateware for ourselves. Caroline used a bent spoon to eat and I found a broken plastic fork. We sat at the corner of the table and chased the spaghetti around in its saucepan. We laughed.

INDEX